TOM SAWYER

TOM SAWYER

a play

by

JOHN CHARLESWORTH

and

TONY BROWN

based on the novel
by Mark Twain

music by Eric Wayman
(published by Chappell & Co.)

HEINEMANN EDUCATIONAL BOOKS

Heinemann Educational Books Ltd
Halley Court, Jordan Hill, Oxford OX2 8EJ
OXFORD LONDON EDINBURGH
MELBOURNE SYDNEY AUCKLAND
IBADAN NAIROBI GABORONE HARARE
KINGSTON PORTSMOUTH NH (USA)
SINGAPORE MADRID

ISBN 0 435 23169 3

Printed and bound in Great Britain by
J. W. Arrowsmith Ltd, Bristol

CONTENTS

ACKNOWLEDGMENTS

We should like to thank Bill Breese for permission to use the cover photographs; Tom Manning for further photographic work; and of course all who helped with the first production of the play, particularly Pam Munro and Sylvia Hill for secretarial help, and Barbara Tobin, who suggested the idea originally.

The piano score for the music of the play is available from Messrs. Chappell & Co., 50 New Bond Street, London W.1.

INTRODUCTION

Long lazy summer days, paddle-steamers passing on the river, half the children eagerly looking forward to the annual Sunday School picnic, the other half ready for any mischief or adventure that presents itself . . . and Aunt Polly's fence needs white-washing. In short, it's a summer like all the others Tom has known. Until he and Huck decide to take a dead cat up to the graveyard at midnight. . . .

Everyone remembers the spirit of Mark Twain's book, and it is this rather than the strict story-line that we have tried to preserve in adapting it for the stage. Also its good humour and gentle probing of the uncomfortable choices presented when dream adventures become real. Inevitably there is much that we have had to transpose or leave out, notably the Becky Thatcher episodes. This last was a decision made with great regret. As the novel is episodic, and a play needs a stronger structure, the Injun Joe plot seemed to offer the best foundation. We also wanted to design a vehicle for large numbers of young actors, and making room for several scenes between Tom and Becky would have meant having to cut out the gregarious fun of the Gang and Sunday School Picnic episodes. Finally, Tom's part is already a taxing one, and to ask a young actor to sustain a further complex relationship with Becky besides those with Aunt Polly and Huck would have been asking perhaps too much.

As a foil to the 'crowd scenes' of the play, however, we have tried to develop the relationship between Tom and Huck more fully. Tom is a natural leader, impulsive, wildly romantic, full of schemes that are sometimes heroic and self-sacrificing and at others foolish or self-centred; Huck is an outsider, common-sensical, sometimes selfish and sometimes with a more instinctive humanity than Tom. 'Can't either of us get very far on our own perhaps' may be felt to reach out further into the play, therefore, than simply getting Injun Joe's treasure-chest out of the caves.

What also comes through, more strongly in performance perhaps than on the page, is the way that Huck's friendship with Tom gradually draws him into 'civilization', from which he narrowly escapes at the end again to the woods and the river.

Tom Sawyer is a play with music, the music written with young people of no special musical ability in mind. The songs are within anyone's capability, and a piano can do the rest.* If a producer feels reluctant to take on the musical numbers, however, *the play could be performed simply as play*, with the music omitted. It will 'work' without the songs.

Naturally though, we feel the play will be a thinner experience without its music. Certainly the songs contributed enormously to the enjoyment of both actors and audiences in the first production. As the play was envisaged with music from the start, some of the scenes also depend on it to make their full effect and would have been handled differently without it. This is particularly so with the Prelude, the Celebration Day scene, and the Finale. There the short exchange between Tom and Huck relies for most of its impact on the contrast with the surrounding musical jollity. Some of the audience may find it sad that Huck should reject his final acceptance by the community; others may find it heartening that he preserves his independence. But either way, like the nature of Injun Joe's death, it is an essential feature of Mark Twain's lack of sentimentality, and something we could not leave out. 'Well, I ain't everybody, Tom, and I couldn't stand it.' It is the voice of truth to individual feeling in the face of mass opinion.

But that way lies another book, and perhaps another play. Good luck with your production!

*See the Music Notes, p. 77.

To the young people
who gave
their time and talents
so generously
both on stage and behind the scenes
to the first production
of this play

Tom Sawyer was first presented at Spalding Grammar School on 13 December 1973 with the following cast:

TOM	John Fidler
SID	John Day
AUNT POLLY	Carole Guttridge
BEN RODGERS	Richard Hurst
JOE HARPER	Michael Harpham
JEFF THATCHER	Russell Harman
DAVE RICHARDS	Tony Heil
JOHNNY MILLER	Bruce Turner
HUCKLEBERRY FINN	Steven Green
DR ROBINSON	Dick Shutt
INJUN JOE	John Clark
MUFF POTTER	Nigel Cope
THE MINISTER	Stewart Boyle
WILLIE	Michael Thurston
LITTLE GIRL	Sally Catcheside
MRS RODGERS	Judith Gedney
MRS HARPER	Katherine Anderson
JUDGE THATCHER	Geoffrey Daw
CLERK TO THE COURT	Alan Pitts
PROSECUTING ATTORNEY	Richard Wells
MR RODGERS	Denis Hall
DEFENDING ATTORNEY	Alan Bowell

OTHER MEMBERS OF TOM'S GANG: Jeremy Baker, Benny Blom, Les Britton, Martin Cook, Tim Forman, Richard Teeuw.

x

BOYS AND GIRLS: Richard Beaumont, Stephen Byford, Heather Chubb, Simon Coaton, Nick Crosby, Julie Deaton, Sheona Frith, Kenneth Greetham, Linda Hawes, Gillian Kitchener, Linda Lee, Kathryn Molesworth, John Molson, Kim Nelson, Jane Savage, Debbie Sinnott, Paul Smalley, Angela Smith, Susan Strickland, Elaine Swan, Stephen Taylor, Charles Thompson.

TOWNSFOLK: Alan Aistrup, Howard Beeken, Jeanette Burgess, Rowena Burton, Wendy Burton, Mark Chamberlain, Martin Chiappini, Jenny Dillon, Mark Eggleton, Richard Gledhill, Nicholas Grief, Julia Hartley, Philip Harwood, Patrick Johnson, Tim Kitchener, Rachel Noyes, Isobel Slator, Kim Smith, Sandra Smith, Kevin Storey, Jill Tinkler, Sue Wells, Suzette Wells, Russell Willerton.

Producer: John Charlesworth. *Musical Director*: Eric Wayman. *Band*: Alan Forman, Paul Gray, Aidan Huxford, Graham Lake, Charles Lulham, Stewart Milton, Nicholas Pitts, Christopher Quinton, Graham Rouse, Roger Selby, Kevin Smith.

CHARACTERS

TOM *Chris*
SID, *his brother* *David*
AUNT POLLY, *their aunt* *Kathryn*
BEN RODGERS *Susannah*
JOE HARPER *Richie*
JEFF THATCHER
DAVE RICHARDS } *Tom's friends*
JOHNY MILLER
HUCKLEBERRY FINN *Paul*
DR ROBINSON *Katie Machennan*
INJUN JOE *David*
MUFF POTTER *Jack*
THE MINISTER *Jennifer*
WILLIE
LITTLE GIRL
MRS RODGERS *Laura*
MRS HARPER
JUDGE THATCHER
CLERK TO THE COURT *Jenni H*
PROSECUTING ATTORNEY
MR RODGERS *Laura*
DEFENDING ATTORNEY
Other members of Tom's Gang *Richie, Vicky, Ross, Joe*
Boys and girls *Vicky*
Townsfolk *Me, Janet*
Bible Basher Mavi.

Time: about 1850
Place: St. Petersburg, Missouri

xii

TOM SAWYER

Paula Lord

Paula

PRELUDE

*The Prelude is a kaleidescope of Tom's harum-scarum ways, and
the set should be flexible enough to accommodate the rapid
changes of location. Apart from the opening fishing episode
and the final pirates' one, the order of the episodes can be
altered to suit the staging and production, and episodes
subtracted or others added. The episodes are separated
musically. After the fishing episode everything must move
with great speed and liveliness.*

*Summer. A street in the little town of St. Petersburg, Missouri, on
the banks of the Mississippi.*

TOM *is fishing, almost asleep in the hot afternoon sun. He is
barefoot, and playing truant. From the distance is heard the
'call' for the first time.*

Don't sing.

MUSIC NO. 1 — TOM SAWYER

GIRLS (*distant singing*): Tom Sawyer! Yoooo, Tom!
Tom Sawyer! Where you gone?

AUNT POLLY's *voice is heard calling over the singing.*

AUNT POLLY (*off-stage, distant*): Tom! (TOM *doesn't stir.*) Tom!

TOM (*sitting up*): Comin', Aunt Polly! (*He looks ruefully in the
direction of the shout, casts out his line, tips his hat over his
eyes and settles down to doze again.*)

AUNT POLLY (*nearer*): Tom! (TOM *sits up.*) Tom! Tom! (*Nearer
still and more urgent.*)

3

TOM *quickly stows his line and runs off, as other voices join in the shouts. They die away and* TOM *returns. He is either walking on his hands or runs on and does a forward or backward roll, remaining with his legs in the air. He finds the* MINISTER *standing over him and rights himself in some embarrassment.*

MINISTER: Now, Thomas, why aren't you in school this afternoon?

TOM: I'm . . . I'm just on my way, sir.

MINISTER: Like *that*?

TOM: Well, sir, my big toe, sir. It's mortified, sir . . . and, and Dr Robinson, he said, sir. . . .

MINISTER: Thomas!

TOM (*beaten*): Going , sir!

He starts to run off nimbly, stops, looks round at the Minister, and moves off limping heavily. The MINISTER *is joined by a group of* TOWNSFOLK, *who sing, then move to one side.*

TOWNSFOLK (*sing*):

1. Who is out a-foolin', when he should be schoolin'?
   Swimmin' in the creek instead of workin' hard?
   Who torments the girls and always pulls their curls and
   Makes himself the terror of the whole school yard?

Don't sing

School. A row of PUPILS, *including* TOM.

TEACHER: Now, Thomas . . . (TOM *stands up.*) . . . what were the names of the first two disciples that Jesus appointed?

TOM (*sheepishly*): Well . . . er . . .

TEACHER: Now don't be afraid. The names of just the first two . . .

TOM: David and Goliath?

The class jeer and TOM *runs from the room.*

CLASS (*sings, jeeringly*): Tom Sawyer! Yoooo, Tom!
Tom Sawyer! Where you gone?

Don't sing

TOM, *running, comes face to face with a new boy. He stops and looks him up and down.*

TOM: You're new, ain't yer?

JEFF: What if I am?

TOM: I can lick you!

JEFF: I'd like to see you try it!

TOM: What's your name?

JEFF: 'S none of your business.

TOM: Well, I 'low I'll make it my business, if you say much more.

JEFF: Much more — much more — much more — much more . . . !

They fight, rolling on the ground. The CHILDREN *gather round. Enter* SID *and* AUNT POLLY.

SID (*pointing*): Why, there he is, Aunt Polly, and he's fighting! After you'd told him not to.

AUNT POLLY *picks* TOM *out by his ear.*

AUNT POLLY: Now I've got you. (*She raises a stick to tan* TOM.)

TOM: My! Look behind you, aunt!

AUNT POLLY *whirls round and* TOM *escapes, chased by her and* SID. *More* TOWNSFOLK *enter.*

TOWNSFOLK & CHILDREN (*sing*):

2. Who's been playin' hookey? Who just stole a cookie?
   Fought another boy and blacked his eye?
   Who can bait the teacher, irritate the preacher?
   Who can tease his aunt until she hopes to die?

HUCK *sitting smoking on his hogshead. During the above verse* TOM *has rushed on and dived inside.* HUCK *nips down and sits in front. Enter* SID *and* AUNT POLLY, *panting. The 'call' is sung quietly on stage, with the following dialogue above it.*

AUNT POLLY: Oh, Huckleberry. Have you seen my Tom go by?

HUCK: No, ma'am.

SID: You're not going to believe Huck Finn, are you, aunt?

HUCK: Well, he ain't gone *by* — I'm sure of that.

5

AUNT POLLY *tosses her head and she and* SID *hurry off.*
TOM *emerges from the barrel.*

TOM: C'mon, Huck. (*They run off in the opposite direction.*)

TOWNSFOLK & CHILDREN (*sing*):

3. Who is it that glories in adventure stories,
   Highwaymen and pirates, Robin Hood?
   Who is it that's readin' when he should be sleepin'?
   He'll ruin his eyes, but — boy! — it sure is good

Pirates. TOM *stands, feet apart, with sternly folded arms and a lath sword in his belt.* HUCK *is at the wheel or tiller.*

TOM: Hard a-port!

HUCK: Aye, aye, sir!

Enter JOE HARPER, *also with lath sword.*

TOM: Galleon, ahoy! Name your name. I'm Tom Sawyer, the Black Avenger of the Spanish Main.

JOE: Joe Harper, the Terror of the Seas.

TOM: Board her! (*He and* JOE *fight spectacularly. During this any of the cast not yet on enter.*) Fall, fall! Why don't you fall?

JOE: Fall yourself — you're gettin' the worst of it!

TOM: *I* can't fall — cos that's not the way it's written in the book! (*He 'kills'* JOE *with a magnificent flourish, and backs away triumphantly, his sword above his head.*) The Black Avenger strikes again! (*Right into* AUNT POLLY's *arms.*)

ALL (*sing, triumphantly*): Tom Sawyer! Yoooo, Tom!
                    Tom Sawyer! GOTCHER now, Tom!

4. Plagues you when you're busy, chase him till you're dizzy.
   Though he's twice as slipp'ry as an eel,
   Minute that we spy him, then we'll rope and tie him —
   Gotcher, Thomas Sawyer! Now you come to heel!
      (TOM *makes a break for it, but is caught.*)

5. Who is always sorta needin' soap and water?
   Says that water's useful only for a thirst?
   Local residents say he'll be President may-
   be, but only if they haven't hanged him first!

ACT ONE

SCENE 1

Village street, outside Aunt Polly's house. Cat asleep in the sun.
AUNT POLLY *holding* TOM. *The scene continues straight on from the previous one as the rest exit.*

AUNT POLLY: Now, Thomas Sawyer, just explain yourself.
(*The Black Avenger folds his arms defiantly.*) The schoolmaster tells me you weren't in school Thursday afternoon, or Friday either. (*The Black Avenger deflating into* TOM.) Playing hookey, I'll be bound.

TOM: Oh, aunt, I felt like I was *dying.*

AUNT POLLY: Well, a good dose of pain-killer will deal with that, sir! Sid! Bring me that bottle of pain-killer off the kitchen shelf.

SID (*off-stage, in delight*): Yessir, ma'am!

TOM: Oh not *that,* Aunt Polly. It just about burns your guts out.
Enter SID *with bottle and spoon.*

AUNT POLLY: Now, Tom, open your mouth. (*She pinches* TOM's *nose and gives him a spoonful.*) And you'll take another spoonful in five minutes, for good measure, when that one's settled. D'you hear?

TOM: Yes, aunt.
She bustles off, leaving SID *spying on* TOM *and the bottle and spoon with* TOM. TOM *notices the cat sitting on the fence or window-sill. He strokes it. The cat miaows and purrs.*

7

TOM: Now look, Puss, don't you ask for it unless you're sure you want some. (*Miaow.*) You're *really* sure? (*Miaow.* TOM *pours out a spoonful.*) Now if you don't like it, you mustn't blame anybody but your own self.

    He gives the spoonful to the cat, which shoots off-stage like a thunderbolt, yowling. Sounds of smashing glass and general chaos from off-stage. AUNT POLLY *rushes on and* SID *emerges from hiding.*

AUNT POLLY: Tom, what *have* you done to that cat?

TOM: Nothing, ma'am. Cats always act like that when they're having a good time.

AUNT POLLY: That just ain't so — and you know it! Forty times I've said that, if you didn't stop your tricks, I'd skin you. What your poor dead mother would have done with you, I don't know.

TOM: Aw, aunt. . . .

AUNT POLLY: Now come on, tell me — what did you do to that cat?

TOM: I wasn't doing. . . .

SID: He dosed it with his medicine, aunt.

TOM: Why, you. . . .

SID: I saw him, I saw him.

AUNT POLLY: How could you be so cruel, Tom?

TOM: Cruel? It done him *good*, aunt. Honest! I've never seen him get around so nice. . . .

AUNT POLLY: Tom! I'm just obliged to punish you for this. Spare the rod and spoil the child, as the good book says. The front fence needs whitewashing, and that is what you'll do this very morning.

TOM: Aw, aunt, it's Saturday morning. Nobody works on a Saturday morning.

AUNT POLLY: Well, you're one person who will. That way I can be sure you'll be out of mischief for one morning at least. (*Going in.*) The whitewash is in the shed.

SID: And the brushes hanging up behind the door! (*He exits up the street, grinning.*)

TOM (*calling*): Siddy, I'll lick you for this!

> As TOM *goes in for the whitewash and brushes,* BEN
> RODGERS *is heard off-stage chuffing and hooting like a*
> *paddle-steamer. He enters, arms revolving in big circles. He is*
> *boat and captain and engine-bells combined. He is also eating*
> *an apple!*

BEN: *Ch*-ch-*chow*-wow, *ch*-ch-*chow*-wow, *ch*-ch-*chow*-wow, etc.
Hoo-oo-oot! Slow ahead! Ling-a-ling! *Ch*-ch-*chow*-wow,
ch-ch-*chow*-wow. (*He slows almost to a standstill, as* TOM
enters with two buckets and four brushes, and starts to
whitewash the fence, in an angry, slapdash way, then flings
the brush into the bucket.) Starboard paddle astern! Ling-a-ling!
(*Right arm moving in slow, large circles.*) Chow! *Ch*-ch-*chow*-wow,
ch-ch-*chow*-wow! Astern on the larboard! Ling-a-ling-ling!
(*Left arm slow circles.*) Chow! *Ch*-ch-*chow*-wow! Stop 'em
both now! Ling! (*As* BEN *edges expertly into the quayside,*
TOM's *face lights up with an idea and he resumes whitewashing*
the fence — slowly, artistically.) Get that headline out there!
And the spring-line! Stir yourselves! Stand by for the stage now!
Let her go! (*Turning gauge-cocks.*) Sht! S'sht! Sht! (*Berthed at*
last, BEN *stares for a moment at* TOM, *who takes no notice.*)
Hey-there! You're up a stump, ain't you! (*No answer.* TOM
stands back to survey his work, then gives it another artistic
touch.) Hey . . . . Tom! You gotta work this morning?

TOM: Oh, it's you, Ben! I didn't notice you.

BEN: I'm going swimming in a minute. Bet you wish you could —
'stead of having to work.

TOM (*after a look at* BEN): Depends what you call work.

BEN: Well, *that* is, ain't it?

TOM: Maybe so, maybe not. (*Resuming whitewashing.*) Suits me,
anyway.

BEN: Oh, come on now, you cain't let on you like it.

TOM: Like it? I don't see why not. Does a boy get a chance to
whitewash a fence every day? (TOM *continues whitewashing,*
artistically, absorbed. BEN *gets more and more drawn towards*
it.)

9

BEN: Say, Tom, let's have a go.

TOM (*as if about to consent, then thinking better of it*): No. I'd like to, honest I would, Ben, but Aunt Polly's mighty partic'lar about this fence. I reckon there ain't but one in a thousand, maybe two thousand, that can do it the way it's gotta be done.

BEN: Go on, Tom. I'd let *you*, if you was me. I'll let you have my apple core.

> *He tries to take the brush. Enter* JOE HARPER.

TOM: Hey! No, Ben! I'm scared Aunt Polly. . . .

BEN: You can have it *all*! (*He takes a brush and starts, artistically.*)

TOM: Well, maybe . . . (TOM *takes the apple, and starts to work alongside* BEN. *After a pause . . .*)

JOE: Hi, Tom! Ben!

TOM AND BEN (*preoccupied*): Oh, hello, Joe. Hi!

JOE (*sarcastically*): You enjoying yourselves?

TOM: Sure!

JOE: You're joking, *must* be!

BEN: Well, 'tisn't every day a couple of *boys* gets the chance to whitewash a fence.

TOM: Right here on the street.

JOE: I guess not. D'you reckon I could have a try?

TOM: What you got?

JOE: A dog's collar. (*Seizing* TOM's *brush.*)

TOM: All right, but take it slow. . . .

> *The three work. Enter* JEFF THATCHER *and* DAVE RICHARDS. *They stare amazed.*

JEFF (*nudging* DAVE): The St. Petersburg chain-gang!

JOE: Chain-gang!

BEN: Aunt Polly's mighty partic'lar about her fence.

JOE: Bet she wouldn't let a couple of slouches like you two. . . .

JEFF: Who you calling slouches?

> *They rush for brushes, but* TOM *grabs them by their collars.*

TOM: What's it worth?

DAVE: Couple of marbles?

JEFF: Or a kitten without an eye?

TOM: Make it three marbles, and you can have my brush.

DAVE: Done!

The goods are handed over and TOM *retires to watch, meeting* JOHNNY MILLER.

TOM: You got a whitewash brush at home?

JOHNNY: Yes.

TOM: I could sell you a go for. . .

JOHNNY: A piece of chalk?

TOM: Yes.

JOHNNY *hands his chalk over and runs off to get his brush. Other* BOYS *are by now flocking in with brushes. They offer a key, a spool-cannon, the handle of a knife, a frog, etc. in exchange for the chance to whitewash.* TOM *sits at the receipt of custom.*

MUSIC NO. 2 – PERSPICACITY

TOM (*sings*):

1. When the weather's boilin' and you're goin' swimmin',
   But you're set to toilin' by these pesky women,
   Then you need to hatch a plan to set you free.
   That's the time to use your PERSPICACITY.

BOYS (*sing*):

2. When troubles multiply and cares attack,
   And difficulties are immense,
   We always find we're on a cheerful track,
   Slappin' whitewash on a fence.

TOM (*sings*):

3. First you start a-thinkin', then you mulls and chews it,
   No good standin' blinkin', you've a mind so use it.
   Suddenly you find you've had a great idee –
   All because you used your PERSPICACITY.

11

BOYS (*sing*):
4. There ain't no occupation half as grand,
    Or one that touches it for sense,
    As workin' with a paintbrush in your hand,
    Slappin' whitewash on a fence.

TOM (*sings*) and the BOYS (*hum*):
5. Folks have queer ideas what constitutes a pleasure,
    Work can never please, so if it does, it's leisure,
    So you all can learn from my philosophy,
    If you'll only use your PERSPICACITY.

BOYS (*sing*):
6. You may not think it's art — but (boy!) it's fun,
    Producing happiness intense.
    And oh the satisfaction when you've done
    Slappin' whitewash on a fence.

TOM (*sings*):
7. Folks have queer ideas what constitutes a pleasure,
    Work can never please, so if it does, it's leisure,
    So you all can learn from my philosophy,
    If you'll only use your PERSPICACITY.

BOYS (*sing*):
8. Why is the White House, Washington, D.C.,
    The home of all our presidents?
    So they can all relax like you and me,
    Slappin' whitewash on a fence.

(simultaneously)

   At the end of the song, exit BOYS *with brushes and
   buckets, leaving* TOM *to survey the finished fence.*

TOM (*calling*): Aunt Polly! Can I go and play now?

AUNT POLLY (*off*): What, already? How much of that fence
   have you done?

TOM: I've finished it.

AUNT POLLY (*off*): Now, Tom, don't tell lies.

TOM: Honest, aunt — it *is* done.
   Enter AUNT POLLY. *She is astonished.*

AUNT POLLY: Well, I never! Now if you'd work like that more
   often, you'd happen find it more rewarding.

12

TOM: You're right, Aunt Polly. That's the way it was this morning!

AUNT POLLY: You *certainly* can work when you've a mind to. But I must say it's powerful seldom you've a mind. Yes, go along and play. But don't let me ever catch you doing a thing like that to the cat again.

TOM: But, Aunt Polly, I only gave it a dose of the medicine you gave me.

AUNT POLLY: Well . . . I suppose . . . what hurts a cat *could* hurt a boy as well. So, off you go. (*He starts to leave.*) But don't let me catch you playing with that Huckleberry Finn. He's idle and lawless, you know that, and bad. I've warned you now. . . .

TOM: Yes, aunt.

    Exit AUNT POLLY *to house.* TOM *is running off the other side, when* HUCK *enters.* TOM *looks round to see if the coast is clear before starting the conversation.* HUCK *has a dead cat with a string round its neck.*

TOM: Hello, Huckleberry.

HUCK: Hello, yourself, and see how you like it.

TOM: What's that you got?

HUCK: Dead cat.

TOM: Lemme see him. (HUCK *holds up the cat.*) My, he's pretty stiff. Where'd you get him?

HUCK: Bought him off'n Joe Harper.

TOM: What did you give?

HUCK: Four marbles and a bladder that I got at the slaughter-house.

TOM: What'll you take for him?

HUCK: Well. . . .

TOM: I got a pinch-bug. Want to see him? (*He takes out a small box and lets* HUCK *look inside it.*)

HUCK: Where'd you get him?

TOM: Out in the woods.

HUCK: I don't know. It's a mighty small pinch-bug.

TOM: Oh, anybody can run a bug down that don't belong to them. This is a pretty early pinch-bug, I reckon. It's the first one I've seen this year. He's good enough for me. I wouldn't swop him for anything.

HUCK: Well, that suits me. I'm happy with this cat, I reckon.
Pause.

TOM: What's a dead cat good for, anyway?

HUCK: Good for? Cure warts with.

TOM: I never heard of that. I take mine off with a bean.

HUCK: Yes, bean's good. I done that, but a dead cat's better.

TOM: Yes? How's it work?

HUCK: Why, you take your cat and go and get in the graveyard, long about midnight, where somebody that was wicked has been buried; and when it's midnight a devil will come, or maybe two or three; and when they're taking that feller away, you heave your cat after 'em and say, 'Devil follow corpse, cat follow devil, warts follow cat, *I'm* done with ye!' That'll fetch *any* wart.

TOM: Sounds genuine. Have you tried it yet?

HUCK: No, but old Mother Hopkins told me.

TOM: Well, it must be right then, because all the folks say she's a witch.

HUCK: *Say!* Tom, I just *know* she is. She witched pap once. He was coming along one day, and he saw she was witching him, so he took up a rock and threw it at her. If she hadn't dodged, he'd a got her. Well, that same night, he rolled off'n a shed where he was layin' drunk, and broke his arm.

TOM: That's awful, Huck. But how did he know she was witching him?

HUCK: Well, pap says that when they keep looking at you right steady, that's when they're witching you — specially if they mumble. Because when they mumble, they're saying the Lord's Prayer backwards.

TOM: Huck, when you going to try the cat?

HUCK: Tonight, I guess. I reckon they'll come after old Hoss Williams tonight.

TOM: Why didn't they get him last night?

HUCK: How you talk! Devils don't slosh around much on a Sunday, I don't reckon.

TOM: Yes, that's so. . . . Say, can I go with you?

HUCK: Of course — if you ain't scared.

TOM: Scared! That's likely! Just when I'm thinkin' of forming a band of robbers, with a hideout and weapons and an oath like they have in all the pirate and robber books.

HUCK: When's it gonna start?

TOM: Well, er . . . Now! C'mon, let's round up Joe Harper and Ben Rodgers and the others.

They run off, just as AUNT POLLY *enters from the house, with a shopping basket on her arm. She catches sight of them as they exit.*

AUNT POLLY: Now was that Huckleberry Finn with Tom? I never know what he's up to. He never plays his tricks two days alike. Sid don't ever try my patience like Tom does. But, then, Sid'd never have done the fence so nice. I reckon Tom's a kind of a singed cat, as the saying is — better'n he looks. But I often wonder if I'm doing my duty by that boy, and that's the Lord's truth, goodness knows. Every time I raise my hand to him, he knows he's only got to make me laugh and it's all over. I just can't hit him a lick.

MUSIC NO. 3 — BRINGIN' UP A BOY

AUNT POLLY (*sings*):

1. Bringin' up a boy is tough when you're alone,
   Specially when he's not your own, the work of your hand.
   Is a mother's love a thing uniquely grown?
   Does the pain of birth forge links I don't understand?
   Perhaps he don't think the things I do,
   Perhaps I don't love him like I should,
   Perhaps what I'm telling him ain't true.
       (*Spoken*) I just wanna do the best,
   So his life can be some good.

2. If he could behave, how easy it would be,
   Never tell a lie, and never a hair out of place,
   Never tear his clothes and never climb a tree,
   Never do a thing to cause his aunt disgrace.
   But Tom and the dream are far apart —
   Maybe that's the way it oughta be —
   And Tom's got an open, lovin' heart:
      (*Spoken*) Pray God he keeps it!
   How much of that love's for me?

3. P'raps I oughta be more hard than I have bin.
   Am I doing right? Spoil the child by sparin' the rod?
   Which way can I turn? He's got no other kin,
   No-one he can trust. So I'll put my faith in God.
   But Tom isn't really bad, I know,
   Even his tricks is only pranks.
   Each night I pray the Lord will show him
      (*Spoken*) How much I love him.
   I don't want no other thanks.

   She exits to the village. Re-enter TOM *and* HUCK, *with*
   JOE HARPER, BEN RODGERS, JEFF THATCHER, *and*
   other BOYS.

TOM: Now I'm gonna start a band of robbers. The hideout's in
   the quarry cave. It'll be called Tom Sawyer's Gang, and
   everybody that wants to join'll have to take an oath and write
   his name in blood. Is everyone agreed?
GANG (*variously*): We don't know yet. We ain't heard the oath.
   Yes. Sure. Let's hear it. What's it say?
TOM (*producing piece of paper from his pocket*): Well, every
   member of the gang must swear to stick to the band. And if
   anybody does anything to anyone in the gang, whichever boy
   is ordered to kill that person and his family must do it and
   afterwards hack a cross in their breasts, which is the sign of the
   gang. And nobody that doesn't belong to the gang can use that
   mark, and if they do they must be sued; and if they do it again,

they must be killed. And if any member of the gang tells its secrets, he must have his throat cut and his name blotted off of the list with blood, and never mentioned again by the gang, but have a curse put on it and be forgot for ever.

JOHNNY: Gee, Tom, that's a real beautiful oath. (*General agreement.*)

JOE: Did you make it up out of your own head?

TOM: Well, some of it. The rest was out of pirate books and robber books. Every gang that amounts to anything has it.

JEFF: *I* reckon we ought to kill the *families* of anyone that tells the secrets as well. (*General agreement.*)

TOM: Well, I'm agreed.

JOE: But Huck ain't got a family we can kill. What you gonna do about him?

TOM: He's got a father, hain't he?

BEN: 'Cept you can't ever find him these days.

JOHNNY: 'Course you can. He's always laying drunk with the hogs in the tan-yard.

JOE: Used to be, you mean.

JEFF: He ain't been seen around for more'n a year now.

BEN: So he can't come in.

JOE: But it ain't Huck's fault.

JEFF: That don't matter. Every boy has to have a family or some-body to kill, or else it wouldn't be fair and square for the others.

HUCK: What about Muff Potter? He gives me food sometimes. You could kill him.

BOYS (*variously*): Oh, he'll do, he'll do. That's all right. Huck can come in.

TOM: Yes, Muff'll do for a family.

DAVE: So that's settled.

BEN: Now what's the line of business of this gang?

TOM: Nothin' only robbery and murder — suchlike high-toned stuff. We're kinda highwaymen. We stop stages and carriages on the road, with masks on, and kill the people and take their watches and money.

JOHNNY: Do we always kill the people?

TOM: 'Course we do. Except for some you bring to the cave and keep them till they're ransomed.

BEN: Ransomed?

TOM: That means we . . . we keep them till they're dead.

BEN: Ransom them to death, huh? . . . And a bothersome lot they'll be too, eatin' up everything there is!

JEFF: Why can't we take a club and ransom them straight off?

TOM: Now do you want to do things the reg'lar way or not?

BEN: Well, it seems a fool way to me. Say — do we kill the women as well?

TOM: Well, Ben Rodgers, if I was as ignorant as you I wouldn't let on. Kill the women? Who ever heard of anything like that? You fetch 'em to the cave, and you're always as polite as pie to them. And by-and-by they fall in love with you and never want to go home any more.

BEN: So, mighty soon we'll have the cave so cluttered up with women, and fellers waiting to be ransomed, that there won't be any place for the robbers. But go ahead, I ain't got nothing to say.

TOM: Well, that's the way they do it in all the books, and that's the way it's gonna be.

JOHNNY: When do we start the robbing?

TOM: Well, we gotta spy out the land first — everybody does that — and then we can start next week, and rob somebody and kill some people.

BEN: I can only manage Sundays.

JOE: But 'twouldn't be right to kill people on a Sunday.

OTHERS: Not on Sunday. Course not.

BEN: Well, the only other time's this afternoon.

TOM: Right! This afternoon then! Up on Cardiff Hill. Bring your swords and pistols. And the password's 'BLOOD'.

JEFF: And the counter-sign?

TOM: 'MORE BLOOD'.

> *Enter* AUNT POLLY *with* DR ROBINSON. *She sees* TOM *and calls him across.*

TOM (*calling*): Yes. (*To the* BOYS) Two o'clock this afternoon on Cardiff Hill.

>TOM *crosses to* AUNT POLLY *and* DR ROBINSON. *The* BOYS *drift off home, leaving* HUCK.

TOM: Morning, Dr Robinson.

DR ROBINSON: Morning, Tom. Fine job you made of the fence, I see.

AUNT POLLY: Now you've not been talking with Huckleberry Finn, have you? I warned you about mixing with that boy. No good'll come of it.

TOM: Not exactly, Aunt Polly. We didn't ask him. He ain't one of us, really.

AUNT POLLY: I should hope not. (*Exit* HUCK.) Well, Dr Robinson, I'd like to stand and talk with you, but I've got my house to run and two boys is more than a handful for an old body like me.

DR ROBINSON: I understand, ma'am — though I'd never agree that you're old.

AUNT POLLY: Oh, get on with you, doctor.

DR ROBINSON: Good-day to you, ma'am.

AUNT POLLY (*going*): Tom, there's wood needs chopping.

>*Exit* AUNT POLLY, *followed by* TOM. *As* DR ROBINSON *starts to walk across to exit, he meets* INJUN JOE, *who has just entered.*

DR ROBINSON: Oh, Injun Joe . . . You're just the man I was hoping to see.

INJUN JOE: Yes?

DR ROBINSON: There's another — a — job that could bring some money your way. Four or five dollars perhaps. Tonight.

INJUN JOE: Same as before?

DR ROBINSON: Yes.

INJUN JOE: Too risky. It's full moon just now, and there's no damn cover up there . . . and it's grisly work at the best of times.

DR ROBINSON: You know it isn't something that can wait.

INJUN JOE: Course I know that. But it's dangerous work, and I don't see why I should risk myself on account of your benefit.

It was *your* father had me jailed for a vagrant — more than once. Remember? And that ain't all, not the hundredth part of it! The last time he did it, the judge had me horse-whipped. Horse-whipped in front of the jail, like a nigger! With all the town looking on! What makes you think I'd risk myself for you?

DR ROBINSON: Because the money's easy. And Injun Joe's not the one to say no to a chance of easy money. Anything else is in the past, and gone.

INJUN JOE: But not forgotten. Anyway, who's the other guy you've got to help do the liftin' . . . or are you goin' to dirty your hands yourself this time?

DR ROBINSON: Muff Potter.

INJUN JOE: That drunken idiot! It was difficult enough to keep him sober last time.

DR ROBINSON: Maybe so — but at least he knows the ropes.

INJUN JOE: *And* fool enough to get 'em knotted up! And drunk enough to trip the lot of us! Have you any guarantee he'll turn up even, never mind anything else — and where's my four or five dollars then? No, it ain't worth the bother.

DR ROBINSON: Not even if I pay you now?

INJUN JOE: No. . .

DR ROBINSON: And yours to keep, suppose the job's called off?
    INJUN JOE *hesitates, but* DR ROBINSON *is already counting four dollars into* INJUN JOE'S *hand.*

INJUN JOE: *Five.* (DR ROBINSON *adds another dollar.*)

DR ROBINSON: Half-past eleven tonight. And Potter'll be there.

INJUN JOE: He'd better be, 'cause I ain't goin' alone.
    They go their separate ways. DR ROBINSON *exits, but* INJUN JOE *steps aside into the shade when he hears drunken singing off-stage.* MUFF POTTER *enters supported by* HUCK.

HUCK: Come on now, Muff. I'm takin' you home.

MUFF POTTER: Not goin' home. Got a ver' important job to do tonight. I'm goin fishin'. (*Laughs drunkenly.*) Fishin' for dead bodies.

HUCK: *Your* most important job is to get home.

MUFF POTTER: Now, wait a minute, boy. Wait a minute. I gotta present for you, a present for good ol' Huck. (*He fumbles in his pocket and brings out a length of fishing-line.*) A bit of fishin'-line. Catch some fishes for yer pussy-cat.

HUCK (*holding up the cat*): His fishin' days is over, I guess. He won't be catchin' many where he's gone . . . Maybe cookin' a few, though.

MUFF POTTER: Well, keep it all ' same, Huck.

HUCK: Thanks.

MUFF POTTER: You keep a secret too, boy? I'm lookin' for Dr Robinson. C'n you take me to him?

HUCK: You're not sick, are you, Muff? Why d'you want a doctor? (*INJUN JOE steps forward.*) Oh Lord, here's Injun Joe.

INJUN JOE: Shut up, Potter!

MUFF POTTER: Wha' . . .?

   INJUN JOE *slaps his face viciously.*

HUCK: C'mon, Muff, I'll get you home.

INJUN JOE: You get home, boy.

HUCK: But I don' want him to be hurt.

INJUN JOE: You want to watch it isn't you that's gittin' hurt, boy — pokin' your nose into things that don't concern you . . . Now, git.

HUCK: But. . .

INJUN JOE: Git! (*Then, as HUCK stands his ground, he steps to him, grips him by the shoulders and wrenches him round, then, still holding his shoulders, speaks quietly, but with such menace that HUCK shrinks a little.*) Boy . . . I said go home, and I mean *go home.* And keep outa my way — or, so help me, when I'm done with you they'll have to take you home in a wheelbarrow. *Now get goin'.* (*He pushes HUCK violently away. HUCK is about to stand his ground, but thinks better of it and runs.*) Now, you fool, can't you stay off the drink even for one day — this one in particular?

MUFF POTTER: Come, Joe. I ain't really drunk. I only had. . .

INJUN JOE: Not really drunk! You smell like a brew-house! (*He draws his knife and, holding MUFF, puts the point to MUFF's throat.*) Listen . . . I ain't gonna lose my profit on tonight's work for *anyone,* least of all you. You better get sober real quick, or I swear to God I'll use this on you. 'Twouldn't be the first time.

> *He grips* MUFF's *arm and roughly leads him off.* CHILDREN *start to assemble from all sides, all with lunch baskets and dressed in their Sunday best. Much excitement and decorous horse-play. Enter the* MINISTER. *The whole of this episode is used to cover the set-change to Cardiff Hill.*

MINISTER: Come along, children, we don't want to lose any of this beautiful afternoon. It's not every day we have our Sunday School Picnic. Now is everybody here? Stand still while I count. (*He counts, with some difficulty.*) Now where's Willie got to? Has anyone seen Willie? (*Someone squeaks a balloon, as* WILLIE *enters carrying an enormous picnic hamper.*) Well, now, Willie, are you going to eat all that?

WILLIE (*proudly*): Yes, sir, Mr Minister!

MINISTER: You'll be sick.

WILLIE (*proudly*): Yes, sir, Mr Minister!

MINISTER: Well . . . (*With energy*) Well, line up in twos. And shall we all sing our happy little song as we walk along?

ALL: Yes, sir, Mr Minister!

> *The* MINISTER *leads them into the song.*

MUSIC NO. 4 — NATURAL SALVATION

MINISTER and CHILDREN (*sing*):

1. The songs of the birds as they play in the trees,
   The tender refrain of the hard-working bees,
   And we must not forget the melodious breeze,
   As they all sing the praise of our Saviour.

2. The eagle it flies up above in the sky,
   While fish in the ocean swim happily by.
   We love them — they love us — and we all know why:
   It's because we all love our dear Saviour.

22

3. The smallest black beetle, the largest of whales,
   The donkeys and grizzly bears, gophers and snails,
   On the sea or the prairie, o'er hills or in dales,
   All laugh for the love of our Saviour   (*They exit singing.*)

SCENE 2

Cardiff Hill. Enter Tom Sawyer's GANG, *less Tom and Huck.
They are equipped with lath swords and broomstick pistols.
They are plainly expecting Tom.* TOM *bounds on stage.*

BOYS (*challenging*): Blood!

TOM (*excitedly*): More blood! Quick — there's a whole parcel of
   Spanish merchants and rich A-rabs coming up the hill. Get
   your masks on! (*The* GANG *start to tie handkerchiefs over
   their noses and their mouths.*) And there's elephants and
   camels and over a hundred mules, all loaded with di'monds.

JOHNNY: Won't they be too much for us?

TOM: Course not. They haven't got no more than forty guards.
   We'll ambush them, and kill the lot and scoop the di'monds.
   Now, hide — and wait for me to give the signal.
        They hide about the stage. After a moment or two, enter
   HUCK, *without sword, etc., but with dead cat. He looks a bit
   lost.* TOM *whispers urgently from hiding.*

TOM: Blood! (HUCK *looks round, puzzled.* TOM *emerges,
   crouching low.*) Blood!

HUCK: Oh, *there* you are, Tom — if you want me in the gang still.

TOM: BLOOD!

HUCK: Where? (*Examining his face, etc.*)

TOM: No, the *countersign*!

HUCK: Oh — More blood!

TOM: Quick! There's a great caravan of elephants and A-rabs
   coming up the hill. (*He drags* HUCK *into hiding.*)

HUCK (*bobbing up*): Where's the elephants and A-rabs? (*He is suppressed.*)

The Sunday School Song is heard in the distance. Enter the Sunday School crocodile, all very neat and proper. It winds its way round the stage, still singing. The MINISTER *in charge.*

MUSIC NO. 4A – NATURAL SALVATION (*reprise*)
MINISTER and CHILDREN (*sing unaccompanied*):

1. The sun every morning with glorious ray
   And his sister, the moon, turning night into day,
   Both join in the chorus of this round-e-lay
   That we're singing in praise of our Saviour.

2. Oh glorious Nature, we see thee all round,
   And where there is nature, sure God will be found.
   All nature rejoices to hear the glad sound
   Of a song sung in praise of our Saviour.

MINISTER: Now wasn't that nice? Let's sit down, children, shall we? (*He dusts a place, the* CHILDREN *dust their places, and they all sit down.*) That's it. First, I want to say how happy it makes me to see so many bright, clean little faces on our picnic today. There's one thing I want you to remember though, children; and that is, that all the time we're here in the countryside we're surrounded by God's little creatures. So treat them kindly and greet them with a smile. And now it's nearly picnic-time. (*A scramble to open picnic baskets, etc.*) Ah-ah! Grace first! Now close eyes . . . hands together . . . (*He does so, and the* CHILDREN *follow suit.*) For what we are about to receive, may the Lord make us truly thankful.

TOM *yells 'Charge!' and the* GANG *rush out. Chaos* WILLIE *climbs into his hamper for safety and the* MINISTER *tries to shepherd his charges away. The Sunday School party is routed, and the* GANG, *except for* BEN RODGERS, *re-assembles.*
GANG (*variously*): How many did you kill? I killed sixteen. Etc.
TOM: Count up the booty, men. (*They do – a prayer-book, a rag-doll, napkins, various odds and ends.*) How's that for bales

24

of silk and slathers of di'monds! Now let's see what's in the
treasure-chest. (*They open the hamper and discover* WILLIE.)
A spy! (WILLIE *is chased off; then* BEN *appears with a tearful*
LITTLE GIRL.)

BEN (*roughly pushing her forward*): And here's the women!
(*Sobs and wails.*) Dying to fall in love, I guess!

TOM: No, that ain't no way to go on, Ben. You've gotta be polite.
You'll see how they love it. (*To the* GIRL, *with an enormous
bow.*) I sure beg your pardon, ma'am, for this inconvenience
(*more wails*) but . . . but would you do me the honour to
accept this here bullseye? (*Wails.*) It ain't beeen sucked but
only once. (*Devastating yells and stamps.*) . . . Why'd you have
to bring her, Ben?

> The BOYS *gather in a puzzled huddle.*

JOE: What we gonna do? Take her to the cave? (*More wails.*)

BEN: Take her back to her mammy, more like.

TOM: 'Tain't in the books exactly, but . . . (*further wails*) . . .
anyone got five cents? (*Someone has, and* TOM *gives it to the*
LITTLE GIRL.) Take her home, Joe.

JOE: But, Tom. . . .

TOM: Take her home. The Chief commands. (JOE *exits with the*
LITTLE GIRL.) And shift the booty to the cave.

> They all start to move off, but HUCK *lingers.*

HUCK: Tom . . . (TOM *returns.*) Tom, I didn't see no elephants
and A-rabs and things.

TOM: There was loads of them there.

HUCK: Why couldn't we see them then?

TOM: Enchantment, of course. The other side had got magicians,
and they called up some genies to help them.

HUCK: Couldn't *we* have got some genies and licked the other
crowd?

TOM: How you talk! You gotta have a ring to rub or an old tin
lamp. Then thunder and lightning rips around, and the genies
have to do whatever you command. Maybe build a palace forty
miles long, out of di'monds, and fill it full of chewing-gum, or
anything you want.

HUCK: Well, the genies *are* a pack of flat-heads! Why don't they keep the palace for themselves?

TOM: Shucks, it ain't no use to talk to you, Huck Finn. You don't seem to know anything, somehow. You coming to the cave?

HUCK: Well, it's gettin' on for dark, and your Aunt Polly'll be out looking for you soon, and if she has to do that you'll never get away tonight.

TOM: Tonight?

HUCK: You ain't forgotten, have you, Tom? The graveyard? At midnight?

TOM: Oh that? 'Course! Sure! You still got the cat?

HUCK (*holding it up*): Most of it.

TOM: Well, I'll get along home then.

HUCK: And I'll come and miaow outside your window when it's time.

TOM: O.K. I'll be waiting. . . . How'd it go again? (*As they exit*) 'Devil follow corpse, cat follow devil, warts follow. . . .'

MUSIC NO. 5 — CHANGE OF SCENE

SCENE 3

Neglected graveyard. Near midnight. Broken fence, leaning round-topped boards marking graves, a worm-eaten cross or two. Hoss Williams's newly-heaped grave concealing a trap-door or something similar. Faint wind moaning. TOM *and* HUCK *enter,* HUCK *carrying the dead cat. They search about nervously for Hoss Williams's grave, then conceal themselves. Wind. An owl hoots.*

TOM: Hucky, do you reckon the dead people like it for us to be here?

HUCK: I wisht I knowed. It's awful solemn like, ain't it?

TOM: I bet it is. (*Pause.*) Say, Hucky, — do you reckon Hoss Williams hears us talking?

HUCK: O' course he does. Least his spirit does.
  Pause.

TOM: I wish I'd said '*Mister* Williams'.

HUCK: A body can't be too partic'lar how they talk about these yer dead people, Tom.
  Pause. Then faint sounds of men approaching from off-stage.

TOM (*seizing* HUCK's *arm*): Sh!

HUCK: What is it, Tom? (*They cling together, terrified.*)

TOM: Sh! There 'tis again! Didn't you hear it?

HUCK: I. . .

TOM: There! Now you hear it!

HUCK: Lord, Tom, they're coming! They're coming, sure. What'll we do?

TOM: I dunno. Think they'll see us?

HUCK: Oh, Tom, they can see in the dark same as cats. I wish I hadn't come.

TOM: If we keep perfectly still, maybe they won't notice us at all.

HUCK: I'll try to, Tom, but. . .

TOM: Look! See there! What is it?

HUCK: It's devil-fire. Oh, Tom, this is awful!
  Enter DR ROBINSON, INJUN JOE *and* MUFF POTTER.
  The DOCTOR *carries a lantern and* INJUN JOE *and* MUFF
  POTTER *carry a hand-barrow between them, with spades and
  a coil of rope. They stumble uncertainly about the graveyard.*

HUCK: It's devils, sure enough. Three of 'em! Lordy, Tom, we're goners! Can you pray?

TOM: I'll try. (*He shuts his eyes and starts to pray.*)

MUFF POTTER (*stumbling drunkenly*): Damn this ground! Why couldn't we come in the daytime?

INJUN JOE: Fool!

HUCK: Tom, they're *humans*! One of 'em is, anyway. One of
'em's old Muff Potter's voice.

TOM: No — 'tain't so , is it?

HUCK: What'll you bet?

MUFF POTTER: Whoa, there!

HUCK: Still drunk.

INJUN JOE: What you want now? You're making noise enough
to have the whole blame graveyard rising round our ears.

MUFF POTTER: Save us a lot of diggin' if they did. (*He laughs
drunkenly.*)

TOM: It's Injun Joe, with Potter.

HUCK: That's so. I'd ruther they was devils any day.

TOM: And Dr Robinson.

HUCK: What can they be up to?

MUFF POTTER: Sorta resurrection — eh, Doc? (*They have now
reached the grave.*)

DR ROBINSON: Here it is. And we're in luck — it's not been
properly filled in.

    INJUN JOE *and* MUFF POTTER *put down their load.*
MUFF *holds the lantern, while* INJUN JOE *starts to dig.*
DR ROBINSON *crouches down towards one side of the stage,
keeping a wary look-out. After a moment or two. . .*
Come on, hurry up with it, the pair of you! The moon might
come out at any moment, and anyone passing by would see
you plain as daylight.

MUFF POTTER: I'd laugh if the Minister was passing by.
(*Stepping forward and raising his hat.*) Evening, Mr Dobbins,
I guess you'll find the Day of Judgement's got here sooner than
you thought!

DR ROBINSON: And so will you, unless you hurry.

    MUFF POTTER *cuts a knot off the rope and passes it down
to* INJUN JOE. *When it's round the 'coffin'. . .*

INJUN JOE: Now the dern thing's ready, Sawbones. (*Climbing
out of the grave.*) And you'll just out with another five dollars,
or here the coffin stays.

DR ROBINSON (*getting up*): What do you mean?

INJUN JOE (*approaching*): You know what I mean.

MUFF POTTER (*also approaching*): Grave-robbin's a pretty
    serious business.

DR ROBINSON: Now look here, you asked for your money in
    advance, and I've paid you what you. . .

INJUN JOE (*interrupting*): Another five, or the coffin stays
    exactly where it is.

MUFF POTTER: And you can shovel the earth back yourself.

DR ROBINSON: Look, boys, I thought we could trust each other.
    You wouldn't be turning frauds, would you?

INJUN JOE: Cut the humbug! You're fraud enough yourself,
    ain't you? Stealing here at dead of night, with men whose
    hands you'd be ashamed to shake in daylight. Call that fair and
    open? Sure, smile and raise your hat to all the women in the
    town, but will you let 'em smell the earth and corpse-sweat
    stinkin' on your hand?

DR ROBINSON: How else can I get a body to dissect, with the
    damn-fool law as it is? I don't enjoy the role of graveyard
    jackal, I can tell you.

INJUN JOE: D'you think we do?

DR ROBINSON: You're not paid to enjoy it. You're paid to do
    a job of work.

INJUN JOE: *And* break the law.

DR ROBINSON: Since when have you been so dainty about
    breaking the law? If the people in this town have a doctor who
    knows how the human body works, it's because he's not afraid
    to dirty his hands. When I began in St. Petersburg, the only
    remedy a doctor offered was pious words — that and a clutch
    of leeches sucking out your life-blood. D'you want the town to
    slip back to that?

INJUN JOE: I couldn't give a dime if it slipped into the river!
    What doctoring do *I* get outa your corpse-knowledge? Or Muff
    here, or Josh Riley, or that scarecrow kid of Old Finn's. The
    unrespectable ones. Don't we smell sweet enough for you?

MUFF POTTER: We don't smell of money, may be.

INJUN JOE: I didn't notice you handin' out any of your fancy
    cures when I was sick last winter.

DR ROBINSON: Did you come to see me?

INJUN JOE: And be kicked away from the door like a dog? Walked over as if I didn't exist — 'cept when there's dirty work wants doing.

DR ROBINSON: Now, Injun Joe. . .

INJUN JOE (*interrupting*): Injun, Injun, Injun! Never Joe on its own, is it? From any of you! Always shouldered out of my white man's name by 'Injun'. As if you're all ashamed your precious white blood's got mixed with red and I've one of your names to prove it. Think I don't notice? Don't feel? D'you think an Injun's flesh don't bruise and bleed under the lash like anyone else's? And go on aching for revenge? (*Slowly.*) And now you've given me the means to do it. Just one word from me, and the successful Dr Robinson. . .

DR ROBINSON: I could have you jailed any time I want.

INJUN JOE: You already have done. When your father had me jailed and horse whipped for a vagrant ten years ago, who was the kid that told him I was begging at the kitchen-door? Remember? I don't forget. I ain't got Injun blood for nothing. And now the time's arrived to settle.

DR ROBINSON: The settlin'll be at your hanging.

INJUN JOE (*slow, quiet, intense*): The settlin's now.

INJUN JOE *beckons* MUFF *with a slight movement of the head. They advance slowly on* DR ROBINSON, *who retreats.*

DR ROBINSON: You dirty half-breed. . .

INJUN JOE: Yes? (*Deliberately*) Doctor . . . *Whitey* Robinson?

DR ROBINSON *suddenly strikes out at* INJUN JOE *and lays him on the ground.*

MUFF POTTER (*putting down his knife*): Here, now, don't you strike my partner!

POTTER *and* DR ROBINSON *fight.* INJUN JOE *picks up the knife and circles round, waiting for an opening. The* DOCTOR *breaks free, snatches up a spade and fells* MUFF. INJUN JOE *springs and stabs the* DOCTOR, *who collapses.* INJUN JOE *stands over the two forms.*

INJUN JOE: That score's settled, damn you.

INJUN JOE *robs* DR ROBINSON's *body. As he does so,*

TOM *and* HUCK *steal out of the graveyard, terrified, leaving the dead cat behind.* INJUN JOE *puts the knife into* POTTER's *hand, and sits down to wait.* POTTER *comes round, confusedly.*

MUFF POTTER: Lord, what happened, Joe? (*He looks at the body, then discovers the knife in his hand, horrified.*) No, it warn't me, Joe. (*He puts the knife down, and scrambles away in terror.*) That kinda story won't wash. (*He rubs his head, dazed.*) Tell me how it was, Joe. My head's all muddled. I shouldn't ever have taken any drink tonight. It's all the whisky. (*He shakes his head unbelievingly.*) I've never used a weapon in my life before. There's no-one that won't say that. (*He scrambles across to* INJUN JOE *and remains on his knees before him.* INJUN JOE *watches impassively.*) You won't tell, will you, Joe? I've always stood up for you in the past. You remember that? You won't tell, Joe? Say you won't. (*He buries his head in his hands. Pause.*) I'll bless you for that as long as I live.

INJUN JOE *stands.*

INJUN JOE: Come on, now. This ain't the time for hanging around. (MUFF POTTER *gets up.*) You go off one way and I'll go the other. Move, now, and don't leave any tracks behind you. (MUFF *exits.* INJUN JOE *crosses to the grave and picks up the lantern.*) Fool! He's so fuddled with whisky and the knock he took he won't think about his knife, till he's gone so far he'll be too scared to come back. . . . Not here! (*He exits.*)

MUSIC NO. 6 — CHANGE OF SCENE

31

SCENE 4

Night. A broken-down corner of building or fencing next to the town jail. Enter TOM *and* HUCK *out of breath, as if having run non-stop from the graveyard a mile away.*

TOM: Stop now! It'll be safe here. (*They collapse on the ground, panting. Pause.*) Say, Huck, what do you reckon'll come of this?

HUCK: If Dr Robinson dies, I reckon hanging'll come of it.

TOM: Yes, I guess so.

HUCK: I *know* it.
    Pause.

TOM: Who'll tell? Us?

HUCK: What are you talking about? S'pose something happened and Injun Joe didn't hang, why he'd kill *us* some time or other, just as dead sure as we're lying here.

TOM: That's just what I was thinking, Huck.

HUCK: If anybody tells, let Muff Potter do it, if he's fool enough. Or drunk p'raps.
    Pause.

TOM: Huck, Muff Potter don't know what happened. How can he tell?

HUCK: Why's that?

TOM: Because he'd just got that whack when Injun Joe done it, and it laid him right out. D'you reckon he knew *anything* after that?

HUCK: By hokey, that's so, Tom!

TOM: So you and me are the only ones that saw what happened. . . . Us and Injun Joe. (*Pause.*) Hucky, you sure you can keep it to yourself?

HUCK: Tom, we *got* to. You know that. S'pose we squeaked about this thing and they *didn't* hang him, what then? That Injun devil wouldn't make any more of drownding us than . . .

than a couple of kittens. Now, look, Tom, we got to swear to one another — that's what — swear to one another never to say a word.

TOM: I'm agreed, Huck. We'll swear an oath.

HUCK: There orter be writing 'bout a big thing like this.

TOM: And blood.

>TOM *finds a crumpled piece of paper in his pocket and a stub of pencil.* HUCK *looks over his shoulder as he writes.*

TOM: 'Huck Finn and Tom Sawyer swears they will keep their lips sealed about this and wish they may drop down dead in their tracks if they ever tell and rot.'

HUCK: I've got a pin.

>HUCK *takes a pin from his jacket and they prick the balls of their thumbs. Much squeezing needed to produce the blood.*

TOM (*signing*): T . . . S . . . Now you.

HUCK: I . . .

TOM: Look, like this. . . . H . . . F . . . (TOM *shows* HUCK *how to make the letters.*) Now. (TOM *folds up the paper and hides it in the woodwork, while* HUCK *shyly, proudly, traces out his initials again on the box.*) It's hidden now.

TOM and HUCK: Barley-corn, barley-corn, hid in the ground,
Blood-oath secret, never be found.

>*They spit in each other's palms, then shake hands solemnly. In the distance is heard the sound of the* TOWNSFOLK, *in lynching mood, drawing nearer and nearer.* TOM *and* HUCK *peer out. They speak above the introduction to the song.*

HUCK: It's Muff they've got, not Injun Joe! Tom, Tom, don't you see what's happened? *They reckon Muff Potter did it!*

TOM: Oh lordy!

HUCK: Does the oath keep us from telling — always?

TOM: Of course it does. We'd drop down dead if we ever said a word.

HUCK: Oh *lordy!*

>*They watch appalled as* MUFF *is dragged onstage. The* TOWNSFOLK *have pitchforks, a rope, sticks and guns, lanterns and torches.*

MUSIC NO. 7 — HANG HIM, HANG HIM!

TOWNSFOLK (*sing*):

1. Why don't we lynch him?
   Lynch him for murder!
   Get a rope, string him up to the nearest tree —
   Hangin's too good for him!
   Let's see him dancin',
   Dancin' on air!
   Let him die the death, swingin' high.
   Hang him, hang him, *etc.*
       (POTTER *is manhandled by the mob.*)

2. Don't waste time, hang him!
   Yes, hang him now!
   Have some fun, see some old-fashioned justice done,
   Make a bad end of him.
   Bind him and mount him,
   Mount him on horse-back.
   Whack its rump, and then watch him jump.
   Hang him, hang him, *etc.*
          (*Law Officers intervene to secure* POTTER.)

3. Don't want no court-room,
   We're judge and jury.
   Law's O.K., but we've got us a better way
   Set up for such as him.
   Rope is our sentence,
   Sentenced to hang.
   Knot it well, send him off to hell.
   Hang him, hang him, *etc.*
       (POTTER *is flung into jail at the climax of the song, and
       reviled. Resentfully the mob turns to leave,* TOM *and*
       HUCK *with them.*)

4. Why don't we lynch him?
   Lynch him for murder!
   Get a rope, string him up to the nearest tree —
   Hangin's too good for him!
   Let's see him dancin',

34

Dancin' on air!
Let him die the death, swingin' high.
Hang him for murder . . . ad lib.

The TOWNSFOLK *leave and the singing fades into the
distance.* MUFF *is left sitting terrified and despairing in the
jail, picked out by a single spot. He is alone. The spot fades.
Then dawn breaks and the lights come up.* CHILDREN *laugh
and shriek tauntingly round the jail, then exit.* HUCK *and*
TOM *enter and approach the jail cautiously.*

TOM: Muff . . . Hey, Muff. . . .

MUFF (*looking out*): Hello, Tom . . . Huckleberry.

HUCK: We got a bit of tobacco for you, Muff.

TOM: And some matches. (*They pass them through the bars.*)

MUFF POTTER: You're mighty good to me, boys. I've been
saying to myself, 'I used to mend all the boys' kites and things,
and show 'em where the good fishin' places was . . . and now
they've all forgot old Muff when he's in trouble.' But Tom
don't, and Huck don't — *they* don't forget him. Well, boys, I
done an awful thing, and now I got to swing for it, and it's
right . . . Leastways, I hope so, anyway. . . .

TOM: Muff, are you sure you really. . .?

MUFF POTTER: Well, we won't talk about that. I don't want
to make *you* feel bad. But I will say this: don't *you* ever get
drunk, then you won't ever get here.

HUCK: We just thought. . . .

MUFF POTTER: Now stand a little over there. (*They move.*)
That's it. It's a prime comfort to see a couple of friendly faces
when a feller's in such a muck of trouble. Come here now, and
shake hands. That's it. Your hands'll come through the bars,
but mine are too big. (*They shake.*) You hands are only little
and weak — but they've helped Muff Potter a power, and
they'd help him more if they could, I know. (*They move
guiltily away from the jail.*) Goodbye, boys.

TOM and HUCK: Goodbye, Muff.

TOM (*awkwardly after a pause*): Huck, d'you reckon we should
tell?

HUCK: Tell? We shouldn't be alive two days if that got found out. *You* know that.

TOM: I know, but . . . I wish we could get him out of there.

HUCK: My! We couldn't get him out, Tom.

TOM: You're right, of course. All the same, I hate to hear folks calling him the bloodiest-looking villain in all the county, when he never done — that.

HUCK (*nods, then. . .*): He ain't ever done anything to hurt anyone. Just fishes a little to get money to get drunk on — and loafs considerable. But everybody does that — preachers and suchlike. He give me half a fish once, when there wasn't enough for two. And lots of times he's kinda stood by me when I was out of luck. (TOM *nods.*) I reckon he's a goner now.

TOM (*cautiously*): Huck, they couldn't anyone *get* you to tell, could they?

HUCK: 'Course not. Hain't I said so?

TOM: No, it's not that . . . it's just that . . . Oh, I don't know!
He runs off. HUCK *follows, puzzled.*

SCENE 5

Two weeks later. The Courtroom — with bench, dock and witness-stand, but so overflowing with spectators that it is not clear where the jury-box, if any, ends and the public begin.
CLERK, PROSECUTING ATTORNEY, DEFENCE ATTORNEY; TOM *and* HUCK. *The court is reassembling after the lunch-hour recess. As the courtroom is set up, the* CROWD *pours across the front of the stage talking excitedly. Enter* AUNT POLLY *and* MRS RODGERS.

AUNT POLLY: Well, I hope we'll be luckier this afternoon and get a seat near the front.

MRS RODGERS: I thought I would have been early enough this morning, but simply everybody seemed to be here.

BOTH (*meeting* MRS HARPER): Afternoon, Mrs Harper. Sarah.

MRS HARPER: Afternoon. Seems to be more people here than ever

AUNT POLLY: Mrs Rodgers and I was just saying. . . .

MRS RODGERS: Did you see the way Muff Potter looked this morning?

MRS HARPER: All kinda dazed.

AUNT POLLY: I couldn't help feeling kinda sorry for him, weighed down with all those chains. And that defence lawyer not putting up any sort of fight for him at all. It's a positive shame, I'm sure.

MINISTER: It's a judgement, Miss Watson; *His* hand is here.

PASSING MAN: Besides, ma'am, it ain't much good being a defence lawyer if you haven't got any defence to offer. And Muff did the killing all right. He confessed as much himself.

AUNT POLLY (*as they pass on into the court*): Well, I don't know. I think he ought at least to try. . . .

> MUFF POTTER *brought in. Buzz of conversation swells up.* JUDGE THATCHER *enters and the* CLERK *calls for everyone to stand. The* JUDGE *sits; everybody sits.*

JUDGE: The hearing is resumed.

CLERK: The prosecution will continue its case.

PROSECUTION (*rising*): Your honour, gentlemen of the jury. . . . This morning you heard testified in this court a number of highly suspicious circumstances relating to the accused. Let me remind you . . . of how, when the body of Dr Robinson was found stabbed in the graveyard, the accused was discovered washing in the brook at a very peculiar hour and how he immediately sneaked away when seen; of how the knife there on the table was found next to the body of Dr Robinson; and of how this same knife had often been seen in the possession of the accused. These are *facts*, your honour, all testified to by sundry worthy citizens of this town. To complete the case for the prosecution, we have just two more witnesses to call, gentlemen of the jury.

JUDGE: Proceed.

CLERK: Call Henry Bartholomew Rodgers. (MR RODGERS *takes the stand.*) Repeat the oath.

MR RODGERS: I swear by Almighty God to tell the truth, the whole truth and nothing but the truth.

PROSECUTION: Henry Bartholomew Rodgers, storekeeper in this town. . .

MR RODGERS: Yes, sir.

PROSECUTION: Were you one of the crowd that went up to the graveyard when news was brought of the discovery of Dr Robinson's body?

MR RODGERS: That's right, sir.

PROSECUTION: And did you see the accused there at that time?

MR RODGERS: Yes, sir. He was brought there by the Sheriff.

PROSECUTION: Now will you describe to this court how the accused looked when the Sheriff brought him forward?

MR RODGERS: He was pale and kinda fearful. And shaking. And when the Sheriff asked him if that was his knife, he collapsed and would have fallen right over if one or two hadn't been holding him up.

PROSECUTION: And what, if anything, did you hear him say at this point?

MR RODGERS: Well, Injun Joe was there, and he said to Injun Joe. . .

PROSECUTION: As exactly as you can recall it.

MR RODGERS: He said, 'Tell 'em, Joe, tell 'em — it ain't no use any more.' (*The court erupts and the* JUDGE *bangs for silence.*) And then Injun Joe said. . . .

PROSECUTION: Thank you, Mr Rodgers. (*To* DEFENCE) Take the witness.

DEFENCE: I have no questions to ask him.

    Disappointed buzz. MR RODGERS *retires.*

1ST CITIZEN: Ain't he even goin' to *try* to defend him?

2ND CITIZEN: Hasn't asked a single question yet.

3RD CITIZEN: If he doesn't say something soon, poor Muff's as good as hanged already.

CLERK: Call Injun Joe. (INJUN JOE *takes the stand.*) Repeat the oath.

INJUN JOE: I swear by Almighty God to tell the truth, the whole truth and nothing but the truth. (TOM *glances at* HUCK.)

PROSECUTION: Is your name Injun Joe?

INJUN JOE: Yes, sir.

JUDGE: Is that the witness's real name?

INJUN JOE: That's the name everybody thinks fit to call me by, your honour, and I don't reckon I've ever known any other.

JUDGE: Proceed.

PROSECUTION: This court has just heard that, on the morning in question, after people had assembled in the graveyard to view the body of Dr Robinson, the accused turned to you and said, 'Tell 'em, Joe, tell 'em.' Will you now tell this court as clearly as you can what you then said?

INJUN JOE: I told them what happened in the graveyard in the early hours of that morning, when I'd gone there with Dr Robinson and Muff Potter. (*Buzz.*)

PROSECUTION: And that was. . . ?

INJUN JOE: That Dr Robinson and the accused got in a fight on account of some money. They was pitching into one another pretty fiercely for a while. Then Potter grabbed up his knife and . . . jammed it into Dr Robinson.

MUFF POTTER (*protesting*): But, Injun Joe, you said. . .

INJUN JOE (*interrupting, cold and hard*): I saw that clearly.

PROSECUTION: And the spade. . . ?

INJUN JOE: Oh, yeah. It was at that moment that the Doc hit Potter with a spade, and knocked him out. Right out, I guess. I was too scared to stay longer after that.

MUFF POTTER (*inarticulately*): He's lying.

PROSECUTION: Thank you. That's all. (*To the* DEFENCE) Take the witness.

MUFF POTTER (*trying to attract the* DEFENCE's *attention*): You gotta help me!

DEFENCE: I have no questions to ask him.

Angry outburst from the spectators. INJUN JOE *steps down, and* MUFF POTTER *sits down in despair.*

SPECTATORS (*variously*): Whose side are you on? Call yourself
   a lawyer? etc.

   Fists are shaken, and only after prolonged banging can the
   JUDGE *make himself heard.*

JUDGE: If another outburst of that sort occurs, I shall clear the
   court. Defence Counsellor is an able and experienced lawyer,
   who is doing his best for his client — and you're not making it
   any easier for him.

   Abashed rumbling, but ultimately silence.

PROSECUTION: That concludes the case for the prosecution,
   your honour. After the testimony of the last witness no
   question can remain in anybody's mind. By the oaths of
   citizens whose simple word is above suspicion, we have
   fastened this awful crime beyond all possibility of doubt upon
   the unhappy prisoner in the deck. 'Tell 'em, Joe, tell 'em,' he
   said. And we have heard now what there was to tell. We rest
   our case here.

   He sits. The DEFENCE ATTORNEY *rises, to some
   resentful murmuring.*

DEFENCE: Your honour — in our remarks at the opening of this
   trial, we outlined our purpose to prove that our client did this
   fearful deed while under the influence of a blind and
   irresponsible delirium produced by drink. We have changed our
   mind. (*Buzz.*) We shall not offer that plea. (*To the* CLERK)
   Call Thomas Sawyer. (*Amazement.*)

CLERK: Thomas Sawyer.

   TOM *goes into the box fearfully, amidst a general hubbub,
   from which arise the* PROSECUTION'*s objections. Uproar.
   Silence restored with difficulty.*

PROSECUTION: Your honour, YOUR HONOUR . . . I must
   object to the introduction of this witness. The Prosecution has
   received no notice that he was going to be called.

JUDGE: Well, Mr Defence-Lawyer?

DEFENCE: Your honour, it's true no notice has been given, but
   this witness has only this morning come forward. In any case,
   I never heard of a case where a defendant couldn't call *any*
   witness to prove his innocence.

JUDGE: Objection over-ruled. Proceed.

CLERK: Do you, Thomas Sawyer, swear by Almighty God to tell the truth, the whole truth and nothing but the truth?

PROSECUTION: Your honour, how can the Court expect to hear the truth from someone such as this young man, this . . . youth, this . . . boy, this . . . whipper-snapper?

AUNT POLLY (*angrily from the body of the court*): That ain't so. He's a boy alright, but he ain't no whipper — no, nor yet no snapper either.

JUDGE: Are you the boy's mother, ma'am?

AUNT POLLY (*stands*): Well, in a manner of speaking, your honour. I'm his mother's sister, and I've brought him up since his mother and father were taken to an early rest — God rest their dear souls.

JUDGE: And is he a truthful lad? Does he know the meaning of the oath?

AUNT POLLY: Indeed he does.

PROSECUTION: And never goes telling long, romancing tales, like all boys of his age?

AUNT POLLY (*hesitating, torn between the truth and her desire to defend* TOM): Well . . . I wouldn't say . . . I . . . Oh dear, I . . . (*She is very near to tears.*)

PROSECUTION (*quietly*): Your honour, when even the boy's own aunt can't vouch for his honesty. . .

JUDGE: Mr Prosecutor! (*Kindly, slowly*) Ma'am, is your boy truthful?

AUNT POLLY: Well, your honour, I ain't saying he never tells a lie. If he's played hookey from school, or snitched some cookies from the jar, or tormented the cat — well, he'll wriggle out of it any way he can. But (*as the realization dawns on her for the first time*) he ain't ever told me a lie over a *big* thing — not even . . . no, not even if it meant he'd be in trouble for telling the truth. He ain't a bad boy, your honour. Like I said, he's just . . . just a boy.

JUDGE: Would you swear to what you've just said, ma'am?

AUNT POLLY: Your honour, I wouldn't trust my Tom with a

pot of strawberry jam, but I reckon I'd trust him with my life! I'll swear to that if you want me to.

JUDGE: Then that's good enough for me. (AUNT POLLY *sits.*) Let the witness take the oath.

CLERK: Do you swear by Almighty God to tell the truth, the whole truth and nothing but the truth?

TOM: I do.

JUDGE: Now listen, my boy. Your aunt's a fine woman to stand up for you in that way.

TOM: Yes, sir.

JUDGE: And you ain't going to let her down by saying *anything* but what's true?

TOM: No, sir.

JUDGE: No matter what it costs?

TOM *looks at* INJUN JOE, *who looks piercingly at* TOM. TOM *is visibly affected and, turning to the* JUDGE, *says, 'No matter. . .', but his voice cracks. Then, after a pause in which he droops and looks down, squaring his shoulders, he lifts his head and says quietly, but firmly and clearly. . .*

TOM: No matter what it costs.

DEFENCE: Now, Thomas, where were you on the seventeenth of June, about the hour of midnight?

TOM (*glances at* INJUN JOE *and falters, then. . .*): In the graveyard. (*Buzz.*)

DEFENCE: A little louder, please. Don't be afraid. You were. . .

TOM: In the graveyard.

DEFENCE: Were you anywhere near Horse Williams's grave?

TOM: Yes, sir.

JUDGE: Speak up just a trifle louder.

DEFENCE: How near were you?

TOM: Near as I am to you.

DEFENCE: Were you hidden or not?

TOM: I was hidden behind one of the head-boards near Hoss Williams's grave

DEFENCE: Anyone with you? (HUCK *is petrified.*)

TOM (*glancing at* HUCK): Yes, sir. I went there with. . .

DEFENCE (*interrupting*): Wait . . . Never mind mentioning your companion's name. (HUCK *relieved.*) We will produce him at the proper time. (HUCK *petrified again.*) Did you carry anything there with you?

TOM *hesitates, then looks confused.*

JUDGE: Speak out, my boy. Don't be diffident. The truth is always respectable.

TOM: Only a . . . a . . . dead cat.

Ripple of amusement. THE PROSECUTING ATTORNEY *springs to his feet.*

PROSECUTION: Your honour, this is absurd! Can the jury really believe that this boy was in the graveyard at midnight, giving (*heavily sarcastic*) Christian burial to . . . a *dead cat*? (*Loud laughter.*)

DEFENCE (*triumphant*): We will produce the skeleton of that cat! Now, tell us everything that occurred. Tell it in your own way. Don't skip anything, and don't be afraid, my boy.

TOM: Well, sir, we hadn't been there long when we saw three others coming, three men. They was Dr Robinson, Muff Potter and . . . Injun Joe. I reckon. . .

PROSECUTION (*interrupting*): He reckons! He reckons!! Your honour, I object to this — I won't call it evidence — this farrago, this catalogue of nonsense. (*Viciously.*) He reckons indeed! He can see in the dark, can he?

TOM *wilts under this attack and glances appealingly at* DEFENCE *and the* JUDGE.

DEFENCE: Your honour, is my witness to be allowed to testify without bullying and interference, or is he not?

PROSECUTION: Any witness who tells such fairy-stories *deserves* to be bullied! What this boy is saying . . . (TOM *near to tears now.*)

JUDGE: Mr Prosecutor, sit down.

PROSECUTOR: But, your honour. . . .

JUDGE: SIT DOWN, SIR! Or shall I commit you for contempt of court? (PROSECUTION *reluctantly sits. The* JUDGE's *voice becomes kindly.*) Now, boy. What did you do when you saw these men coming?

TOM: Hid, sir.

JUDGE: Where?

TOM: Behind some bushes and head-boards, sir.

JUDGE: Well, you can't see through a head-board. Could you see through the bush?

TOM: Not very well at first, sir, but when they drew near. . .

JUDGE: How near?

TOM: Near as I am to you, sir. Well, then we could see pretty good.

JUDGE: But it was dark, wasn't it?

TOM: Not what you'd call *real* dark, sir. The moon had come up, an' you could see clear enough to recognize folks.

JUDGE: That seems to clear the matter up. Proceed. (*Nods to* DEFENCE.)

DEFENCE: And you plainly saw Injun Joe with the Doctor and Muff Potter?

TOM: Plain as the wart on your nose, sir . . . I mean . . . yes, sir.

DEFENCE: Then proceed, my boy, and tell us in your own words what you saw — (*glaring at* PROSECUTION) I trust without further interruption!

TOM: Well, Injun Joe and Muff Potter started digging out the grave. They were just about to haul up the coffin, when a fight broke out. About some money, I think it was. The Doctor knocked down Injun Joe, then Muff Potter goes for Dr Robinson. Dr Robinson strikes out with a spade and catches Muff a pretty heavy blow that knocks him down. But, at that moment, just when everything looked over, up springs Injun Joe, holding a knife, and. . .

INJUN JOE: Liar!

He springs for TOM, *struggling with the* DEFENCE ATTORNEY, *who blocks his way. Screams, shouts. Chaos.* INJUN JOE *draws back. Several* MEN *advance towards him. He draws a knife to hold them at bay, but is disarmed from behind after a struggle. The* MEN *advance again. He looks round*

44

desperately, cornered, then picks up a chair and throws it at the MEN. *Chaos, as he leaps out of the courtroom.*

CURTAIN

MUSIC NO. 8 — END OF ACT ONE

ACT TWO

SCENE 1

Two weeks or so later. Some out-of-the-way corner of the town. A broken-down fence, boxes. GIRLS *and a few* BOYS *are playing at Sunday School, including* JOE HARPER, SID *and* JOHNNY MILLER. *One boy is imitating the Minister and is leading the children in a parody version of the Sunday School Song as the curtain rises.*

MUSIC NO. 9 — NATURAL SALVATION (*reprise*)
CHILDREN (*sing unaccompanied*):
1. The songs of the birds making hay in the trees,
   The tender refrain as they twitter and sneeze,
   And we must not forget the melodious cheese,
   As it chirps a sad song for Old Dobbins.

2. The elephant flies up above in the sky,
   While a fat stick of rhubarb swims happily by.
   We love it — with custard. . . .
   TOM, HUCK *and the rest of the* GANG *rush on.*
TOM: Has anyone seen Joe, or Johnny Miller? (*They identify themselves.*) Hey, d'you know what? There's been another robbery. Old Man Rodgers's shop.
BEN: 'Sright — two hundred dollars or more. Got in through the window.
JOHNNY: That's the third in two weeks.

46

BEN: They've gotta catch him soon.

SID: Criminals always make mistakes.

JEFF: And then there'll be a trial.

DAVE: Just like Muff Potter's.

BEN (*the lawyer, to* HUCK): Now, sir, do you recognize this alibi?

HUCK: Yes, your honour, I lost it last Monday.

JEFF: Silence in court! (*He bonks* HUCK *on the head with a mallet.*)

JOE: Hey! Muff Potter's trial!

TOM: Not again. Pirates is better. (*Loud preference from the others for the trial.*) Well, count me out, then.

JOHNNY: Then can I be Tom?

> *They quickly rearrange themselves and start.* JEFF THATCHER *plays the Judge,* JOE HARPER *Muff Potter,* HUCK *Injun Joe,* BEN RODGERS *Defence Attorney,* DAVE RICHARDS *Prosecuting Attorney, and* JOHNNY MILLER *Tom.* TOM *sits to one side, and* SID *hangs about on the fringe. It is a rowdy, melodramatic travesty of the original.*

BEN: And where were *you*, Thomas Sawyer, on the seventeenth of June, at the dreaded hour of midnight?

JOHNNY (*melodramatically*): In . . . the graveyard, your honour.

> *Gasps and shouts from the* CHILDREN. JEFF *bangs for silence with his mallet.*

BEN: Were you . . . *alone*?

JEFF: Don't be different, my boy. The truth is always detectable.

JOHNNY: You've come in too soon. You've got to give me a chance to be silent first.

BEN: Your honour, I beg to suggest that you're . . . just an old flat-head!

JEFF (*furiously*): Ben Rodgers, we'll settle that one out of court. And I'll black your eye! Proceed.

BEN: What did you take to the graveyard?

JOHNNY: A dead cat, your honour.

DAVE: Your honour, I . . . am . . . objectionable! I never heard such *tom*-foolery. (*He smirks.*) A *dead cat?* (*Jeers and whistles from the crowd.*)

BEN (*cutting across the noise magnificently*). We will produce the skeleton of that cat! Now, boy, tell us in your own words just what happened.

JOHNNY: Well, after Huck and me got there with the dead cat. . .

BEN (*repeat performance*): We will produce the skeleton of that cat!

> *Jeers, during which* INJUN JOE *enters. He is disguised as an old Spaniard, apparently blind and dumb. He stands listening.*

JOHNNY: . . . we saw these three men approaching. They was Muff Potter, Old Sawbones and (*gesturing dramatically*) . . . Injun Joe. (HUCK *snarls.*) And just when Muff and Injun Joe was about to lift the corpse from its gruesome coffin, they turned on Dr Robinson. 'Give us another dollar, you mean old Frankenstein!' says Injun Joe. 'Not if I can help it!' says he. Just then, the moon came out from behind a cloud, and with a snarl Injun Joe. . .

> *With a snarl* HUCK *leaps forward and grabs a wood dagger. Screams.*

HUCK (*brandishing the dagger*): Just you wait, Tom Sawyer! I will be revenged!

> HUCK *snarls, and leaps away to the accompaniment of shouts and screams. He runs almost into the arms of* INJUN JOE, *and freezes. The other children see what has happened and the shouts die. The children shrink away from the sinister figure of the blind and dumb Spaniard. Most exit.* TOM *hides and* HUCK *stands petrified, as* INJUN JOE *taps his way off-stage.*

TOM (*emerging from hiding*): Huck, *that* was close!

HUCK: My heart most jumped out of my mouth when I saw the Spaniard standing there.

TOM: Who *is* he? No-one seems to know.

HUCK: Been hanging round the town for a week now. He's dumb as well as blind, folks say. He's up to something, Tom.

TOM: Scares me — almost as much as when I think 'bout Injun Joe. It's all right in the daytime, but. . .

HUCK: Same with me, Tom.

TOM: . . . but at night I keep thinking I can hear Injun Joe come creeping up the stairs to cut my throat. Leastways, that's the way it seems. I wish they'd hurry up and capture him.

HUCK: I don't ever want to lay eyes on him again.

TOM: I reckon I ain't ever going to draw another safe breath until I've seen him — dead.

HUCK: Well, you didn't have to.

TOM: What?

HUCK: Let on we was in the graveyard.

TOM: But, Huck, if. . . .

HUCK: We swore an oath, didn't we?

TOM: Look. . .

HUCK: And signed it in blood, and swore never to tell, and then you went and let on, told it all in public, and Injun Joe's just biding his time now somewhere, waiting to murder us.

TOM: Don't, Huck. Don't talk like that! Every night I wish I'd never said a word, but when I see Muff Potter next morning, free and happy and so grateful, we just couldn't have 'lowed him to be hanged and let that murderin' half-breed go free.

HUCK: Well. . . . p'raps not. But (*sighs*) life ain't . . . easy, any more.

TOM: No.

HUCK: I can't just sit and smoke, or go for a swim like I used to, without worrying.

TOM: I wish I could go right away . . . and become a hermit, or a clown. Or run away to sea and dig up treasure.

HUCK: Pap used to say there was treasure buried somewhere hereabouts.

TOM: Where?

HUCK: He never said. And I wouldn't take much stock in what my Pap said, anyway. He was almost always drunk.

TOM: Let's look for it this afternoon.

HUCK: But where?

TOM: Well, it's usually buried underneath a blasted oak, or near a haunted house. Every haunted house has treasure buried somewhere, and a ghost to guard it.

HUCK: You mean our haunted house has got a load of treasure too?

TOM: Sure! All we gotta do is dig. Can you get a spade?

HUCK: I reckon so.

TOM: We'll go this afternoon, then. See you up on Cardiff Hill.

HUCK: O.K. (*Exit* HUCK.)

MUSIC NO. 10 — TOM'S SONG

TOM (*sings*):

1. Sometimes when life gets on top of me, and
   It ain't easy no more,
   I've got a system to take things in hand,
   Makes 'em better for sure.
   I become
   In imagination most anything,
   Like a highwayman or maybe a king —
   Cares just vanish in a minute.

2. First I'm a pirate, a brave buccaneer,
   Fearsome, bearded and bold.
   Treasure-ship captains who see me appear
   Feel their blood running cold.
   There I am,
   Scourge and terror of the whole Seven Seas,
   Stolen gold and silver up to my knees.
   Hooray for the Jolly Roger!

3. Then I'm a clown in a big circus ring,
   Grease-paint, red nose and all,
   And though there's lions and everything
   Major attraction is me.
   See the crowd!
   Hear 'em swear that I'm the funniest sight,
   Watching me until they laugh with delight —
   I'm the centre of attraction.

4. So, when I'm lonely, unhappy and down,
   This is just what I do.

Soldier, highwayman or pirate or clown
Always will see me through.
So I bet,
Now you've heard my scheme for clearing the blues,
You all wish you could step into my shoes —
Don't you now? Come on, be honest!
Exit TOM, *as* AUNT POLLY *hurries on, followed by* SID.

AUNT POLLY: Now where did you say he was?

SID: About here, aunt.

AUNT POLLY: With Huckleberry Finn?

SID: That's right, Aunt Polly.

AUNT POLLY: If I've told him once, I've told him a hundred times. . . . (*Enter the* MINISTER.) Oh, Mr Dobbins, have you seen my Tom anywhere?

MINISTER: No, Miss Watson. I was just on my way to have a word with you about Tom myself. We missed him from Sunday School yesterday, and a little bird tells me he was down by the river fishing.

AUNT POLLY: I've a notion to skin that boy alive! I saw him off to Sunday School sure enough.

MINISTER: And I fear I must mention another distressing circumstance. Our annual Sunday School Picnic, Miss Watson, was attacked. The dear little boys and girls and I were enjoying the beauties of Nature, when we were rudely set upon by a group of rough and raucous boys, and. . .

AUNT POLLY: It wasn't Tom?

MINISTER: I am sorry to say it was, Miss Watson.

AUNT POLLY: Now, Sid, just go and find that boy at once and bring him here. Sure as he's born. . . .

SID (*with pleasure*): Yes, Aunt Polly! (*On his way out, he meets* MRS RODGERS *and* MRS HARPER *hurrying in. He lingers.*)

MRS RODGERS: Oh, there you are, Miss Watson — Good morning, Mr Dobbins — I hope you won't be offended, but. . .

MRS HARPER: It's Tom.

MRS RODGERS: Playing at Muff Potter's trial. Over and over every day.

MRS HARPER: And making all the rest join in.

MRS RODGERS: I just shudder to think what's happening to my Ben.

AUNT POLLY: How can you be sure?

MRS RODGERS: I wouldn't have told you if I hadn't seen it with my own two eyes.

SID: It's true, Aunt Polly.

MRS HARPER: He has them gloating over all the dreadful details.

MINISTER: Most sordid and unnatural!

MRS RODGERS: The knife and all the blood. . .

MRS HARPER: And digging up that coffin. . .

MRS RODGERS: And the corpse. . .

MRS HARPER: We can scarcely bear to think about it.

MRS RODGERS: . . . lying ghastly in the moonlight.

MRS HARPER: Talking 'bout such matters ain't right for young folks.

AUNT POLLY: Nor for grown ones neither.

MRS HARPER: And it's got to stop before your Tom has led them all astray.

AUNT POLLY: I know Tom ain't no angel. . .

MINISTER: He might be if he came to Sunday School more often, ma'am.

AUNT POLLY: . . . but he ain't no devil either. Goodness knows, he saved Muff Potter's life.

MRS RODGERS: *And* won't let anyone forget it.

AUNT POLLY: Now, Ethel Rodgers, how can you say such meanness? (*Enter* TOM *with a spade. He starts to back out when he sees everybody.*) It ain't easy for a boy. . .

SID: There he is, aunt!

AUNT POLLY: Tom.

TOM: I'm just going.

AUNT POLLY: Thomas Sawyer, come here to me. (*He does so.*) Now, Tom, look at me. I want to hear you say it just ain't true what Mr Dobbins here was telling me.

MRS HARPER: Play-acting that trial.

AUNT POLLY: Don't crowd him, Sarah Harper. Now, Tom, I

know you'll tell the truth to me. It's like the Judge said at the trial: the truth is always respectable. Now let me hear you say it. You weren't amongst the boys who attacked the Sunday School Picnic three-four weeks ago . . . were you?

TOM (*reluctantly*): Yes, aunt.

AUNT POLLY: Oh Tom, Tom, you seem to try every way you can to break my old heart with your outrageousness. Why did you do it?

TOM: We was only playing a game, aunt. Me and Joe Harper and. . .

SID: Huck Finn.

AUNT POLLY: *Huckleberry Finn*! Tom Sawyer! (*She boxes his ear.* SID *sniggers, and she boxes* SID's *ear.*) And that's for you, sir, for telling! Tom, I will not have you playing with that boy. Where he is there's trouble. It was him that got you into that graveyard mess. He's dirty, lazy, wicked. . .

MRS HARPER: And he smokes!

MINISTER: The Devil finds work for idle hands.

MRS RODGERS: It's true.

MRS HARPER: Indeed.

MRS RODGERS: It's just what you'd expect. He's got no home.

MRS HARPER: And sleeps in a barrel.

AUNT POLLY: With no-one to see he goes to school.

MINISTER: Or church.

MRS RODGERS: He'll end up just like his father.

AUNT POLLY: It was him that put you up to that attack.

MRS RODGERS: It's just the sort of thing he'd do.

MRS HARPER: Getting up a violent gang. . .

MINISTER: Frightening innocents. . .

MRS RODGERS: Giving them nightmares. . .

MRS HARPER: Making them cry. . .

AUNT POLLY: It's got Huckleberry Finn written all over it.

TOM (*shouting*): It wasn't Huck! It was *my* gang. And Huck was only in it 'cos I wanted him.

AUNT POLLY: You wanted him! (*She subsides on to a box.*)

TOM: Yes. *That's* the truth. There's nothing wrong with Huck,

however much you carry on. I'm seeing him again this
afternoon . . . and I'm not coming back! (*Exit* TOM.)
AUNT POLLY: Tom!

MUSIC NO. 11 – RIP-RAPSCALLION
AUNT POLLY & OTHERS* (*sing*):

1. Well, did you hear that? (Yes we did, yes we did.)
   Was that my Tom I heard speakin'?
   I just can't credit it was really him as said it —
   Why, he's justa kinda low-down, high-falutin,
   Under-handed, badly-mannered,
   Rip-rapscallion boy — yes, he surely is!

2. Why, he plays such tricks (Yes he does, yes he does.)
   He sets my head all a-reelin'.
   And I do declare I've had more than I can bear,
   When he tries those cunnin' little, round-the-houses,
   Monkey-artful, foxy-minded,
   Plain mischievous pranks, all the live-long day.

3. Why, this town ain't safe (No it ain't, no it ain't.),
   This town ain't safe from his nonsense.
   He's here and there and he's ev'ry-kinda-where,
   With a head full of rip-rapper, fire-cracker,
   Merry-weather, now-or-never,
   Penny-dreadful schemes, always going wrong.

4. Well, it just ain't right! (No it ain't, no it ain't.)
   Ain't gonna stand it no longer!
   He's a slipp'ry eel, but I'll lay him by the heel.
   When I catch him, I'll hog-tie him, hornswoggle,
   Double-wallop, tan his backside,
   Pack him off to bed, till he mends his ways.

5. Now I heard him say (Yesterday, yesterday.)
   That he don't like church on a Sunday.

*All the TOWNSFOLK can join in this song, if wished.

54

And you know in school that he always plays the fool,
Till the class is grass-hopper, gob-stopper,
Natter-natter, what's-the-matter —
Who's the culprit? Bend over, touch your toes!

6. If he had a Pa (If he did, if he did.),
Then it might be a diff'rent story.
But it's hard for me to be all that I should be —
Oh, he'll turn out a hellion, a whipper-snapper,
Artful dodger, jolly-roger
Box-of-monkeys — sure, and he'll land in jail!
Enter MR RODGERS.

MR RODGERS: Was that Tom I just saw running out of the back?
AUNT POLLY: What's the matter now?
MR RODGERS: He's run off with my spade.
SID: The truth is always respectable!
Outraged chatter, as all exit.

MUSIC 11A — CHANGE OF SCENE

SCENE 2

*The Haunted House that evening, about sunset. Dusty, derelict.
A rickety staircase, a broken chair and a box with a lantern.
Silence. Pause.* TOM *and* HUCK *are heard approaching and
enter with spade and pick. They look round circumspectly.
Both are weary.*

HUCK: D'you reckon treasure's always as hard to find as this?
TOM: All the best sort is. Gold and di'monds just don't lie around
for folks to stub their toes against.
HUCK (*lighting lamp*): Well, I hope you're right about it this
time.
TOM: What do you mean?

HUCK: Well, we didn't get much more than a rag-doll and a ratty prayer-book off that load of Spaniards and A-rabs.

TOM: That was because of the magicians, I tell you.

HUCK: Maybe so, but it had all the marks of a Sunday School to me
    HUCK *starts to fill his pipe. Enter* JOE HARPER.

JOE: How much longer we staying, Tom?

TOM: Well, we gotta wait an hour or two yet, so as we can see where the shadow of the pine-tree falls at midnight.

JOE: Midnight?

TOM: 'Course. 'Cos where the shadow falls'll be where the treasure's hid. I should've thought of that before.

HUCK: I didn't reckon on no midnight, Tom.

JOE: I don't like haunted houses, Tom. They're a dern sight worse'n dead people.

HUCK: Dead people might talk maybe, but they don't come sliding around in a shroud when you ain't noticing, and peep over your shoulder all of a sudden and grit their teeth the way a ghost does. I couldn't stand that, Tom.

JOE: Sh! What's that?

TOM (*scared*): What? . . . Where?

JOE: By the door. I thought I saw a bit of a grey shape floating around. It's . . . it's. . .

HUCK: It's only mist, I reckon.

TOM (*much relieved*): Well, that's all right. There hasn't ever much been seen around this house, only some blue light slipping by the window — no regular ghosts.

HUCK: If there's blue lights flickering around. . .

JOE: You can bet there's a ghost mighty close behind.

TOM: I reckon three of us'll be enough to take it on (*Owl hoots. The* BOYS *cling together in terror.*) maybe. (*Changing the subject.*) Say, Huck, will you teach us how to smoke?

HUCK: Sure. (*He passes his pipe to* TOM, *who tries gingerly.*)

TOM: Joe? (*He nods doubtfully, and* TOM *passes the pipe.* JOE *takes a puff and hands it back to* TOM. *They carry on passing the pipe round.*)

TOM: Why, it's just easy! If I'd a knowed *this* was all, I'd a learnt long ago.

JOE: So would I. It's just nothing.

TOM: I don't feel sick, even a little bit.

The only light now comes from the lantern and a little moonshine through the door.

JOE: Neither do I.

TOM: *I* could smoke this pipe all day, but I bet you Jeff Thatcher couldn't.

JOE: Jeff Thatcher! Why, he'd keel over with just two draws.

TOM: And Johnny Miller! Just one little snifter would fetch him.

JOE: 'Deed it would.

TOM: Say, I wish the boys could see us now.

JOE: Yeah.

TOM: I know. We'll not say anything about it, and some time when they're around I'll say to you, 'Joe, got a pipe? I'd like a smoke.' And you'll say, kinda careless like, 'Yes, I got my *old* one. Hope my tobacker's *strong* enough for you.' And then we'll just light up, all calm and casual.

JOE: That'll be great, Tom. I can't wait to see their faces.

TOM: Yeah. . . . They'll be looking kinda green . . . with envy.

(TOM *and* JOE *are beginning to feel sick.*)

JOE: Yeah . . . I guess so. . . .

TOM: No question of it. . . .

JOE: Yeah. . . . ⎫
TOM: Yeah. . . . ⎭ (*Continue as long as situation will take it.*)

JOE: Yeah. . . . . I . . . er . . . I've left my knife outside. I reckon I'd better go and find it. (*He gets up.*)

TOM: I'll help you. (*He gets up too.* HUCK *is also getting up.*) No, you needn't come, Huck — we can find it.

They both rush out, leaving HUCK *smoking serenely in silence for a bit.* TOM *returns, looking pale and subdued. He sits down. Pause.*

HUCK: Find it?

TOM: Joe's still . . . still looking.

Enter JOE *rather shakily. After a moment something catches his attention outside.*

JOE: There's something coming up the hill. (HUCK *goes to look out of the door.*) A sort of flickering light.

HUCK: It's coming this way.

TOM: What is it?

JOE: Ghosts?

HUCK (*returning*): It's making for the fence.

JOE: Oh my! Let's run!

HUCK: No. Hide . . . up the stairs. Sh!

They hurry up the stairs, taking the lantern, and crouch or lie down where they can see the room.

TOM: Put the lantern out. (HUCK *does so.*)

In the silence a tapping can be heard approaching, then INJUN JOE *appears in the doorway, still dressed as the Spaniard. He carries a lantern. He enters, pauses, looks cautiously around.*

TOM (*whispered*): It's the blind and dumb Spaniard!

HUCK (*whispered*): What's he want a lantern for, if he's blind?

INJUN JOE: Damn boys! Playin' round here all day, stopping me from gettin' in to pick the goods up.

HUCK (*whispered*): He ain't dumb! . . . (INJUN JOE *takes off his hat and wig and dark spectacles.*)

JOE (*whispered*): Or blind!

HUCK (*whispered*): It's Injun Joe!

TOM (*whispered*): Oh, lordy!

INJUN JOE: They may be back again tomorrow, so I'd better get the stuff out of here tonight . . . and take it to the other hideout. (*He tries to open the trap-door (or boarding) with his fingers, fails, looks round, sees the pick and uses that. He lifts out a small chest and takes it to the box, opens it, and fingers some of the gold and silver within.*)

TOM (*whispered*): There *was* treasure, after all. (*The* BOYS, *straining to see, make some slight sound.*)

INJUN JOE (*looking up*): What's that? (*He stands.*) Can't be anyone around . . . though, come to think of it, that pick had fresh earth on it. I wonder . . . (*He takes his knife out, and starts to mount the stairs, to the boys' consternation. A step or two up, he hears something outside, and goes to look out.*) Just an old stray dog. Dawn's not far off, though. (*He starts to put his disguise back on.*) It'll take me a while to get this over to Hideout No. 2, so I'd best be moving. . . . Give myself another day or two after that for my revenge. . . . Then for Texas!

    INJUN JOE *leaves with the treasure-chest. The* BOYS *descend cautiously and peer through the chinks at his departure.*

JOE: What we gonna do?

TOM: If only we'd have searched around *inside*!

HUCK: He talked about revenge.

TOM: And that means us, Huck.

HUCK: Oh, don't.

TOM: Well, me, at any rate. It was only me that testified.

HUCK: Then I reckon we should tell Judge Thatcher and
    Mr Rodgers, they'll know what to do.

JOE: That's it.

TOM: Let's get back to town. (*Exeunt.*)

MUSIC NO. 12 — CHANGE OF SCENE

SCENE 3

Near dawn. A room in Aunt Polly's house. A table, chairs, lamp. AUNT POLLY *and* MRS HARPER *are weeping,* SID *looking subdued.*

MRS HARPER: The dawn's lightening up a lot now. We ought to
    try to get a bit of sleep.

AUNT POLLY: I just couldn't have gone to bed with Tom not turning up last night. Oh, if anything has happened to him. . . .

MRS HARPER: If they was anywhere about, I reckon the two of them'd been found by now.

AUNT POLLY: I never thought Tom meant it when he said he wasn't ever coming back.

MRS HARPER: I guess they've run away.

SID: Or got drowned.

AUNT POLLY: He was the best-hearted boy that ever was. No more responsible than a colt perhaps, but. . . .

SID: I hope Tom's in a better place.

AUNT POLLY: Sid! Not a word against my Tom, when we may not see him any more. Oh, Mrs Harper, I don't know how to give him up.

MRS HARPER: The Lord giveth and the Lord taketh away. Only yesterday Joe put a shooting-cracker right under my nose . . . Oh, I'd bless him if he did it now.

AUNT POLLY: Like me with Tom. Poor dead boy, dead boy . . . but he's out of all his troubles now. The last words I ever heard him say was. . .

TOM, JOE *and* HUCK *rush on.* HUCK *is very much left to one side in what follows.*

TOM: We're back, Aunt Polly!

AUNT POLLY: Tom! Thank god you're safe!

TOM *and* JOE *are smothered with kisses and hugs.*

AUNT POLLY: Tom, how could you worry me like that?

JOE: We've been treasure-hunting.

MRS HARPER: Joe, *you're* the only treasure that I have.

AUNT POLLY: Praise the Lord from whom all blessings flow! (*She makes for the door.*) Oh, I just gotta tell everybody you're back.

TOM: But, Aunt Polly, I haven't told you who we've seen.

JOE: You gotta hear the news.

AUNT POLLY: Oh, that'll keep! Ain't nothin' so important as lettin' people know you're safe.

MRS HARPER: Folks have been out searching.

AUNT POLLY: They've gotta be told.

TOM: But I tell you. . .

MRS HARPER: You boys must be starving.

AUNT POLLY: The Judge, he rode as far as. . .

JOE: But you don't know who we saw.

MRS HARPER: As long as we can see *you* — that's what matters.

AUNT POLLY: I just can't say another word . . . I'm so thankful that you're . . . Where've you been? I never thought to see you again. I figured maybe you were drowned. . .

MRS HARPER: Or run away. . .

AUNT POLLY: Or got lost in the caves . . . or . . .

TOM: LISTEN! . . . *Will you listen*! WE — FOUND — INJUN — JOE!

AUNT POLLY, MRS HARPER, SID (*variously*): Injun Joe! What! Still about? Where? I can't believe you're still alive! He might have killed you!

AUNT POLLY: We've got to tell Judge Thatcher and the men. They'll know what to do.

MRS HARPER: Come on, Joe. The sooner that red devil's behind bars. . .

JOE (*going*): He was in the Haunted House.

    MRS HARPER, JOE *and* SID *hurry out into the street. They can be heard shouting 'Joe's home. Tom and Joe are back! Wake up, everybody! Injun Joe's been found!' It fades into the distance.*

AUNT POLLY: Oh, Tom, why ever did you do it? Making me think you'd run away. Why'd you hurt me so?

TOM: I didn't think to hurt you, aunt.

AUNT POLLY: Oh, Tom, I guess you're just so full of the old scratch, that I wonder if you ever think at all . . . how much I love you.

TOM: I'm sorry, aunt. (*He snuffles a tear.*)

AUNT POLLY: I could forgive you a million times. (*She hugs him.*) Now, let's see what's going on out there. I guess I won't be the only one who's glad to know you're safe.

    They exit, leaving HUCK *alone. He looks around the room,*

*bemused, touches the lamp, runs his fingers wonderingly over
the table-cloth. This is the first time he's ever been in a
'civilized' home. He looks 'lost' in a way we've never seen
before.* TOM *suddenly appears at the door.*

TOM: Hey, Huck! C'mon! Aunt Polly says you should be in on
the celebration, too. (*They run off.*)

SCENE 4

*This scene 'evolves', like the impromptu celebration itself,
starting in the street and ending on Cardiff Hill. The early part
should be used to cover the scene-change. People rush on
echoing Mrs Harper's shouts from the previous scene. Cheers
and excitement develop. Hints of music.* JUDGE THATCHER,
in nightshirt, is seen talking to MR RODGERS.

MR RODGERS: Who'd have thought that was Injun Joe walking
about the town bold as you please this past week?
JUDGE: Murdering villain! We gotta catch him now. Can you
get a party of men up to the Haunted House and pick his trail
up from there?
MR RODGERS: I've half-a-dozen all ready to go.
Bunting starts to appear.
JUDGE: I'd go myself, but it looks like there's a little celebration
needs presiding over here.
MR RODGERS: Soon as we find anything, I'll let you know. (*He
exits.*)
A group of CHILDREN *swirl round the Judge.*
JUDGE: Hey, hold on a minute! Now is everything ready?
CHILDREN (*variously*): The baskets are being packed, Judge.
Aunt Polly's got a coupla bacon-pies in the oven. And
pancakes on the griddle. Amos Carter's got some jars of
sasparella. Somebody's raiding the melon patch.
JUDGE: Well, now — you just give me time to get my clothes on,
and I'll bring along a couple of dozen of Mrs Thatcher's cream-

buns. And perhaps there's a block or two of ice-cream in the ice-house.

The CHILDREN *cheer and the* JUDGE *exits. The excitement builds into a song.*

MUSIC NO. 13 — CELEBRATION DAY

ALL (*sing*):

1. Oh, St. Petersburg, Missouri, has been taken by the heels,
   And it's hard to say exactly just what everybody feels,
   But with Tom, Joe and Huck back then it's surely safe to say
   That St. Petersburg has got a celebration day.

2. From St. Joseph in the west there to St. Louis in the east,
   And from Jackson up to Milton they will hear about the feast,
   For the whole town's out now, and they're crowdin' in the street —
   You can hear the fiddles tunin' for their tappin' feet.

3. Oh, you never seen the like of all the things there'll be to eat,
   There'll be cornpone bread and hominy and pies and sausage meat,
   There'll be lemonade there, and then ice-cream by the quart,
   So no matter how much people eat we'll not run short.

4. Can't you hear them fiddles callin'? Listen to that banjo play!
   It sets your feet a-tappin', and it makes you start to sway.
   There'll be jigs and reelin' and a stampin' to the beat
   Of a celebration square-dance in the open street.

The JUDGE *has re-appeared, dressed fully, during the song.* HUCK *is seen at the side, a bit out of things.* AUNT POLLY *catches sight of him.*

AUNT POLLY: You enjoying yourself, Huckleberry?

HUCK: Yes, ma'am.

AUNT POLLY: Because this doesn't happen every day.

JUDGE: And now, folks, take your partners for a square-dance.
(*Cheers. The* JUDGE *will act as caller during the dance.*)

MUSIC NO. 14 — SQUARE-DANCE

*Towards the end of the dance, one or two people enter
with stone jars of lemonade and baskets of mugs.*

WILLIE (*calling*): The lemonade's arrived! Gallons of it!

MRS HARPER: There's plenty for everybody.
People flock across for lemonade. Enter MR RODGERS
to JUDGE THATCHER.

JUDGE: Find anything?

MR RODGERS: 'Fraid not, Judge. Just about put Cardiff Hill
through a corn-riddle, the nine of us, and haven't found a
cent.

JUDGE: Injun Joe's an Injun all right. Seems he's covered his
tracks pretty well. . . . Could he have made for the river?

MR RODGERS: Fred Miller and his men would have picked
him up, if he had.

JUDGE: Well, where. . . . What about McDougal's Cave?

MR RODGERS: You could be right, Judge. But we could search
through there all day and never find him.

JUDGE: And he won't come out before nightfall, so let the kids
enjoy their fun, and we can go up there this evening, and wait.
They retire, talking. The MINISTER *takes over.*

MINISTER: And now it's the children's turn. Is everybody ready
for a little game of hide-and-seek? (*The* CHILDREN *gather
round.*) Now which two shall have the privilege of being the
first two to be 'on'? I know — the two brave little boys in
whose honour we're having this little celebration: Joseph
Harper and Thomas Sawyer.

TOM: And Huck!
The THREE BOYS *stand centre and the rest of the*
CHILDREN *hide.*

MINISTER: There's one little boy peeping, I see! (*It's* HUCK!)

MUSIC NO. 15 — ALL HID?

THE THREE (*sing*): All hid?

REST (*sing*): All hid. — *2 counts*

THE THREE (*sing*): Five, ten, fifteen, twenty,

ALL (*sing*): All hid.

   1. Old Uncle Ned fell out of bed,
      Cracked his head on a piece of lead . . .

         (CHILDREN *caught and game restarts.*)

THOSE 'ON' (*sing*): All hid? — *2 counts*

REST (*sing*): All hid.

THOSE 'ON' (*sing*): Five, ten, fifteen, twenty,

ALL (*sing*): All hid.

   2. Way down yonder in jaybird town,
      Devil knocked my daddy down . . .

        (*Same again, only* TOM *and* HUCK *have gone.*)

THOSE 'ON' (*sing*): All hid? *2 counts*

REST (*sing*): All hid.

THOSE 'ON' (*sing*): Five, ten, fifteen, twenty,

ALL (*sing*): All hid.

   3. Sixteen birds sitting in a row,
      The big black crow is Injun Joe . . .

        (*The game is over. The* ADULTS *count the* CHILDREN
        before setting off home.)

ADULTS (*sing*): All here?

CHILDREN (*sing*): All here.

ADULTS (*sing*): Five, ten, fifteen, twenty,

ALL (*sing*): All here.

AUNT POLLY: No, wait a minute. Tom's not here. (*Calling.*)
   Tom!

JEFF: And where's Huck?

SEVERAL (*calling*): Tom! Huck!

AUNT POLLY (*agitated*): Oh dear!

MUFF POTTER: They can't be far away, Miss Watson.

JUDGE: Now who saw Tom and Huck last?

MINISTER: They were here at the start of the hide-and-seek.

JEFF: Huck found me.

OTHERS: And Tom me. And me.
AUNT POLLY (*calling*): Tom! Tom! (*Others take up the call, which turns into the musical call with which the play began.*)

MUSIC NO. 16A — TOM SAWYER (*reprise*)

JOE: I wonder if he might have hidden in the caves.
JUDGE (*uneasily*): McDougal's Cave?
JOE: That's just the sort of thing Tom would do.
AUNT POLLY: If he's lost in there, he'll never get out alive!
BEN: Tom knows the caves better than most.
AUNT POLLY: You know how those caves run into each other till it's all a tangle of openings and passageways.
MUFF POTTER: Now don't you worry, Miss Watson. We'll find him.

MUSIC NO. 16B — TOM SAWYER (*reprise*)

The call bursts out again fortissimo, and continues as they set off for the caves, moving offstage. The lights fade.

SCENE 5

McDougal's Cave. The early part of this scene is played on the forestage or in the auditorium, whilst the cave is being set behind the closed curtains. Enter TOM *and* HUCK *with candles.*

TOM: Boo! That scared you. (*They fool about.*)
HUCK: Wheeee! I'm a bat.
TOM: I bet no-one's been down this passage before.
HUCK: I reckon not — hidden behind that kinda waterfall of stone.
TOM: We're explorers! May never get out. And in a hundred years' time someone'll discover our whitened bones. And they'll call the cave Tom Sawyer's Cave.

HUCK: Sh! Look!

TOM: What?

HUCK: Bats! Hundreds of 'em!

They are attacked by bats.

TOM: Whew! Nearly lost the candles then.

HUCK: I can do without meeting them again.

TOM: If they put the candles out, we'd be really in a fix.

HUCK: How long d'you reckon we've been down here, Tom? Maybe we ought to be going back now.

TOM: Yes, perhaps we better.

HUCK: Can you find the way? I'm all mixed up now.

TOM: Yes, I reckon so. It's . . . it's this way. (*He sets off in the wrong direction.*) Sh!

HUCK: What?

TOM: Sh! . . . I thought I heard a noise.

HUCK: Nothing . . . only water dripping somewhere.

Sound of 'Tom!' shouted in the distance.

TOM: There it is!

They move towards the sound, but it comes from various places outside the auditorium, so that TOM *and* HUCK, *in attempting to follow it, get thoroughly lost.*

TOM: Blame it! I'm all confused.

HUCK: Tom . . . Tom, d'you reckon we're lost?

TOM: I don't know . . .

The shout comes again, from the direction of the stage — the curtains have opened again by now. In hurrying towards it, TOM *stumbles and falls to the ground with a cry.*

TOM: Oooh! Oooh! My arm! (HUCK *examines it.*)

HUCK: Can you bend it?

TOM: I don't know, I . . . (*Agony.*)

HUCK: I reckon you've broken it, Tom. Have you got a handkerchief? (*He fixes up a makeshift sling for* TOM.) How'd it happen?

TOM: I guess I must have tripped over that rock there.

HUCK: That ain't no rock, Tom. (*Examining it.*) It's a box.

TOM: It's Injun Joe's treasure-chest! (*They open it.*) My, but we're rich, Huck! Let's not fool around here any longer, but snake it out.

HUCK: I can't hear the shouts any more.

TOM: That doesn't matter.

HUCK: Maybe not — so long as we keep walking *upwards*.

They struggle along with the treasure-chest, but it is heavy. At one point they nearly step off into a void. HUCK *holds out his candle and looks down.*

HUCK: The floor kinda drops away.

TOM: D'you reckon it's bottomless?

HUCK: I don't know. It's just blackness, Tom. Lordy, I wish we was out of here.

They struggle on further, but TOM *stumbles and bangs his arm agonizingly.*

HUCK: You all right?

TOM (*unconvincingly*): Yes . . . 'course.

HUCK: Blame it, Tom! Why don't we leave the box and just get out of here?

TOM: Leave the treasure! . . . You must be nuts, Huck Finn. You could become a steamboat captain or a judge or a clown or anything with what's in there.

HUCK: We'll pretty soon be corpses if we don't get out of here. The caves go on for miles, and the candles won't last much longer. What'll we do then? We're lost, Tom. Cain't you see? Folks ain't lookin' for us any more. We could wander around for days and never find a way out. And all you can think of is foolin' around with a load of treasure — stuff that ain't even ours.

TOM: But can't you see their faces when we spring it on them?

HUCK: Who?

TOM: Mr Rodgers and the others that's been stole from.

HUCK (*exasperated*): Aw, dry up, will you? What about the fix we're in? Ain't you got the sense to see? Why're you always fancifying things? Dressing things up like something out of a book?

TOM: Cos there's got to be some . . . some *grandness* sometimes.

HUCK: This ain't the time for anything but the truth. And that's pretty ugly for us right now.

TOM: If we'd only thought of *us* before, Muff Potter would have been hanged.

HUCK: That was different. That was a man's life we was risking ours for. This is just a box of money.

TOM: Just because it isn't yours. You're pretty selfish, ain't you?

HUCK (*turning away in disgust*): Selfish yourself.

TOM: Thinking of yourself all the time.

HUCK (*swinging back*): Are *you* thinking of Aunt Polly right now? How she'll feel if you die down here? Are you thinking of me? Or just the glory of handing back the money? If you're so concerned about the treasure, you can get it out yourself.

TOM: All right!

HUCK: Right!

TOM: Right! . . . And let me have the other bit of candle back. (TOM *tries to move the box on his own and fails. Pause.*) Huck, you know I can't shift it.

HUCK: Can't either of us get very far on our own perhaps.
The shouts are heard again, faintly, to one side of the stage.

TOM: There they are!
They shout back and go on towards them. Suddenly, as they are approaching an alcove, INJUN JOE *appears, knife in hand.*

INJUN JOE: Keep quiet, you little devils! Or I'll slit your throats!
TOM and HUCK shrink back, terrified, and all three listen to the shouts pass across the back of the stage. TOM, *with rescue slipping from their grasp, grows more and more desperate. As the shouts start to die away, this is too much for* TOM, *who yells out.* INJUN JOE *lunges towards him with the knife, but* HUCK *hinders him. There is a fierce struggle, with* INJUN JOE*'s efforts divided between the two boys. It is important that at some point the actions of the two boys help each other. Agonized cries from* TOM *with his broken arm.*

Finally a long despairing scream from INJUN JOE *as he falls into the pot-hole. Silence — broken only by* TOM's *sobbing.*

HUCK: Are you all right, Tom?

TOM: Yes. Are you?

HUCK: I guess so. (*He gingerly approaches the edge of the pot-hole.*) He. . . . Dead now, I reckon. Could've been us.

TOM: Don't, Hucky.

HUCK: C'mon, let's shout.

They shout. No reply. Again. Answering shouts from the rescuers, who appear with lanterns — MUFF POTTER, JUDGE THATCHER, MR RODGERS, AUNT POLLY, SID, *other men and one or two boys.*

AUNT POLLY: Oh, Tom, Tom, praise God you're safe! Even if your arm is . . .

JUDGE (*interrupting*): Well, that should keep him out of mischief for a while, Miss Watson.

SID: His clothes is awful dirty, Aunt Polly, and look at his pants.

AUNT POLLY: Sid Sawyer, you're a trouble-maker (*hits him*), a tell-tale (*again*), and a sneak (*again*). All that matters is he's safe. (*To* TOM) I guess I'm the gladdest body alive just to see you safe and sound.

TOM: Ain't you glad to see Huck, too, Aunt Polly? Somebody's gotta be glad to see him.

AUNT POLLY: And so they shall! Poor motherless boy! (*She embraces* HUCK, *much to his embarrassment.*) I guess all he needs is a proper home. I reckon we can make room for him.

TOM: Yippee!

AUNT POLLY (*to* HUCK): Happen with someone to look after you and see you go to school . . .

HUCK (*reluctant*): Well, ma'am . . .

AUNT POLLY (*interrupting*): No, no thanks, Huck. It's settled.

JUDGE: What's that box you've got there?

TOM: That's our surprise! We found it. It's . . . Go on, Huck.

HUCK: It's the money that was stole. Mr Rodgers's and Widow Douglas . . .

MR RODGERS *opens the chest and people crowd round.*

MR RODGERS: And many more besides. (*On his knees at the box.*) I'm mighty grateful to you boys. Makes up for the spade and no mistake!

JUDGE: And what can't be traced to its owners will be yours, boys.

MUFF POTTER (*as they start to leave*): So all's well that ends well, Miss Watson.

As the others go, the JUDGE *detains* MUFF.

JUDGE: Ended well *this* time maybe, Potter, but there's others like Tom and Huck, and it mightn't do so next time. We've a plain duty to see that no-one else gets lost in these caves. (*They start to leave.*) And there's one sure and certain way of doing it. . . . Nail up the entrance, Muff Potter!

They exit. As heavy hammer blows resound from the wings, INJUN JOE *is seen, cut and bruised, crawling towards the entrance, a broken leg dragged behind him. The lights fade.*

FINALE

The music takes up the hammer blows. Enter the WHOLE CAST. TOM *and* HUCK *are going home in triumph on a 'wagon' — twirling parasols make the wheels.* TOM's *arm is in its sling.*

MUSIC NO. 17 — YIPPEE-I-AY

ALL (*sing*):

1. Here they both come, yes it's Tom and Huckleberry comin'
   up to their door,
   Back from the grave, when we thought that we would never
   see them again no more.
   But now the storm is over, sun's come out again,
   Drivin' off the rain-clouds we had before.
       Shout out hooray! Yippee-i-ay halleluiah!
       For all St. Petersburg!

2. Indian Joe thought he'd got away with it and reckoned he
   got us beat,
   But two gallant lads put a stop to him because they would
   not admit defeat.
   So now it's jubilation! Everyone is here,
   Come from far and near on their happy feet.
       Shout out hooray! Yippee-i-ay halleluiah!
       For all St. Petersburg!

3. If it's a fact that a body's mighty lucky when ev'rything
   come right,
   Then we got fortune a thousand thousand times in St.
   Petersburg tonight.
   And all the population shares a single joy,
   Coupl'a golden boys set the town alight!

The music stops, and everybody freezes except TOM *and*
HUCK.

HUCK (*shaking his head*): It won't work, it won't work, Tom.
I ain't used to it. It's friendly of Aunt Polly, but I'd have to
wash, and wear them smothery clothes, and comb my hair to
thunder.

TOM: But everybody does that way, Huck.

HUCK: Well, I ain't everybody, Tom, and I couldn't stand it.

TOM: If you'd give it a try, Huck, I know you'd like it.

HUCK: No, Tom, I like the woods, and the river, and the air.
And my old barrel's good enough for me. I'll see you around . . . .
       HUCK *exits. The song starts up again.*

ALL (*sing*):

4. Stand on the shores of the Mississippi there to shout out
   our words of joy,
   Let 'em all know that our hearts are happy from Ohio to
   Illinois,
   And all you paddle-steamers, let your whistles blow,
   Tell your news when folks holler 'Ship-ahoy!'
       Shout out hooray! Yippee-i-ay halleluiah!
       For all St. Petersburg.

CURTAIN CALLS

ALL (*sing*):

5. A boy and his dreams are far apart,
   And most of his dreams are only play,
   But give him an open, lovin' heart, ~~pause~~,
   Then a dream can point the way.

6. Everyone's here now to join the celebration. Gee, what a
   sight to see!
   All the best stories have got a happy endin' — that's how it
   oughta be!
   We'll tell the world we're feeling joy through all the town,
   Not a single frown left, we all agree.
         Shout out hooray! Yippee-i-ay halleluiah!
         For all St. Petersburg.

                    CURTAIN

PRODUCTION NOTES

Tom Sawyer can be performed almost anywhere, whether with thirty in a classroom or a hundred in a hall. The original production had a cast of seventy boys and girls, and a few notes on the setting may be helpful as starting-points for anyone considering a full-scale production.

Any of the usual forms of staging will be suitable: proscenium, thrust or in the round. All that matters is that the scenes should be able to follow each other without a break and that the actors should be able to move around the acting area with ease. In the Celebration Scene in Act Two, for example, as the excitement at the boys' return builds up, groups of townsfolk ought to be able to group and re-form, run to wake up others and make preparations for the celebration; the game of hide-and-seek needs to be able to scatter round and amongst the actors; and the actors should be able to melt out of the acting area at the end, leaving it empty and abandoned as their voices fade into the distance. Whatever will enable this to happen will do.

With arena staging perhaps there should be a number of locales, each centred on a centre-piece of some kind — a rostrum group, or Aunt Polly's front porch with roses and a fence, or the jail — always with the feel of weather-boarding. Towards one side perhaps the suggestion of a cluster of village houses; at another a higher group of rostra (possibly masking the main entrance) suggesting Cardiff Hill, and later forming the focus of the Court Scene. The intimate scenes, such as Tom's dialogues with Huck, the Haunted House, and inside Aunt Polly's House, need to be isolated in pools of light and if possible take place close to the audience. A fence, a barrel, boxes, bales of cotton, bunting, flags, all easily moved by the actors, can be shifted from place to place to give a local habitation and a name to otherwise neutral spaces.

Whatever the form of staging, some kind of hole will be needed — trap-door or space amongst rostrum blocks — for the grave and the pot-hole in the caves.

The original production was on a conventional proscenium stage (28' x 24') with no wing space. Except for a group of raised levels at the back, we cleared the whole of the stage area. On this, three low platforms on castors, each with a flat screwed to one side, were moved about freely; also a two-sided 'hut' on castors. All four could be pushed to the sides right out of the way, to release the whole of the stage space for big scenes like the Celebration Day, or grouped in various ways with barrel, fence, etc., to produce any of the other scenes. The shifting was usually done during a momentary black-out, by a back-stage team well experienced in blackout quick-changes from our annual revue. Several times the platforms were moved in full view of the audience as part of the action. (Tom, for example, hitched a ride to school on one after leaving the Minister in the Prelude.) We used the body of the hall twice: the Sunday School children departed for their picnic singing down the centre aisle, and Tom and Huck got lost there at the start of the Caves Scene. (As corridors run round two sides of the hall, the searching voices could come confusingly from all over.)

The opening Prelude gives the audience a chance to get to know what to expect. It is a scene that touches in, before the plot starts, Tom's relationships with Aunt Polly, and Sid and Huck and his other friends, his attitude to school, and his imagination; a scene to establish St. Petersburg as a place where a boy can fish and doze on his own, and equally where everybody knows everybody else; but it is also a scene to accustom the audience to the versatility of the setting, the action flowing from block to block or the blocks rolling round the stage as the Black Avenger of the Spanish Main and the Terror of the Seas sail alongside each

other on the moving platforms; a scene to build up in every way —
from silence and a solo actor in a single spot to a blaze of light
thronged with the population of St. Petersburg raising the roof
with 'Gotcher now, Tom!

With a multi-purpose set it is worth going to some trouble to
get costumes and props right, so that neutral platforms and
rostra can be localized by the actors and the props they use. For
similar reasons, the townsfold and children should not be vague
chorus-figures, but blacksmiths, wheelrights, paddle-steamer
officials, negro house-boys, rook-scarers, elder sisters with infants
to look after, and so on.

For the Square Dance one can ignore the purists and simply
combine the showier figures from various dances. Actors who can
move rhythmically to music should be able to master things in
two or three sessions. In arranging the dance, Smalley and
Tether's book *Let's Dance — Country Style* (Paul Elek Books
Ltd) proved an invaluable help to a non-square-dancing producer!

JOHN CHARLESWORTH

MUSIC NOTES

The two things that seemed most important in writing the music were that it should be both simple and tuneful. Although most of the music is original, American folk-song, with its catchy melodies and the kind of syncopation that comes easily to children today, seemed an obvious starting-point. 'All Hid?', in fact, is a Mississippi children's singing-game and there are other traditional tunes in the Square Dance; and 'Natural Salvation' and 'Rip-Rapscallion' are closely based on American folk-songs. Without in any sense trying to write pseudo folk-tunes, we have tried to make the remaining seven songs stand happily alongside the traditional material. We had no expert singers, just an average group of young people. In the event, they took to the songs like ducks to water, much to our delight, and now, over a year later, they are still singing them.

Apart from 'Tom's Song', they can all be sung by varying numbers of singers, from a handful to the whole cast. For example, 'Bringin' Up a Boy' is really a solo, but as our Aunt Polly had been chosen for her acting ability rather than her singing, it proved acceptable to have Aunt Polly's singing supported by a small group of the Townswomen. 'Rip-Rapscallion' presented a similar problem, which we similarly overcame. It is only 'Tom's Song' that really must be a solo.

'Perspicacity' and 'Hang Him, Hang Him!' look at first sight rather more complicated, as there is more than one line of music going on at the same time. This should cause no real difficulty, however. Each line is simple, and most children can after all manage 'London's Burning' as a round in some three or four parts.

The whole show can be accompanied on the piano alone. If a double bass and a drum-kit are available, however, they can be added quite simply, to give a rhythmic lift and impetus to the songs. Moreover, many schools will possess assorted percussion instruments, and will want to use these, too. Blocks, tambourines, chime-bars, xylophones, glockenspiels, etc., can all be added *ad lib* to provide more colour. If the school is lucky enough to have a pair of timps, these can be used to great advantage as well, not only in the music itself, but also to add excitement to, for example, the fight in the cave near the end.

Some schools may wish to be more adventurous, as indeed we were in the first production, and have a band. We chose the band from the talents we had available, and arranged the music accordingly. Basically we used a flute, two clarinets, two trumpets, trombone, double bass, piano, drums, and timps. But when we discovered that our trombonist could play the piano accordion as well, it seemed a pity not to use this in the Square Dance; and so it went on, until by the end, in addition to the basic line-up given above, the music had also made use of a guitar, banjo, violin, French horn, melodica, piano accordion, and assorted percussion. Not bad for eleven players! The great thing is to make use of whatever instrumental talents are available. Perhaps no two productions of the play will have music that sounds quite the same.

The particular instrumentation can add considerably to the effect of each number. The plaintive tones of the melodica in the opening Prelude set the atmosphere for Tom's lazing away his time fishing, with the river rippling away on the piano underneath. For the introduction and interludes to 'Rip-Rapscallion' different instruments were given little stabs of notes, adding to the general air of chaos and exasperation the song is trying to convey.

As schools' musical resources will vary so much, it didn't seem helpful to give the music a straight-jacket of the instrumentation

78

which we happened to use in the first production. The piano score, therefore, offers the following: all the music for the songs and the incidental interludes, arranged so that they can be accompanied on the piano alone, but also with some suggestions for each number of how other instruments can be brought in to add further point and colour to the music.

ERIC WAYMAN

⁂ Paula Low *⁂*

J. I. M. Stewart

THE MADONNA OF
THE ASTROLABE

MAGNUM BOOKS
Methuen Paperbacks Ltd

A Magnum Book

THE MADONNA OF THE ASTROLABE
ISBN 0 417 02190 9

First published in Great Britain 1977
by Victor Gollancz Ltd
Magnum edition published 1978

Copyright © 1977 by J. I. M. Stewart

Magnum Books are published
by Methuen Paperbacks Ltd
11 New Fetter Lane, London EC4P 4EE

Made and printed in Great Britain
by Richard Clay (The Chaucer Press) Ltd
Bungay, Suffolk

A Staircase in Surrey

*   *   *   *

THE MADONNA OF THE ASTROLABE

I

Happy birthday to you,
Squashed bananas and stew!
You look like a monkey,
Go back to the zoo!

JOHNNIE BEDWORTH SANG this as lustily as any of his guests. There was no impropriety in his joining in, since none of the juveniles present retained much awareness of the originating occasion of the party. It was doubtful whether even Johnnie's sister Virginia did. She was crooning the lines broodingly to herself in a corner, and seemed progressively less well-disposed to the festivity as it became more and more of a romp. Indeed, not so much a romp as a rumpus. But this too was in order. The room was called the rumpus room—although a linguistic purist (such as Cyril Bedworth was) might have been prompted to speak of it rather as the rumpus area. For on the ground floor of the Victorian North Oxford house several walls had been knocked down and compensating girders inserted—this no doubt at the expense of our college, which owned the property—in the interest of open-plan living. The boundaries between sitting-room, rumpus room, and kitchen having thereby become merely notional, Mabel Bedworth could talk to visitors in the first and keep an eye on her children in the second without interrupting her culinary activities in the third. The rest of the house, three more storeys and a basement, had presumably been re-modelled on similar principles. Its original design must have equanimously envisaged the doing to death of three or four domestic servants a year.

It struck me that a philosopher (and Mrs Firebrace, who had

7

brought her three sons, was eminent in the university as that) could not fail to find matter for speculation in what was proving the theme-song of the party. Outrage takes on a sharper edge when it travesties or parodies some familiar orthodoxy—as Black Masses and Feasts of Fools witness. Johnnie Bedworth and his friends were on the crest of such an indulgence. The words they chanted were wicked and daring in an extreme, the battle-cry of a heady insurgence. Singly or in couples, these academic infants—all flashing eyes and floating hair—would bear down upon a grown-up, shout their strident and defiant quatrain, and dash away again. I had seen the precise physical manœuvre on television the evening before: a student at some violent confrontation with authority breaking ranks, darting forward to take a swipe at a police-man's helmet (or at the muzzle of a mounted policeman's horse), and darting back again rather more quickly still.

I offered the analogy to Mrs Firebrace, who replied—I felt discouragingly—that it could not be extended through other dimensions of the two affairs. She was a woman with deep-set black eyes operating from behind a tumble of black hair, so that one conversed with her rather as one might have nerved oneself to interrogate a sibyl shrouded in the darkness of a cave. At the moment, I could just see that she was looking at her watch. It wasn't with any uncivil intent. Two of her boys were among the oldest at the party, and she was reflecting that they must be got home in time to be calmed down and persuaded to do their prep. The children at private schools, it seemed, were already shouldering this burden; those enjoying state education (and they were the majority) would still be free of it for some time ahead.

'It appears,' Mrs Firebrace said, 'that birthdays can be significant from a very tender age indeed.' She glanced at me sharply (or I thought she did), as if to confirm that I had made an appeal for, and would be gratified by, rational talk amid the surrounding din. 'In the early days of psychotherapy

8

William Brown was able to elicit memories of people's second, or even first birthday.'

'They say now that they can get at pre-natal memories.'

'But that isn't so remarkable.' Mrs Firebrace was surprised that this should have to be pointed out. 'A random somatic event or sensation in the womb is one thing; an anniversary occasion is quite another . . . I wish Jacob wouldn't pick his nose.'

'Why?'

'*Why*?' Mrs Firebrace, whose train of thought had been interrupted on observing this displeasing action on the part of her eldest son, stared at me blankly. 'It's unhygienic.'

'Then why not stop him?'

'And how am I to do that?'

'Leather him whenever the loathsome practice rears its ugly head.'

'Jacob would bite his nails instead. He's very resourceful.'

'Leather him harder.'

'What good would that do?'

'His resourcefulness would eventually lead him to find satisfaction in some socially inoffensive gesture. Twiddling his thumbs or smoothing down his hair. But you were saying something about birthdays.'

'In its radical sense the concept is a simple one—just the day you came out of mummy's tummy. The tiniest child can understand that.'

'Of course. It's the most natural thing in the world. Nothing in the least odd about it.'

'Mr Pattullo, please do not subject me to banter. It's the worst type of male chauvinism.'

'I'm terribly sorry.' Mrs Firebrace and I were getting along quite well together. 'Do continue.'

'A birthday *anniversary* is quite a complex idea to get hold of. Far more, even, than the concept of a today or a tomorrow. Where does any first grip on it come from? It must be a matter of the deep structure, wouldn't you say?'

9

I thought it wise not to say. The next ugly head to be raised looked like being Professor Chomsky's, and it was improbable that I'd make much of this savant amid the uproar surrounding me. The threat, however, was obviated by my host. Johnnie Bedworth was making a dash at me, his head lowered like that of a charging bull. Oxford children incline to precocity, and although I understood it to be Johnnie's fifth birthday that we were saluting I couldn't be certain that he was incapable of some full-blown fantasy of the successful goring of a matador in an appropriate Spanish setting. Within inches of me, however, he halted and straightened up. He was struggling for breath, for speech. Or was he bottling up enormous mirth? Impossible to tell. His complexion was turning from pink to purple. He spluttered. His whole person seemed to swell under the pressure of whatever it was that was going on in him. He gulped, and I saw that words were again, if briefly, at his command. I was about to be told that I was of simian appearance and had better return whence I had come.

'See you later, alligator!' Johnnie shouted at me. Screaming with laughter, he turned and bolted across the room. He ought, I believe, to have given me a chance to reply 'In a while, crocodile'. That would have been correct. But Johnnie's concern had been with frustrating legitimate expectation. It seemed to him enormously funny and utterly devastating that I should *not* have been told to go back to the zoo. I found myself feeling for Johnnie the respect due to a *confrère*. He had discovered one of the prime mechanisms of comedy.

Except for myself—drawn in as a kind of honorary uncle in consequence of that cordial regard which Cyril Bedworth so undeservedly bestowed on me—the adults present were all, as was natural, parents. There were almost as many fathers as mothers—this because, until the dinner-hour comes round, Oxford dons are the most domesticated of men. Moreover, although of learned or speculative habit, they are prompt and dutiful in joining at need in the activities of their young. Several were now taking part in 'Murder'. This was by way of a *reprise*. 'Murder' having proved the main success of the party, the infants were insisting on going through it again before breaking up. Even a simplified version of the game might have been judged unsuitable for those of such tender years. But there was no doubt of its grip, and it was those children who least understood the root idea who most seriously addressed themselves to a proper comportment during the ritual. I knew little about children; only my brother Ninian's had been much on my horizon, and I had lived abroad too long to see a great deal even of them. The dream children to whom I have occasionally confessed had never, significantly, been proper children at all; they had sprung to life almost within reach of the age of the young people who now occasionally turned up to my lectures. (Perhaps this disregard of two of the Seven Ages of Man was partly a matter of professional prejudice. Children are a dead loss on the stage. Shakespeare himself couldn't manage them, even although he had actual children with theatrical training always to hand.) So it was very much from the side-lines that I judged juvenile assemblies.

There had, of course, been Charles and Mary Talbert, the progeny of those deep, and deeply wedded, scholars who had presided over my early assaults on English literature within the university. I didn't think I had actually been to a birthday party in Old Road; and if such festivities were ever mounted there it was probable that their high-light had been the production of a new educational game of philological character. There had been, too, the children I used to observe in the course of my pilgrimages through North Oxford to my other, and reclusive, tutor, J. B. Timbermill. These, unlike the young Talberts, had scarcely been inhibited, and a certain social motility had been suggested by their pursuit of street games (involving much unsightly chalking of pavements) which would appear to have percolated from other strata of society. What I chiefly remembered of these, however, was again something in a linguistic area: their uniform command of what Timbermill called Received Standard English—a dialect at that time barely to be comprehended by my alien ear. Here, at least, there was a marked contrast between then and now. Johnnie Bedworth, even when bellowing at the top of his voice, produced cockney with the precision of an accomplished character actor: this because his nursery school had provided him with a boon companion (present at the party) who had lately migrated to Oxford from Mile End. Contrastingly, there were two or three children whose complexions suggested regions farther away, but whose accents, far from being answeringly coffee-coloured, were indistinguishable from those of Heads of Houses or Fellows of Lady Margaret Hall.

The darkly shadowed Mrs Firebrace had left me—composedly, although the occasion of her departure was her youngest son's having been sick in some inappropriate place. I continued to reflect on social change as evidenced in infancy. In the Edinburgh of my childhood coloured boys and girls of any variety hadn't existed—not even, so far as I could remember, as a casual phenomenon in the streets. They belonged solely within the sphere of religious education—being frequently represented in a species of Sunday School iconography as awaiting in distant lands enlightenment on Noah's Ark and the Twelve Tribes of Israel. But had one of them turned up while we were ourselves receiving such instruction I doubt whether we should have behaved at all well, so untoward would the irruption have appeared to us. Here at the Bedworths' party the pinko-greys on the one hand and the contrastingly tinted on the other seemed to be a wholly integrated group, confirming the view that racial feeling surfaces only at adolescence. It was true that the parents of almost all the children here present would be firmly anti-racist. Yet that might cut two ways. How antipathetic to the unformed mind must be elders of liberal persuasion who forbid the chanting of 'Ten little Nigger Boys' and banish *Little Black Sambo* from the nursery library!

These thoughts were interrupted by the appearance before me of Virginia Bedworth. She had detached herself from the final game with the air of a conscientious hostess who has adequately discharged a duty and earned an unobtrusive breather for a while.

'Excuse me,' Virginia said. 'Please, may I get my book?' She edged past me, ran a practised eye along a shelf, and possessed herself of a volume which, although slim, was almost as tall as herself. (Virginia was three.) She then turned and showed it to me politely. It was *Babar and Father Christmas*. 'It's rather noisy here,' Virginia said. 'I shall read quietly in my room.' And with this she withdrew from the party.

Her mother was much involved with the celebration still, but by way of an activity at least suggesting the end of the tunnel. Each child was to receive a present on leaving, and Mabel Bedworth was checking these over. At the start of the occasion, Johnnie had received a present from each of his guests. There was no doubt an immemorial, a courtly, an oriental sanction for these punctilious exchanges, but I couldn't confidently remember that it had obtained in my time. At Christmas parties, indeed, everybody had got a parcel from the tree. But hadn't it been felt there was something excessive about taking presents to birthday parties— and certainly about giving others away at the door? Wouldn't this have drawn down the same disapprobation as did the hiring, by parents lacking in decent self-reliance, of a conjurer or ventriloquist 'to make the thing go'? I found myself hazy here, my only clear memory being that I hadn't greatly cared for birthday parties. And my brother Ninian had been at one with me. We may have felt awkward because our manners, as much as our clothes, had not been of an acceptable party-going sort. We were conscious of being held to stand in need of explanation—something sufficiently achieved when it was remembered that our father was an artist, and our mother slightly mad, though 'well-connected'. The last phrase had come to me when I was young enough to associate it perplexedly with the use of the telephone.

These thoughts were interrupted by the return of Mrs Firebrace, who had coped with the emergency presented to her. There was no reason why she should thus seek me out again; we were but slightly acquainted; it might have been more natural for her to switch her attention to one or another of her fellow parents 'sitting in' on the party. I was conjecturing that she perhaps judged me lonesome, and that her action was charitably motivated, when something of a freshly appraising character in her glance prompted me to discard this theory.

'Penny,' Mrs Firebrace said briskly, 'is coming to stay with me.'

My response to this news—or to the manner of its delivery —fails to return to my mind. It may have been as inappropriate as Laertes's 'O, where?' when told of Ophelia's death by drowning. My first feeling, certainly, was irrelevant and trivial, since I found myself resenting so baldly phrased a communication from a person scarcely known to me. This was unjust. Encountering me as she had done at Johnnie Bedworth's party, and equipped with a piece of information I had some title to receive, Mrs Firebrace would have done equally ill either to withhold or to make a business of it. And if 'Penny' had been awkward as suggesting that we were all three of us intimate together it had certainly been the only term at Mrs Firebrace's command. 'Penny Pattullo'—if Penny still called herself that—would scarcely have done, and 'your former wife' wouldn't have done at all.

I heard myself say—on a note of polite interest—that I hadn't been aware Penny and Mrs Firebrace knew each other.

'Oh, yes, indeed. We were at school together.' Mrs Firebrace was displeased by my ignorance. 'And quite close friends in our last two years there.'

'Penny must just have happened never to mention it.' All this information struck me as odd. I knew about Penny's school—a very fashionable school then—and I'd hardly have thought of it as a likely nursery of young philosophers. Still less should I have imagined Penny disposed to choose as a companion a girl already, it might be presumed, showing a precocious interest in Wittgenstein and Ryle. Not that Penny didn't possess a flair for surprising preferences from time to time.

'But later we rather lost touch,' Mrs Firebrace said.

'Ah, yes. Well, Penny and I have lost touch too.'

'You don't often see her?'

'We haven't met since the divorce.'

'That must be unusual nowadays, don't you think?'

'Perhaps so. "Uncivilized" is probably the word.'

'I've been told it's thought friendly to celebrate the making absolute of one's divorce by going to bed together.'

'Penny and I didn't do that.' The mildness with which I said this cost me no effort. I was accustomed to women—mostly at parties, although scarcely parties like Johnnie's—playing up, as they thought appropriately, to my professional character by saying the sort of things that are said in plays. If Mrs Firebrace's effort had been contextually none too felicitous that only suggested that she was more accustomed to seminars and tutorials than to silly chatter. I still didn't think her a bad sort of woman. 'Is it long since you last saw Penny yourself?' I asked.

'Oh, years and years. But we wrote from time to time. And

there's always been an idea she might come and stay with us in Oxford.'

'But she never has—not till now?'

'Not till now.'

'As a girl she used to visit an aged relative in Oxford—a Mrs Triplett. It's where we first met.'

'Yes—I've heard all about that.'

'No doubt.' I was silent for a moment, offended (as I was inclined to be) at the thought of Penny reminiscing about me to persons unknown. 'And Oxford's an attractive place to return to. I know that, since it's only a few months ago that I did it myself. And after years and years of never being near the place.'

'So Penny is following you up.'

'Following me up?'

'Your example, I mean. Coming back to have a look.'

'Yes, of course. When's this due to happen, Mrs Firebrace?'

'Oh, it's vague at the moment. I'll let you know.'

'My dear lady! So that I can skulk in Surrey Quad, and never venture my nose in the street?'

'No, of course not. But occasionally it's disconcerting to run into somebody after a long interval and as a complete surprise.'

'I suppose so. Indeed, I've experienced something of the kind at least once, come to think of it.' I sought to hold Mrs Firebrace's gaze as I said this, since I was wondering whether she could possibly know what I was talking about. 'But I think I can promise not in any circumstances to be particularly disconcerted by Penny.'

'I could discourage the whole thing.'

This seemed to me an extraordinary remark—the more so because Mrs Firebrace hadn't uttered it with any lightness of air. She seemed, indeed, rather perplexed—as if she were a philosopher not of the metaphysical but of the moral sort, confronting an ethically ticklish situation. My conclusion was that there *had* been lightness of air, probably in a letter of Penny's in which her visit to Oxford had been propounded. Mrs Firebrace had some reason—to put it crudely—to suppose her old school-fellow to be harbouring predatory intentions. It wasn't conceivable that on Penny's part this could be other than a passing joke, at least so far as I was concerned. Mrs Firebrace might have failed, however, to interpret it that way.

I was the last guest to leave the party. This might in any case have been correct behaviour in an honorary uncle, but it was also occasioned by Cyril Bedworth's feeling that he had some piece of college business to discuss. He commonly did feel thus at the tail-end of social occasions; he was beginning to take the full weight of his new duties as our Senior Tutor; it might have been said of him—as of Milton's Satan in a similarly tough spot—that on his Front engraven Deliberation sat and public care. His present problem was the resistance being put up by some of our older colleagues to a proposal that the college Dramatic Society should be given permission to use the Fellows' Garden for a production of the first part of *Tamburlaine the Great*. One of these curmudgeonly members of the Governing Body had advanced as a conclusive consideration the certainty that the pampered jades of Asia would cut up the turf in an appalling manner. It was Bedworth's belief that we could defeat this illiberal opposition if we could only make sure of the support of Albert Talbert. Everybody knew that Talbert was the most distinguished of living Elizabethan scholars, so his supporting the undergraduates' application would carry weight. Indeed, not to defer to him on such a matter would pretty well be—didn't I think?—to break one of the unwritten rules of the game.

I replied that my experience of the Governing Body was still limited, but that I thought he was right. So far as my observation went, its proprieties had the edge on its savageries —if only by a fine margin—every time.

Bedworth, although encouraged by this opinion, now produced a further anxiety. Was Talbert, at least to any pronounced degree, an admirer of Christopher Marlowe? Did I remember that lecture on Marlowe which Talbert had given in 1947 or thereabouts, in which he had described the dramatist as being, if not the most talented, at least the noisiest of the contemporaries of Shakespeare? If Talbert came out with something like that to the G.B. it wouldn't—would it?—advance matters at all.

One part of this questionnaire had its awkwardness for me. I must have attended two or three of Talbert's formal discourses at the distant time invoked, since it had been held a necessary act of courtesy to show one's tutor something like that degree of countenance in the lectures he was constrained to deliver for the university. But if as a consequence of this I had heard Talbert pronounce on Marlowe, the circumstance had faded from my mind during the ensuing quarter of a century. To admit this would be to perplex Bedworth; it might even impair the state of pleasurable feeling I could detect in him as arising from the success of Johnnie's birthday party. I concentrated, therefore, on the simple issue of noise. The point was an important one. The majority of our colleagues undoubtedly disliked uproar, the only variety they were at all disposed to tolerate being—oddly enough—that nocturnally produced by high-spirited young drunks. And ever since the college Musical Society, ambitiously attempting Tchaikovsky's *Eighteen-Twelve*, had surreptitiously introduced into Long Field a battery of cannon provided by a former member who happened to command the Royal Regiment of Artillery there had been an alert feeling abroad that any form of artistic expression indulged in by undergraduates was likely to generate uproar by one ingenious means or another.

It didn't seem to me that a performance of the first part of *Tamburlaine* was likely to prove an exception to this rule. It would be a romp before which the one we had just been through would pale. Bedworth and I discussed the problem for some time. I wasn't a wholly distinterested party. Nicolas Junkin was involved in the project, and had contrived to become my pupil during the present term—for reasons academically obscure, and the more perplexing since I wasn't expected to take undergraduate pupils at all. It had to be concluded that he had no other intent than that of ruthlessly exacting my support for the production.

'Of course,' Bedworth said hopefully, 'noise is never so bad in open air. It ascends mercifully to the heavens. We can point that out.'

'Very true, Cyril. It's why band-stands in public parks and places have lids. They keep the racket to ground level.'

'A few years ago we had *son et lumière* in aid of some building project or other. It was because the college has had to over-extend itself alarmingly of recent years in the way of capital expenditure. The prospect of such an affair outside their windows didn't much please our immediate neighbours. But actually it turned out fairly harmless. Perhaps this will too.'

'Perhaps.' I felt that it would be only honest to afford Bedworth at least a hint of the possible worst. 'It rather depends on what tapes they hire.'

'Tapes, Duncan?'

'Of battles, and cities being sacked, and virgins being raped, and so on. You can take your choice. It's a well-developed industry. No need to bring in real cannon now. They come through the post in a cassette. You just clip the thing in, and then amplify according to taste. It could be done so that the effect would be detectable in Wantage or Abingdon.'

'Oh, dear!' Bedworth was dismayed. 'Do you think, perhaps——'

'We mustn't be faint-hearted, Cyril.'

'Of course not.' Bedworth squared his shoulders. 'I'll tackle Albert. I still think he's the key.'

During this conference Johnnie Bedworth had been hanging around. He ought to have been getting ready for bed, but was contriving an effect of helping his mother to cope with the general debris of the party. When I took my leave he was quick to accompany me down the garden path. It was, I felt, a very proper if slightly unexpected attention.

'My daddy says you have a typewriter that works by electricity.'

'So I have, Johnnie.' I was about to add, 'It's my new toy,' but decided that this, although true, might sound over-playful. 'It saves part of the hard work,' I said.

'I'm to have an electric train at Christmas.' Johnnie considered this statement for a moment, and concluded that, as a boast, it wasn't quite adequate. 'We have a very big motor car.' He frowned. 'Two—three—very big motor cars. We have an aeroplane.'

'An aeroplane must come in very handy.' The exhilaration of his party, I saw, was still affecting Johnnie's vision of things.

'With bombs.' As he made this shocking claim, Johnnie craned his neck sideways and went through the action of peering down over his right shoulder. 'Bang, bang, *bang!*' The bombs had hurtled earthwards and exploded. Johnnie, however, didn't pause to assess the damage. 'Does it do the spelling?' he demanded.

'The electric typewriter? No, I'm afraid not.'

'I could write a proper book like my daddy with one that does the spelling.'

'Probably they'll invent that kind one day. But you can come and see mine, Johnnie. We could spell one or two things together.'

'That would be very nice.' Johnnie was polite but unenthusiastic. 'We have a dog,' he said, with a switch to veracity. 'He's called Bruno. Virginia says Bruno is only a name for a bear, but I think it's quite right to call a dog Bruno too. Bruno wasn't allowed to come to the party because sometimes his behind smells.'

On this note of realism Johnnie and I parted, and I made my way back to college on foot. In the University Parks—the plurality of which had long ago become as fictitious as that of the Bedworths' living-quarters—level evening sunshine washed the grass with gold; skimmed it with shadows, as if the gods were bowling inky sneaks on the cricket field at the centre of the scene. The flatness of the prospect was not totally unrelieved. There were benches; there were shrubs reputed to be of superior botanical interest; there was even a small ornamental pond with ducks. The whole area was confined, but art, not of too obtrusive a landscaping sort, had been deployed to suggest further vistas at least to the imaginatively gifted. I was becoming fond of the University Parks, which as an undergraduate I had seldom frequented. I reflected now that they were a paradigm of their circum-ambient academic repose.

That a trite phrase like 'academic repose' could thus remain part of my mental furniture is an index of the force of early impressions and persuasions. This first year of my return to Oxford had not been without incident, and common sense would tell one that cares and passions are no more to be excluded from a college than—as Johnson tells us the poet Pope fondly supposed—from a grotto 'adorned with fossile bodies'. But this last image would be not a bad one to describe an undergraduate view of dons and their habitations. I don't doubt that my first encounter with Albert Talbert had held some hint as of the tap of a hammer upon rock: here suddenly revealed was evidence of the existence of a heroic age of scholarship long ago.

From these musings, which had come to me half-way across the Parks, I was withdrawn by the appearance of Dr Wyborn, who was bearing down upon me from the direction of Keble chapel. Wyborn was among the minority of my new colleagues whom I hadn't, by this time, got to know tolerably well. Even his function was a little obscure to me. He held the title of Pastoral Fellow, whereas the rest of us were plain Fellow and nothing else. It wasn't just because he was a clergyman; several of our number were that, without being distinguished in this peculiar way. Nor was it because he performed the duties of college chaplain. These were entrusted to a recent graduate—it being supposed (without, perhaps, any rigorous scientific verification) that a young man best understands young men. Wyborn was middle-aged, and his contact with undergraduates was confined to tutoring in Theology the rare youth disposed to that exacting mistress. Some special provision made by a benefactor long ago must account, I supposed, for his exclusive title. Oxford is full of such survivals, and no practical significance commonly attaches to them.

'Good afternoon, Pattullo.'

'Good afternoon.' It was surprising that Wyborn had not only uttered a greeting but also come to a halt before me. He was a shy man whose common habit was to glide past with no more than a murmured word or a faint sideways smile. Yet he wasn't dim; wasn't what the young men called 'grey'; on the contrary, he sometimes gave the impression of being highly charged with something on which he was just failing, as it were, to throw in the switch. At times he reminded me a little of my uncle Norman—also a cleric, although of the presbyterian persuasion—but this was perhaps only a matter of mannerism and physique. My uncle suffered from some curious affliction which gave him the appearance of being frequently in tears, and was thus constrained to be perpetually dabbing at his eyes with a handkerchief: as he was by temperament a lugubrious man the effect could scarcely be heartening. Wyborn dabbed correspondingly at a notably sharp and prominent nose. But this being seemingly un-promoted by any physiological necessity, one might conclude the gesture to be a decorous, if faintly irritating, substitute for the bad habit still practised by Jacob Firebrace. Wyborn was performing it now, and for a moment appeared to have nothing to say. 'I've just come from a birthday party at the Bedworths',' I told him. 'Johnnie Bedworth is five.'

These simple statements elicited a mixed response. Wyborn was not merely a bachelor; he was celibate in a thorough-going sacerdotal way, and the mere sudden mention of a domestic occasion confused him. But at the same time he was taking pleasure in it. Family life represented something beyond the compass of his feeling. Yet there had once been a Holy Family; God, like Johnnie Bedworth, had on a certain day been five years old; it was not improbable that the Mother of God had fixed up a party for Him. That Wyborn's mind really worked in this way could be no more than a conjecture; and since it was the first conjecture it had ever occurred to me to entertain about this unobtrusive man it was possibly wrong. But as it couldn't be called an idea that would naturally come into one's head in the presence of an Anglican clergy-man I was inclined to think that some flicker of mental *rapport* had resulted in my getting it right.

'Are you making your way back to college, Pattullo? If so, let me turn round and accompany you. If I have your permission, that's to say.'

'Yes, please do.' The formality of Wyborn's proposal chimed with his manner of addressing me. 'Pattullo' went against college convention. It was months since any of my colleagues there had employed anything but my Christian name. But Wyborn, I remembered, never used that form with anybody—and was in consequence himself 'Wyborn' and not 'Gregory' to all interlocutors. How this had come to pass, or

23

what it told one about our Pastoral Fellow, I didn't know. It seemed the odder because his surname was so unmistakably in the category of those that carry a muted absurdity along with them. '*Why, indeed?*' was a witticism so obvious that he must have been greeted with it, or variations on it, often enough as a boy. Perhaps he had clung to his patronymic as a result.

'Pattullo,' Wyborn said, and walked on in silence. This absence of immediate further communication may have been justified by the manner in which he had again pronounced my name. For a start, he was reassuring himself as to my identity. He was even reassuring *me* as to my identity. Furthermore, he was intimating a deliberative mood, together with a hint of appeal and a suggestion that something confidential and delicate was in the air. The vocal instrument with which Wyborn managed these effects wasn't in itself impressive, being thin, reedy, and troubled by a curious tremor or wobble. This rendered the more notable the weight of implication achieved.

'There is a matter I should like to consult you about,' Wyborn said. We had now left the University Parks and were walking towards the city.

'Yes, of course, Wyborn.' I spoke encouragingly, but only a further silence succeeded. I wondered whether I ought to have said 'Pray do, by all means', or something of the sort, as carrying a heavier assurance of interest. We passed the Clarendon Laboratory of Experimental Philosophy (which is Oxford's way of naming a haunt of nuclear physicists) and then the University Museum (which houses the remains of a creature 150 million years old, splendidly called *Cetiosaurus oxoniensis*). Wyborn was still in no hurry to speak. And as I couldn't very well either say 'Out with it, man!' or advance some random topic of my own the situation remained static. This didn't trouble me. I was far from all agog about what was to come. I had something of my own to chew over. Or I ought to have had. What was perplexing was that I felt no particular impulse that way.

I didn't often think about Penny. I thought about her far less often than about Janet McKechnie, crudely to be called an old flame, or about my cousin Fiona Petrie, who was gaining some title to be considered a new one. This hadn't been striking me as odd. Penny had long ago passed out of my life as definitely as Wyborn and I had just passed out of the Parks. That she was going to pay a visit to Oxford was not a piece of news that I'd have expected to upset me, and I had only been amused by Mrs Firebrace's scarcely veiled assumption that it must do so. What now struck me as curious was the fact that, from the moment of my making a parting bow to Jacob's mother, I hadn't thought of Penny *at all*. I realized that, had I not met Wyborn and been obliged to pay him some attention, my walk back to college would have produced only reflections on the Bedworth family, the weighty matter of Marlowe's rumbustious Scythian shepherd, and whatever problems of lecturing and supervising I was involved with at the moment. So what was not in my mind was a faint sense of apprehension before this anaesthetic patch in my consciousness. I was a child of the age of the depth psychologies; I had been an inquiring boy at a period before these began to give ground before the slobbering of Pavlov's dogs. When my contemporary Martin Fish had fallen into a depression as the consequence of an unpropitious love affair, and when his friends had discussed the possibility of dropping him through trap-doors and assailing him with loud noises whenever he glimpsed the faithless Martine, this sketching of an aversion therapy had been entirely frivolous. What we had really believed was that Fish had suffered some awful trauma which he would repress, but which would intermittently bob up in him for the rest of his days—failing, that was, the attentions of someone like Sigmund Freud. It was in terms of such distant postulates as these that I was capable now of being bothered by the fact that Penny refused to bother me. Some poet—was it Keats?—had been troubled by 'the feel of not to feel it', and something of the kind was assailing me when Wyborn at last got down to business.

'It's Lempriere,' Wyborn said. 'I feel anxious about him. And I know, Pattullo, that you're a relation of his.'

I was anxious about Arnold Lempriere myself, and judged that others might be as well, since it was possible to sense a certain amount of therapeutic effort going on here and there. But a disposition actually to confer about Lempriere had not, so far, come my way. In our common room a man would have to be in considerable disrepair before anything of the sort took place except between intimate friends. And—unless it was Cyril Bedworth's—I was nobody's intimate friend as yet. Why Wyborn, whom I scarcely knew, should feel he ought to discuss Lempriere with me was obscure.

'Lempriere and I are in some sort of cousinship,' I said. 'And he's been very kind to me as a result.'

'I understand he had a most disagreeable experience at the end of last year.'

'Yes, he had.' Wyborn's 'understand' puzzled me for a moment; it seemed to set him at an implausible distance from the episode to which he referred. There could be nobody in college, surely, who didn't know about it in detail. Yet it was plain to me, even on our slight acquaintance, that Wyborn wasn't a man to prevaricate. A good deal must really pass him by. 'It was a quite horrible affair,' I said.

'But in no sense to his discredit?'

'Of course it wasn't to his discredit.' I suppose I snapped this out. 'Nobody has suggested such a thing.'

'There was something about improper photographs?'

'You do seem to know something about it.' I glanced at Wyborn, perhaps thinking to detect in him the hint of a prurient attitude to our topic. But he wasn't that sort of man

26

either. 'There was nothing particularly improper about the photographs themselves,' I said. 'They were simply of Lempriere at a bathing place on the Cherwell. He takes pleasure in swimming, and has kept it up even in old age.'

'That's most sensible.' Wyborn displayed unexpected animation. 'At our settlement—you know that I sometimes work for a university settlement in the East End of London, Pattullo?—I have known it recommended to some of our geriatric cases. Please proceed.'

'What was improper was the motive for taking the photographs. And the manner of their use—in a fugitive rag put out by one of our junior members—was quite disgusting.'

'Does this mean, Pattullo, that there is still a bathing pool on the Cherwell where men go naked?'

'Of course there is.' I was becoming impatient of this odd conversation. 'Do you disapprove?'

'It's a difficult question.' As if to emphasize an impulse to suspend judgement, Wyborn came to a halt half-way down Parks Road. 'But, no—I don't think I do. Certain of the Umbrian painters, I believe, have employed complete nudity to symbolize the New Dispensation, over against the encumbering garments of the Old.'

'It's a relevant consideration, no doubt.' I was wondering what Lempriere—whose fondness for unencumbered striplings had been spot-lit so cruelly—would make of this theological point. 'I think it has been generally supposed,' I went on, 'that Lempriere—who, you will agree, is a proud and sensitive man, and a man of honour as well—must have suffered a good deal from the wretched business. It may have given a forward shove to the ageing process that already had a grip on him. I'm certain I'd be most unhappy if I'd been subjected to such an outrage.'

'Unhappiness can be creative, Pattullo. It's despair that's deadly. Indeed, one is warranted in calling despair a sin. Can we take means—here is the question—to guard Lempriere from that?'

I dislike Christian busybodyism very much—the more so because I am seldom wholly free from the sense that my spirit is rebuked by it. I resented Wyborn's designs upon Lempriere, which presently revealed themselves as being rather naïvely evangelizing. And I certainly didn't see myself—as was being proposed—persuading my distant kinsman to a resumption of his religious duties and a renewed participation in Holy Communion. All this was embarrassing, and at the same time I was ashamed of being embarrassed by it. I inwardly cursed Wyborn (I am sorry to say) for not knowing one man from another, or what was and what was not conceivable in a society in which he preserved at least some token appearance of mingling. I was squaring myself to the necessity of telling him that I was no good for the purpose he had in mind when our walk came rather suddenly to an end. Wyborn—although I had forgotten it—no longer lived in college, having taken on as a subsidiary duty some chaplaincy in a working-class district of the city. So outside the Indian Institute our ways parted, leaving the Lempriere issue unclarified between us.

I walked on in just such a disturbed state of mind as Mrs Firebrace might have occasioned in me but hadn't. I was seeing, I told myself, as much of Arnold Lempriere as I had done before the wretched Ivo Mumford had given his abortive magazine to the world and been most justly turfed out of Oxford as a result. But Lempriere had become more of an unknown quantity to me, all the same. I had accepted my colleagues' almost unanimous profession that what had happened was a nastiness to be ignored even in the most private conversation. As a consequence, Lempriere and I hadn't exchanged a dozen words about Ivo's wretched *Priapus*. I felt that this had been wrong. The proper course would have been to discuss, for example, whether anything could be done for the boy now that he had been sent down.

Lempriere owned more than enough magnanimity to be capable of that. And even a little talk might have cleared the air.

The college was now in view—and so was the subject of these reflections. Lempriere had emerged through the main gate and was crossing the thoroughfare that slopes gently downhill past the west side of the Great Quadrangle. It struck me that in his own regard he was moving briskly ahead. In fact, his stride was so confined that each pace took him forward by no more than half the distance which he probably thought of it as doing. This made perilous his progress through the traffic—a circumstance which he acknowledged at least to the extent of holding one hand shoulder-high as he walked. Dressed—after his common fashion—in shapeless grey tweed, and this to an effect of being hunched or crumpled in person as well as attire, he recalled, particularly as the towering buses and gigantic articulated lorries went by, a hedgehog injudiciously abroad on a very dusty day.

Lempriere gained the farther pavement in safety, and there for a moment paused. I now saw that he was equipped with a pair of field-glasses, something I had never noticed his carrying about with him before. Old fashioned and probably of the most superior make, the bulky instrument was slung round his neck on a thong and so appeared to bow him down with an emblematical suggestion, as monarchs in old pictures are obliged to lug round outsized orbs and sceptres, and the Great Doctors similarly bear hypertrophied commonplace-books, inkpots and quill pens. As prompted by Arnold Lempriere, a man in whom certain gazing instincts were robustly developed, this was a passing fancy perhaps too obvious to record. His appearance made me now call up, however, something from a distant past; the manner in which Uncle Rory's friend Colonel Morrison had never walked the glens without binoculars, and how appalled had been my sense that these might have focused upon certain irregularities of behaviour between my cousin Anna Glencorry and my-self. Suddenly recaptured like this, memories which time ought to have rendered merely amusing can for a moment occasion the actual sensation of embarrassment or discomfiture which had accompanied the original situation.

Lempriere had disappeared. He could be neither advancing towards me nor withdrawing in the other direction. I thought I must have been wool-gathering (as in fact I had been) until I remembered that, directly opposite the college gate, a narrow street runs off at right-angles in the direction of nothing of much consequence. Lempriere must have departed that way. I glanced down this minor avenue when I reached it. Some thirty yards off, my kinsman had planted himself in the middle of the fairway, thus blocking any traffic that might be desiring to pass in either direction. His field-glasses were trained on something high above my head. This could only be the college tower.

The particular spot Lempriere occupied was one of those from which this splendid architectural achievement may most advantageously be viewed. Another is from a corresponding distance within the college, across the expanse of the Great Quad. Any tall structure shows itself as variously fore-shortened according to the particular triangle constituted by its base-line, its apex, and the position occupied by the eye of the observer. The more subtle the design, the greater will be the number of variously pleasing impressions received as the view-point is changed. Most good judges, however, would have concurred in the opinion that Lempriere had chosen the best station of the lot.

Even so, it didn't seem to me probable that aesthetic pleasure could be what he was aiming at. Only late at night would he consider it decent to pause and admire this most precious of our possessions. There must be another explanation, and I thought I had found it at once. Some sort of roof-climbing exploit had been going forward. The tower, technically the very Everest among Oxford's peaks, had been conquered once more. Lempriere was studying some tangible token of the fact.

In coming so speedily to this conclusion I was again being influenced by memories from some time back. Hazardous scramblings on the leads had been in vogue during those immediate post-war years in which I had been an undergraduate. They were unconnected with any increased interest and expertness in rock-climbing and mountaineering, being rather a test of hardihood on the part of youths conscious of having been just too young to fight. The activity had made headway, too, in public schools. I could remember being told by a fellow freshman how he and two companions had scaled the spire of a near-by parish church—a broach spire, ornamented with crumbling crockets, of a type common in Northamptonshire. The ascent took them the greater part of a night, and they reached the top only because too ignorant to assess the grotesque risk they were running. Coming down was harder; they reached ground-level in full daylight and under the fascinated regard of some 600 boys. Their headmaster stepped forward, congratulated them on their achievement and survival, and led them off to suffer in decent privacy a beating unexampled in the history of the school. He felt obliged, one must suppose, to discourage a practice which might result in his having to send a batch of his pupils home in their coffins.

As for our tower, it had long been regarded as almost impregnable; and as there was no record of anybody ever having been killed or injured on it I imagine that actual attempts had been few. But I could remember the morrow of one night on which success was achieved. From the final glittering vane there flew, triumphant and incredible, a pair of rowing shorts and a pennon-like scarf in the colours of another college.

Nothing of the sort was on view now, and I had been astray in nourishing any such expectation. Undergraduates didn't do such things in present-day Oxford; they eschewed heady ambition, an unfriendly observer might have said, and preferred to stump terra firma, waving placards and bawling. Lempriere's observations, therefore, were in some other interest. I went up to him, waited until he had lowered the field-glasses, and then steered him to the pavement.

'Arnold,' I asked, 'what's this in aid of? Have you taken to bird-watching?'

'Temple-haunting martlets—eh, Dunkie?' Lempriere gave his throat-clearing chuckle, but his expression was sombre. He had been changing of recent months, both physically and in manner. One thought of the quizzical and sardonic as his note; that, with flashes of generous feeling on the one hand and arrogance on the other, had outlined his personality. His self-assurance, moreover, had appeared to be of the bred-in-the-bone sort that is indestructible—and inoffensive even when irritating. But nowadays he seldom seemed at any far remove from agitation, and could even betray an eye misdoubting the manner in which people were regarding him. Yet at the moment he looked at me gamely enough. 'Pendent beds and procreant cradles,' he went on. 'We may see them niched in the ruins well before we die. Either of us. For have I told you? I feel it in my bones that I'm condemned to a more than saurian longevity. Come, Dunkie—wouldn't you say I looked like a tortoise?'

'I was thinking of a hedgehog. And I believe they have an ordinary span of life, like the rest of us.' I didn't suppose Lempriere's bones likely to prove particularly good prophets, but at the same time I knew that he must be rallied and joked with—if necessary, to the death. There were octogenarians in our common room and there were youths in their earliest twenties. Within certain limits of discretion we all played at being contemporaries—a convention which worked well.

'But, Arnold, I still don't know what you're talking about. What ruins?'

'See for yourself. Spot the things with your naked eye first, and then take the glass. The top one's gone already. And it wasn't expected to. Not in anything like the time.'

I did now know what Lempriere was concerned about, and I scanned the west face of the tower. Its upper reaches were still bathed in sunlight, and they shone as if built of freshly quarried stone. This was deceptive; it was simply that the superficial masonry had been washed under high pressure less than a year before. It was then that the mischief had been discovered.

My eye had to take its time, for I hadn't performed this exercise before. Lempriere stood beside me patiently, holding the binoculars. Very high up, and from the smooth surface of a great cyma reversa expanse, light winked at me, winked too from lower down—and from lower down again. It was as if here and there small cleft flints had become accidentally bedded in the stone and were glinting down at us.

'Yes, I see,' I said, and took the binoculars. Focused, they revealed the small squares of glass cemented to the stone over a barely visible crack—a mere hair-line, it seemed—in the massive masonry of the tower. The topmost of these squares of glass was cracked from top to bottom. I handed back the instrument. 'It does look as if some minor surgery is required.'

'It was damned folly, giving the thing that Turkish bath. It went on for weeks. Washed out good honest compacting dirt.'

'Perhaps, Arnold. But I don't believe serious damage can be done that way. It's when foundations subside that you get trouble. Even so, think of the campanile at Pisa. That's seen no end of saurians come and go. It looks like a drunk leaning on a bar that isn't there. But it's a perfectly respectable bell-tower.'

33

The tartness of Lempriere's reply to this low humour was satisfactory, since it held something of his old fire. I decided that it had been nonsense on Wyborn's part to suppose that this tough old man would hold any traffic with dejection as the consequence of an insult inflicted by a beardless boy. We walked amicably back to college together. I wondered whether it had become a habit with Lempriere to make the reconnaissance upon which I had stumbled. Old people occasionally develop a phobia about this or that falling down. It may be a tree or a building or a lamp-post or a statue, according to some stray association buried in a remote past. Perhaps a picture had once tumbled from the wall in Lempriere's nursery, or perhaps he'd been secretly terrified by Humpty-Dumpty's irreparable accident. Something like that.

'If you ask me,' Lempriere said as we were about to part before his staircase, 'Edward has been keeping a good deal under his hat. It's a habit of his.'

'About the tower?' 'Edward' was, of course, a senior man's way of naming the Provost, whom I'd have had to agree owned an advanced technique of non-communication at times.

'Yes. But he can't keep it up, you know. There's a surveyor's report, and it comes before the Fabric Committee tomorrow. We'll all have to be given the truth after that.'

'Or what a surveyor supposes to be the truth.'

'Don't quibble, Dunkie. This is going to be a serious thing.'

I accepted the rebuke, and walked on into Surrey. Surveying it, I reflected that buildings do distintegrate. A massive structure I was skirting, known as the New Library because dating only from the earlier eighteenth century, had in my own time developed the habit of dropping chunks of itself on the heads of passers-by: sometimes they had come earthwards as abundantly as leaves from a tree. Was it conceivable that the tower, although behaving in no such fashion, was stricken in some yet direr degree deep at the roots? As if Arnold Lempriere's apprehensions had been catching, I was worried for some time by this thought. As a child—I told myself—I must have been traumatized too. Perhaps in my case it was by the dramatic news that London Bridge was falling down.

Later that night, and clearly as a sequel to my afternoon's experience, I ascended the tower. It was the first time I'd done so. Indeed, only since becoming a member of the college's Governing Body, I supposed, had I been entitled to ask for the key and make the climb. A man called Hardy, whom I only vaguely knew, came with me, and an easy flight of stairs took us to the first chamber, a mysteriously enormous lumber-room. I remembered that some Oxford colleges are celebrated for having accumulated over the centuries an exceptional amount of junk, ironically referred to as treasures, the greater part consisting of gifts from former members of eccentric or ephemeral or tawdry taste: it was presumably such evidences that surrounded Hardy and myself now. For some time we wandered among them, gently amazed. There was a great deal of furniture, nearly all of it elaborately and curiously carved. There were musical instruments, mummies, oil-portraits, pagodas, penny-farthing bicycles, crucifixes, bird-cages, coffee-grinders. One could feel that here, strangely laid away, was everything there had ever been in the world, so that a near-infinity of time would be required for its surveyance. Hardy said 'Pattullo' on a rising inflection just short of the interrogative, and then 'The superannuations of sunk realms', so that I wondered what had made him think of Keats. Suddenly the oppressive multitudinousness vanished, and I was in open air on the leads of the tower. Then, as if executing with perfect timing a planned surprise, Penny stepped from behind a pinnacle and confronted me.

I felt no astonishment. I was simply observant. Penny looked no older than when I had last seen her—or, indeed, than when I had first seen her, which had been well before her eighteenth birthday. And she had retained one habit I remembered vividly: a fancy for bizarre pets. She often visited a zoo-like department in Harrods, and came home with some small odd creature on which she would lavish affection for a week or so before forgetting about it. (I had to find means of disposing of half a dozen of these discarded favourites in a year.) What Penny held in her arms now, however, was quite commonplace and humble: a hedgehog curled up tightly in a ball. Thomas Hardy (for he *was* Thomas) stepped forward and took the hedgehog away from Penny, saying it was his business to see such innocent creatures should come to no harm. This was to prove a wise measure.

But now Penny and I were alone on the tower—or on some tower, since the structure hitherto around us had unobtrusively gothicized itself and now provided a transformed *mise en scène*. It was still, however, the city of Oxford that was on view; leaning on a parapet together in a commonplace way, my wife and I surveyed it like tourists. Penny turned her head and glanced at me; I looked at her dispassionately; it did, however, seem to me odd that her mere extreme prettiness drew nothing into my blood. Penny's lips, which had been closed, parted slightly. It was a tiny sign from the past—and even then it had meant singularly little: not a kiss, not the beginning of simple talk. But in this second, all the same, ungovernable emotion broke into my dream. My head swam; I thought the tower trembled; Penny went wavy before me, as if seen through turbulent water or in some trick-effect on a screen. This appearance faded. Penny's hand went to her hair, and she glanced round with impatience. I knew at once what was wrong. She couldn't find a looking-glass. To Penny it appeared to be impossible to do as all other women did, and keep such a thing somehow about her person. She began a familiar petulant prowl, and in a moment was peering over the edge of the tower. It was in this moment that my dream, as it were, took off—soaring into the absurd, leaving waking possibility behind it. But when dreams do this they can become less rather than more dream-like, at least to the extent that they impress a sharper sense of their reality on the dreamer.

Penny had found her looking-glass. It was the topmost of several sticking out from the sheer face of the tower and reflecting light at us from a clear sky. If its position was untoward it was nevertheless a familiar object: a driving-mirror of the kind more or less standard on motor-cars. Penny judged it would serve her very well; so clear was she about this that she was hanging head-downwards through a battlement-like aperture in the parapet to reach it. I grabbed her by the legs in the instant of its becoming clear that she now had no other support; I hugged them clumsily to my chest; looking past Penny—now vertical and upside-down—I saw not Oxford and its grey quadrangles but, one thousand feet below, the whole vast extent of the Gulf of Salerno from Capri in the east to those tiny specks in the west that I knew to be the temples of Paestum. Penny's skirt slipped down her thighs, fell like a tent over her head, blotted out all Amalfi immediately beneath. I realized that I couldn't save Penny; that her legs were sliding through my arms as if she were freeing herself from stockings or tights. She was gone. Craning over the parapet I saw her plummet like a bomb, shrinking with incredible speed to some vanishing-point still high above the glittering Mediterranean.

But now I myself was floating free in air, the tower—or was it the solid bastions of Ravello?—having dissolved around me. The sensation of being thus turned into a human balloon—even dirigible, I wasn't sure—was delightful; I reflected that the levitations of the saints had probably been a treat accorded them in virtue of their good conduct; I thought

37

it possible that this experience of my own was similarly a reward for praiseworthy behaviour in some immediately preceding exigency which I couldn't now recall. The air was delicate; the sea sparkled far below; I could distinguish on it a little steamer trailing an old-fashioned cloud of white smoke. I did, however, wonder whether there might not be something precarious about my elevated situation, and this made me glad that I now had a companion again. He was a physicist whose name eluded me and with whom I held only a slight acquaintance, but he seemed a suitable person with whom to discuss the scientific aspect of what was, after all, a surprising achievement. I couldn't actually see this timely authority; he hovered as a disembodied presence; but our conversation was nevertheless quite normal. He explained that there had recently been certain changes in what were popularly known as the laws of nature, and that Newton's sufficiency was no longer quite what it had been. I said that of course I had heard of this, and we talked for some time in a measured and learned way. I was conscious of taking satisfaction in being a cultivated layman, able to follow, and even pertinently to question, any lucid exposition even of recondite matters. The laws of gravity, it seemed, had lately been altered to admit certain principles of latency and periodicity. Just occasionally, to put it very simply, the apple failed to fall, and it so happened that I was behaving like such an apple now. I asked my new companion, not without a natural trepidation, for how long these periods of mysterious *stasis* usually lasted. He replied that it was never for more than fifteen minutes, after which period gravity invariably resumed its sway. Having made this clear, he left me—if, indeed, he may be said in any philosophical sense to have been with me at all. Now high above Atrani (and drifting, I thought, towards Maiori), I was seized by terror and woke up.

This dream didn't yield much to the sort of self-analysis that one practises on such things from time to time. I didn't, in fact, get much further than accounting for the presence of Thomas Hardy. Hadn't I been thinking about roof-climbing as a test of *hardihood*? And hadn't Hardy written a novel called *Two on a Tower*? There were other elements in the dream that hitched on to recent waking life, but I found myself without much impulse to work them out. What remained with me hauntingly were Penny's parted lips. Penny was no longer eighteen—or even twenty-seven. But it wasn't certain that her mouth would have ceased to admit of that tiny motion—a motion at once overwhelming in its effect and meaning nothing at all.

II

THERE COULD BE no question of the gravity of the surveyor's report when it was given to the Governing Body a few days later. The document was alarming. The Governing Body, although an assembly the awesomeness of which was such that I hadn't yet ventured to open my mouth at it, was itself awed by the dimensions of the crisis revealed.

At least so far as their constitution goes, Oxford colleges are out-of-date concerns. In theory they are autonomous and self-perpetuating property-owning corporations in quite a big way. Their survival is nobody's concern but their own, and they made do nicely through many centuries in which their financial operations consisted merely in the gathering in of rents from large estates and applying this income to the furthering of education and learning in whatever manner they judged fit from time to time. In the present age this independence has become precarious, and maintaining it an activity more complex and exacting than a collection of scholars and scientists is well-adapted for. When they do make do it is partly because they are intelligent men, accustomed to analytical thinking of one sort or another. It is also because they are able to call upon the experience of faithful former members skilled in the mysteries of the financial world.

I was discovering in these months that I had brought some bad habits back with me to Oxford. There is no vice in seeing the funny side of things; indeed, when the ability comes unforced virtue attaches to it. Pursued in a theatre of entertainment, however, it prompts to frivolity, or at least to an undiscriminating detached amusement as a response to anything that comes along. I fear I reacted in this professional fashion to the Governing Body. Attending the measured deliberations of these fifty-odd persons, intimidated (as I have said) by a decorum and patience which seldom yielded to anything unseemly or indeed lively in any way, I was too much on the look-out for the absurd. At first, at least, I found little that was discussed interesting in itself, so the spectacle ceased to be boring only when it presented, within a narrow spectrum of behaviour, material for what I hoped remained an entirely private grin.

I imagine that our undergraduates, when they knew of the existence of the Governing Body at all, supposed it to be occupied almost exclusively with the surveillance of their own diverse goings-on. Nothing could have been farther from the truth. A visitor from Mars, I had concluded, could sit in on a good many successive meetings of this assembly without so much as becoming aware that they took place within bow-shot of several hundred young men. The problems of these— or these as a problem—were coped with elsewhere. And if any of my colleagues felt a concern (as I am sure many did) over educational issues confronting universities in the contemporary world, they didn't treat the Governing Body as a forum for their discussion. Never having had to give thought to the priorities enforcing themselves upon administrative assemblies, I had judged this perverse and odd. In particular, I hadn't thought of the overriding necessity we were under simply to ensure that we had a roof over our heads. It was the first rumblings from the college tower that brought this home to me.

'Number 15,' the Provost had said unemotionally. The words, as if they had been a test devised by a social psychologist, divided us at once into two categories. This happened a dozen times at every meeting. Papers of one sort and another had been dropping in on us throughout the preceding fortnight. Some of us had sorted them through, arranging them in an order corresponding to the items of the agenda: these had to do no more than turn to the next page in front of them. Others kept everything higgledy-piggledy, and were constrained to rummage every time. The provident—led by the Provost—invariably waited with apparently effortless patience until the last of the improvident had caught up with them. Sometimes, indeed, a member whose business it was to open a discussion would begin to speak, observe a colleague still leafing through his pile, and break off with an apology for having uttered prematurely. Courtesies like this, barbed in a minuscule way, occasionally provided the more eventful moments of an entire three-hour meeting.

Number 14 had been the report of the Donations and Subscriptions Committee, and this had included a proposed grant of £20 towards the expenses of an archaeological expedition preparing to set out for Kafiristan. Several men spoke about this. Might not £10 be enough? Would £40 not be a more decent measure of what might be expected of us? Hadn't there been a similar application a few years ago from the people proposing fresh work at Leptis Magna—and what had we given then? Were any former members of the college known to be involved in this affair? What was the present balance in the Donations and Subscriptions Fund? This went on for some time, during which two or three fellows of really methodical mind, who came to meetings staggering under the weight of filed reports and minutes extending back into their own near-nonage, applied themselves to sifting out from this archival material precedents which they hoped presently to bring to bear in a weighty manner in one interest or another. Then a man called Sanctuary, who knew about Kafiristan but had been holding his fire, delivered himself of what was evidently a prepared speech, tuned up to a high degree of syntactical elegance. What Sanctuary had to say in effect was that these incompetent persons should be sent no money at all. But as Sanctuary happened at this time to be President of the most august of England's learned academies

42

he had to express himself with great circumspection. This he was well able to do, and enjoyed doing. We listened to him for some ten minutes. The Provost, it seemed to me, listened with particular complacence, and when Professor Sanctuary dried up—or came to a euphonious close—he besought Dr Chambers (who was in the same line of business as Sanctuary) to assist the Governing Body with his views. Dr Chambers proved quite willing to do so. He thought we ought to temporize rather than incontinently turn the application down. There were certain technical aspects of the proposed excavations about which one was entitled to have misgivings. At least in an informal way, inquiries might quite properly be made about them. Meanwhile, the matter should be deferred.

At this point my attention wandered, so I don't know on what grounds we decided on the £20 after all. I had been glancing back at some of the items already dealt with. Several involved money. We had voted £200 towards the college servants' annual summer outing. That had taken no time. Nor had deciding to sell a property, once a water-meadow but now an industrial estate, for a very large sum indeed. But Donations and Subscriptions were seldom rapidly dismissed. So the hour was now late—and here in front of us at last was the staggering issue of the tottering college tower. It was not, of course, literally to be described that way, but the surveyor had made urgency a prominent note in his report. He may have felt that he was dealing with people not easy to get on their toes.

I found myself wondering—one often did wonder—if the Provost was up to something. He was presumably responsible —or able to make himself responsible—for the order in which college business appeared before us. And he would not regard the discovery about the tower as other than momentous. So why had it been placed so far down our agenda?

'I shall ask the Estates Bursar,' the Provost said, 'if he will be good enough to take us through the surveyor's report.'

The Estates Bursar did as he was told. He was a quiet man called Geoffrey Quine, and he had come to us, I understood, some years before from a stratosphere of high finance—the rewards of which he had been able to forgo because he was a person of substantial private fortune. These circumstances lent him prestige among us, so that he was effectively a dictator within his all-important sphere. One could never have guessed this from his manner, which was diffident and gently humorous. In the business of maintaining over our educational labours roofs of a not too hopelessly leaky sort he had the air of a conjuror who must modestly suggest himself as being harassingly overtasked, although he is in fact well aware of his audience's conviction that the mirrors will do their job in the end. He now 'took us through' the report in considerable detail, although it was a lucid and non-technical document which scarcely stood in need of explication. Later on, the problems would no doubt turn complex enough, and appeal to that minority among us who were well-acquainted with the laws of gravity and even the strength of materials. But at the moment the main issue was plain. Perhaps we were being given time to digest it.

'May I take it,' the Provost said when Quine had concluded, 'that the subject is now open to debate?' The Provost seldom addressed the Governing Body other than in interrogative form; it was his way of intimating to his colleagues that he was, as he liked to express it, 'in their hands'. I found myself wondering whether prime ministers adopted this technique in the Cabinet Room. It was a question I must one day put to Tony Mumford, Lord Marchpayne, who had lately vacated his place in that *arcanum* as the result of an unfortunate General Election.

There was a pause. When an issue of real weight arose it was the convention that nobody hurried in. It was possible to feel on these occasions that we ought to be on our knees,

44

like a congregation handed over for a time to the activity of private prayer.

Meanwhile, the sun was setting on the college tower. I was among three or four who could enjoy a clear view of this moment in the day through a lofty window at the end of the big room in which we sat. It seemed to me shocking that my nocturnal imagination could have enlisted an object of such tranquil beauty in the bizarre charade of a dream. At this point I moved my head slightly. And the window-glass must have contained a flaw, for the tower appeared to tremble as I looked.

Sanctuary was speaking—now rapidly and nervously, but with much the same command of complex periods as he had exhibited in his previous set piece about Kafiristan. His theme was the imperative need for rapid and decisive action.

'And before those scoundrels at Westminster,' Sanctuary concluded, 'bring in their next Budget, and finally dry up the springs of charity!' He sat back and glanced round the meeting, pleased that this importing of political animus had cause a stir—conscientiously unfavourable for the most part —among his auditory.

'Professor Sanctuary,' the Provost said evenly, 'favours the immediate launching of an appeal. Were we to agree on that, its scope would have to be considered—am I right in thinking?—with the greatest care. Ought such an appeal to be directed simply to our old members, or ought it to be a national affair? It would be necessary, some of us may feel, to deliberate on that.'

'Mr Provost,' Cyril Bedworth said, and paused to collect himself. As Senior Tutor, Bedworth sat on the Provost's right, and it was his business to act as second in command, something that was not yet coming to him easily. 'Mr Provost, I need hardly remind members of the Governing Body that our last appeal to the generosity of old members happens to be of very recent date. The response was as magnificent as it was timely. But the fact does make our present situation a tricky one. I confess to being shocked by the magnitude of the sum that looks like proving necessary. Very tentatively, and if there is to be an appeal at all, I think I'd favour launching it at a national level. Were it to fail—a possibility we must take account of in the present economic state of the country—the effect would at least be less damaging to morale than would a similar failure in which the application had been merely to the loyalty of members of our own society.'

'Mr Provost, I am in agreement with the Senior Tutor.' It was James Gender who was now speaking. 'As between the wisdom of one sort of appeal or the other, that is to say. But I think I heard the Senior Tutor advance a proviso in which it struck me there was much wisdom. "If there is to be an appeal at all." Before we even begin to decide on that, I should much like to hear whether the Estates Bursar sees any other way of meeting the crisis before us.'

'I suppose, Mr Provost, that Mr Gender is asking whether we can borrow a sum somewhere near the million mark.' Quine spoke promptly, and with as near an approach to amusement as the gravity of our debate permitted. 'Of course the answer is that we certainly can. But if the resulting debt were to be extinguished only over quite a long period of time —say twenty years—the college would still find itself on appreciably short commons throughout. Expenditure on the rest of the fabric would have to be cut. Indeed, we'd balance our accounts at all only by both taking an individual cut all round and retrenching on our teaching and research—in other words, what we're here for, Mr Provost.'

This speech, tipping in as it did a distinction not to everybody's taste, produced silence. It was broken by Wyborn. I had the Pastoral Fellow in my head as one of those whom the Governing Body's proceedings passed by. He was always in his place—attendance at these august deliberations

46

was acknowledged as a high priority by all—but I had never seen him open his mouth, or even contrive any decent appearance of much listening to what was going on. But now he went off like a gun.

'What we are here for, Provost, is a most relevant point. It is the furtherance of piety and godly learning. I think I am not in error in recalling that it is precisely so expressed in the Statutes given us by our Founder. Well, this tower may be falling down. It is of interest, perhaps, that it is not the spire of our chapel that is in this danger. The spire is by some centuries older than the tower. It belongs to an age of Faith, whereas the tower may be said to belong to an age of Enlightenment. And of elegance. Yes, precisely that! It is undoubtedly an elegant structure, and I do not quarrel with it on that account. There can be much edification in beautiful things—most of all, perhaps, in those directly granted to us by the Divine Wisdom. Consider the lilies of the field.' As he said this Wyborn looked sternly at the Provost, perhaps as typifying one in particular danger of being insensitive on this front. The Provost (being an ecclesiastical dignitary) could scarcely express impatience before this sudden homily, although it was certainly something to which the Governing Body was unhabituated. So he maintained an air of grave attention. 'It must be a question,' Wyborn abruptly concluded, 'whether we would be justified in pouring out treasure upon an object which does little more than enhance what are already our abundant material amenities. I would, in fact, oppose such an act.'

There was an uneasy silence, which the Provost was in no hurry to break. He looked round the room, ostensibly soliciting further contributions to the debate, but with a certain tautening of the shoulders which signalled to the instructed that he wanted nothing of the kind.

'The Governing Body will have remarked,' he said, 'that the hour is advanced. And a number of items still falls to be considered. Would members agree that this matter be referred to a committee, empowered to consult with the surveyor and other relevant persons, and asked to report, if possible, to the next Governing Body meeting?'

Nobody demurred. Only I heard Lempriere—who nowadays never spoke at G.B. meetings—growl to a neighbour that the confounded thing might tumble around our ears while we yattered. The members of the committee were appointed—a certain number of them being nominated, as was prescriptive, by the Provost. I was surprised to hear myself—the new boy—included among these last, and it was only later that an explanation occurred to me. Apart from Cyril Bedworth I was very probably the only member of the Governing Body who had been admitted to any knowledge of the Provost's designs upon the Blunderville Trust.

I had heard nothing of this mysterious negotiation since the night on which the windfall it might bring the college had first been revealed to me. Of the technicalities of the thing there had then been no explanation: it had merely appeared that at some date not far ahead the trustees appointed by a former Lord Mountclandon were required to disperse enormous sums to charities at their own discretion, and themselves pass out of existence thereafter. Since the college was by law a charity, and since the last Marquis of Mountclandon had been one of its most faithful sons, the propriety of our getting our cut was incontestable. The Provost's sense of this had been sufficiently strong to involve him in parleyings with the senior Mumfords, Cedric and Tony, which couldn't have been at all to his taste. Looking back on these occasions now, I was surprised that I hadn't been more struck at the time by the secrecy attending the whole business. Only Bedworth as Senior Tutor and myself as Tony's oldest college friend had been admitted to the Provost's confidence. And that seemed to be the position to this day; none of my other colleagues appeared to be aware of the existence of a small fortune conceivably in the offing. Edward Pococke was, I had come to realize, a secretive man—inclined to conceal things, in Lempriere's phrase, under his hat. He was quite capable of concealing some early confidential intelligence of the really acute danger in which the tower stood were he convinced that such concealment was in the interest of a grand strategy of his own conceiving. And now he had put a brake on his colleagues' rational disposition to do something immediate and necessarily public about our critical situation. For a fortnight, at least, nothing about it could be bruited abroad. I saw that the Blunderville money must be a factor in all this, but not the necessity for what my friend Nick Junkin would have called a crafty hush. And I was bothered about the tower, as that dream had perhaps obliquely shown. My father's delight in it had been the sole efficient cause of my ever having entered the college. I resolved to ring up Tony and ask him just what was happening to the Blunderville millions.

III

IN HALL THAT night—which was before I put my resolution into effect—I had an irritating conversation with Adrian Buntingford.

'Well met, Duncan!' Buntingford said. 'You can help me. Your views can clarify my mind.'

'I'd like to think so, Adrian. But what about?'

'That boring debate on the tower. Was the gloomy and obscurantist Wyborn really right about it? Put it this way. Suppose the college to have a fairy godmother willing to wave a wand and grant us any one wish we chose. Would saving the tower compete for first place?'

'Possibly not.'

'Or let's be sober. Demythologize the fairy godmother. Turn her into a pious old member, who hands us an enormous cheque with absolutely no strings attached. That's conceivable, isn't it?'

'Certainly it is.' I had glanced suspiciously at Buntingford. But his florid features didn't readily lend themselves to interpretation, and I had no means of telling whether or not he had got wind of the benefaction possibly ahead of us.

'So here is money in the bank, Duncan, and over there is our beautiful but tottering tower. You'd say it's pretty generally agreed to be beautiful?'

'Pretty generally. But beauty remains in the eye of the beholder.'

'An excellent reply—and so the problem. Ought we to pay up in hard cash to preserve this chancy aesthetic experience? You will observe at once that a contextual factor comes in. This place isn't the Louvre or the Uffizi. Even more relevantly, perhaps, it isn't Palladio's Vicenza. As we heard from our pastoral friend, it exists for the diffusion of piety and godly learning. So to what extent should we be justified in pouring unexpected wealth, as if it were so much ready-mixed concrete, into shoring up a mere sense-on-beauty-occasioning object? Consult your own experience before the tower. Would you describe it as intense?'

'At times, yes.'

'But momentary?'

'Aesthetic experience has a fading quality as one of its characteristics. My father taught me about that. You turn away from Piero's *Nativity* and take a prowl to Uccello's fracas at San Romano. Then you go back.'

'Good. And here, of course, we skirt enormous puzzles. Are you a Christian?'

'No.'

'Have you ever been in a battle?'

'No, I haven't.' Rather unwillingly, I was now responding to Buntingford's tutorial method. He was adept at it.

'But these blanks in your experience don't impair your responding to those two masterpieces? I'm told they're masterpieces.'

'Essentially, I think not.'

'Good yet again. So here is what some pundit calls the phantom aesthetic state. A volatile or intermittent experience, and radically indefinable.' Buntingford's pudgy hand deftly manipulated a small fork on the dish before him. 'Rather like swallowing an oyster. That's what an occasional dekko at the tower is like.'

'It's rather an extreme view, Adrian. Do I understand that you would demolish this unsatisfactory tower, and allocate that pious old member's money to further excavations in Kafiristan?'

'Not precisely to that. What I have in mind is certain areas of advanced neurological research.'

'I don't believe you know any more about that sort of thing than I do.'

'Probably far less, my dear Duncan. But I glance through popular expositions from time to time. And it's almost as if the lore of the phrenologists is returning into vogue.'

'Feeling bumps?'

'Not exactly. But it seems that chaps are learning to stimulate, or otherwise practise upon, very precise areas of the brain. Fix up your guinea-pig—your human guinea-pig— with the right electrodes or whatever they are in the right place and you can generate not merely a diffused euphoria— which a decent brandy will do—but specific pleasurable sensations, whether coarse or refined. Sexual pleasure, for example, in a very high degree.'

'What utter balls!'

'Excellently said, Duncan.' Buntingford startled our neighbours by a sudden shout of laughter. 'But aesthetic pleasure too—that phantom state. It will simply be on tap— as freely as the shocking stuff they now call beer. Coin-operated, it could be, like the things you get cigarettes or aspirin from. Where the tower was, we could have an inexpensive little dispensary of such delights, democratically open to senior and junior members alike. And we'd devote our windfall to furthering neurological research in just such interesting areas. Like the tower itself, it would only be moving with the times.'

Around us at High Table men had been conversing rationally about their cars and television-sets. For this I felt there was much to be said, since I was becoming a little restive before set pieces. Below us in the body of the hall, the three hundred or so undergraduates dining that night were talking about I didn't know what, although I'd have much liked to. Memory didn't help. I could recall the occasion upon which Bedworth and I, sitting at that now vanished institution the Scholars' Table, had discussed the novels of Dostoyevsky at conscientious length. I could recall—but in no sort of useful detail—chatter of a more high-spirited sort: sometimes of a sort, perhaps, to suggest more high-spiritedness than we had actually at command. Many of the young men before me now seemed to judge it quite in order to look serious, or even a little glum. Did they discuss weighty athletic occasions, politics, vacation jobs, the economics of keeping alive on a student's grant? I didn't know. Did they discuss their lengthening sexual histories—about which I had gathered little, except that they were not exclusively of an old-fashioned auto-erotic order? At this still early hour, and sitting in rows as they were, such topics were probably as tabu as they would be in a nunnery.

I gave up this speculation—and at the same time any thought of going into common room for dessert. I'd decided to try to get Tony on the telephone at an immediate after-dinner moment, and have it out with him about the present state of the Blunderville negotiation. It was I who had insisted that it was up to him to weigh in—the implication being that he had a spot of family bad behaviour to atone for to the college. Tony had taken this, and it seemed reasonable to suppose he wouldn't resent a little badgering.

So as soon as the Provost had said grace I walked down the empty hall—the undergraduates' more meagre repast having been concluded some time before—and into the Great Quadrangle. The tower was at least in its customary position. If it stirred it was only as the Chinese jar stirs in the poem, moving perpetually in its stillness—and this I fancied it did even when thus viewed merely in semi-silhouette against a late-evening sky. Walking on towards Surrey, I reflected with dismay that Buntingford's nonsense did no more than caricature a philistinism not always absent from the make-up of even the worthiest men. Suppose the tower had to be dismantled, new foundations laid, the whole structure built up again with fresh-hewn stone. The cost would be, in popular language, astronomical; even as much money as we could imagine coming to the college from the Blunderville Trust would scarcely cover it. Wouldn't there be others besides the fanatical Wyborn who felt that, in our day and age, here simply wasn't the way to use money? It was true that we were under a legal as well as a moral obligation to preserve the tower. We happened to own it, just as a landed proprietor may happen to own a notable tithe barn or wool loft; and like him we must sustain the cost of preventing a scheduled building of historic interest or artistic importance from falling down. But laws of that sort, designed to protect mediaeval things, were of mediaeval character themselves: parliament enacted them, but their enforcement was another matter. Were we to represent ourselves as wretched scholars with an empty purse—or, for that matter, as stiff-necked philistines—it was probable that nothing much could be done about it.

It will be seen that what may be called the tower-theme had lodged itself firmly in my head. Perhaps I'd dream about the tower once more—as it was perfectly proper to do about so phallic an object. Or perhaps it would simply stick in my head through a sleepless night, in which case dawn would find me groping round it as the pivot of a play. This thought amused and alarmed me; I wondered how popular I'd be if I turned out a mini-version of *The Master Builder* on the basis of my present surroundings. Which of my colleagues would make a colourable Halvard Solness?

Passing under the archway that gives on Surrey, and crossing the grass leading to my own staircase, I tried to banish such idle speculation from my mind. And presently I was assisted in this by running into a sequence of small episodes which, besides delaying my telephone call to Tony, had nothing to do with the sober problem my wits were threatening to play the fool with. Or so I judged. The fullness

54

of time was to prove the supposition fallacious in a curious way.

In front of Surrey Four, and lit by the lantern above its entrance, there was parked one of those small trucks or hand-trolleys used by the quad-men for their miscellaneous occasions and frequently borrowed by undergraduates for trundling round their baggage. A removal appeared to be going on. The last occasion upon which I had come upon any nocturnal activity of the sort here had been when the disgraced Ivo Mumford had enlisted a number of his acquaintances in a noisy clearing out of his possessions from the rooms above my own. But on that night the modest vehicle now before me had been represented by his father's ministerial limousine, impudently commandeered for the purpose. Now, as then, there was a certain amount of racket, although this time of a minor sort. It was represented by sundry bumpings and puffings which seemed to be fading upwards on the staircase.

I took a turn round the quad before going indoors; I suppose because the library, with its great pillars softly lit through windows witnessing to scholarly endeavours still going on inside, is an attractive object to look at for a while. It isn't the tower. But it's quite something, all the same.

As a result of this delay, I bumped into two young men as I got back to my own door. They had tumbled downstairs with the needless and hazardous expedition characteristic of their kind. One was Junkin, dressed in the bleached jeans and combat-jacket he favoured at that time. The other, like Junkin slim and fair, I recognized as a recent arrival on the staircase: he had taken over Ivo's rooms. I glanced at him and saw that it was doubtless for socially impeccable reasons that he was wearing a correct London suit. But both youths were smothered in dust.

'Hullo, Duncan,' Junkin said. He was not above showing off a little with this now reasonably legitimate manner of address. 'This is Mark.' Junkin spoke rather as one elderly man, meeting a contemporary in St James's or thereabouts, might thus casually identify a juvenile nephew whom he is taking out to tea.

'How do you do, sir? I'm Mark Sheldrake.' Mark spoke promptly and only a shade stiffly. He was a freshman, and clearly held Junkin in high esteem.

'How do you do?' I said. 'I hope you're comfortably settled in above me.'

'Thank you, sir.'

I took a second glance at this standard public-school boy, with the bizarre consequence that I felt it would be positively impertinent to take a third. Mark Sheldrake was as good-looking as that. He is going to be very hard to evoke or describe, certainly in a word. 'Handsome' is useless. 'Beautiful' is little better, because carrying too many wrong associations. But the phenomenon lay in that area, and was transcendent of its kind. Even so, I'd scarcely have been telling myself not to stare but for a topographical circumstance attending the encounter. My rooms, outside which we were standing, had been Henry Tindale's rooms, and it was awkwardly true that I sometimes felt a certain Tindale aura to linger in them. Mark Sheldrake was very much the sort of young man whom Tindale would have enjoyed seeing tumble through his window. Moreover Tindale, whom in my undergraduate time I'd known only slightly, had later (as will transpire) re-entered my life in circumstances leaving me with a lively residual sense of the disastrousness that can be scattered around by men prompted to take a third glance at any Mark Sheldrake. It was only fleetingly that I was conscious of this odd bobbing up of something from the past. But I was conscious, too, of some further and elusive fact about the young man without which nothing of the kind might have come to me. At the moment I had no leisure to hunt after it.

'Duncan's my tutor,' Junkin was explaining. 'For this

term, that is. It's because I've become very interested in drama from the historian's point of view.'

Mark Sheldrake seemed impressed by this specious statement. It was left to me, however, to make the next remark.

'But what on earth are you both interested in at the moment, Nick? You look as if you'd taken on a rubbish cart.'

'It is that, more or less. We've been giving the Troglodyte a hand shifting some of his junk. He didn't seem to have anybody to help. It was Mark's idea. Mark's absolutely the Boy Scout. He's been expensively educated, and all that.'

Mark didn't seem discomposed by this, but I felt it must be ignored.

'The Troglodyte?' I asked. 'Who's he?'

'He's an old party called Dr Burnside. But we call him the Troglodyte because of his having these attics.'

'Troglodytes don't have attics, Nick. They have caves.'

'They're rather like caves, sir.' Mark Sheldrake felt startled that I should thus venture briskly to correct the eminent Junkin, and he was moving up in polite but firm support of his friend. 'I think I've heard that Dr Burnside is the college archivist. And he's been moving everything of that sort to the rooms at the top of our staircase. He doesn't seem to care to trust the stuff to the porters and people. So he's been very kindly allowing us to help.'

'I see.' A certain social sophistication, I felt, was involved in thus describing what appeared to have been the imposition of a species of *corvée* upon these young men. 'And I've heard about it. Dr Burnside really works in the British Museum. But he has taken a term off in order to get things straight for us.'

'You mean he isn't even a don?' Junkin asked. He spoke as if feeling that his labour might have been requisitioned on false pretences.

'No, he isn't even a don.'

'Then I don't see how he can be college thingummy.'

'It's probably an honorary appointment,' Mark Sheldrake

said, suddenly with the confidence of the well-informed. 'He's an old member. He was up with my grandfather.' Having got this clear, the young man appeared to feel that tutor and pupil might now with propriety be left together. 'I'm going to shake off the dust of battle,' he said—not without a glance at Junkin's warlike jacket. 'I've been up to town, and that gets one mucky too. But I'll shove that trolley away first, Nick.' And with this, Mark took his leave.

'Well!' I said. 'A remarkable acquisition.'

'We all think that.' Junkin grinned cheerfully, having picked up a fragment of sub-text in my comment. 'And then, you see, there's his brother.'

'Mark has a brother?'

'A twin brother—named Matthew by their resourceful parents. Matthew's equally dazzling. They came up last term, and were doubled up in Howard. But they felt it might be less confusing for people if they put a quad between them, which is why Mark's had himself shunted into that pitiful Mumford's old rooms here. They're not fraternal twins, you see, Mark and Matthew. They're monozygotic.'

'Good Lord!' I didn't pause to be impressed by Junkin's unexpected command of this learned word. 'And you say Matthew's exactly like Mark?'

'Two peas. They have a problem.'

'I suppose so.' It seemed a point at which to leave the subject. 'Is Dr Burnside up there now?'

'Oh, yes. Mucking in like mad.'

'I think I'll venture to go up and introduce myself, Nick. I'm curious. I used to know that attic.'

It was apparent from a blank space on the name-board at the foot of Surrey Four that Cyril Bedworth's first home in the college was no longer regularly tenanted, but it hadn't occurred to me to find out whether it had been appropriated to any other purpose. Bedworth had done more for my

Latin there than Buntingford in his casual tutorials; and the graphs and time-tables and reading schedules with which he had adorned the walls of the place had earned from me more respect than I'd ever cared to acknowledge. So the scene of all that attic-varletry may have constituted a minor focus of nostalgia for me. Some explanation of the sort, at least, was necessary to explain why I was climbing to the top of the staircase now instead of getting on with my telephone call to Tony. I hadn't met Burnside and had no reason to suppose he had heard of me, or owned any disposition to make my acquaintance if he had. He was reputed a thoroughly eremitical man. Although his duties as archivist brought him occasionally into residence for substantial periods, he hardly ever dined, it seemed, or entered common room. He contrived, in fact, a condition close to invisibility.

A knock on the door brought a deep-toned command to enter. My first impression was confused. Bedworth's sitting-room, although low-hutched, had proliferated in various nooks and corners, and was thus, as he liked to say, commodious. But this effect now showed itself much enhanced, since the chamber had been opened up into several others running under the leads. What first confounded me, then, was a sense of having walked into something unexpected but equally familiar and even more nostalgic: the enormous upper room in Linton Road which had been the scene of my instruction in Anglo-Saxon and much else by J. B. Timbermill. Burnside wasn't in the least like that preternatural scholar. But for a moment it was almost as if it were Timbermill who had risen to receive me.

There was, however, another and more severe bewilderment. Timbermill's retreat had been promiscuously cluttered not only with books and papers and journals but also with a congeries of objects of antiquarian regard collected from the kitchen middens of our ancestors. This place was cluttered too, but on an altogether larger scale. Burnside's conception of 'archives' seemed to run to anything sufficiently useless that had ever drifted into the college. I was staggered, for example, to find myself contemplating, perched on a shelf, that befeathered hat, ambassadorial in suggestion, which my father on a notable occasion had politely declined to don at the invitation of 'Blobs' Blunderville, Lord Mountclandon, and which I had in consequence been obliged to entertain the Provost's guests by putting on myself. This was sufficiently astonishing. Yet more remarkable was the circumstance that I was back with my dream. Here was the disordered museum which my slumbering mind had sited half-way up the college tower. Or so, let us say, it for some seconds over-whelmingly appeared. Intimations of precognitive experience are commonly evanescent. And now I was obliged to explain myself.

'Dr Burnside?,' I said. 'My name's Duncan Pattullo. I'm the college's junior fellow at the moment, and I thought I'd like to call on you. I hope it isn't an inconvenient time.'

'How do you do?' Having first brushed some dust from his fingers, Burnside shook hands with gravity. He was an elderly man whose extreme mildness of manner ought, one felt, to have gone with a light tenor voice rather than with the *basso profondo* I was now hearing. 'And how very kind! I fear I have been sadly remiss as a social being of late. Only, you see, there is a great deal of work on hand.'

'It seems so,' I said, glancing round the room. 'I've just been talking to a couple of young men who have been doing some portering for you.'

'Yes, indeed. I was most grateful to them—and a little struck by the appearance of the younger, as I judged him to be. *O formose puer*—I was almost prompted to exclaim—*nimium ne crede colori!*' Burnside produced a deep but very gentle laugh. 'Only the warning might have been a little out of turn.'

'I suppose it might.' Burnside had succeeded in surprising

60

me, although I don't think it had been in the least his aim.

'But I really must try to see rather more of my colleagues, as they very kindly regard themselves. I shouldn't like to fail to convey the great pleasure it is to return to the college from time to time, quite apart from the intense interest of the work. Do you know that I might have stayed on in a fellowship? After taking Greats, that is—which was a long time ago. The examiners were kind to me, and placed me above my deserts.'

'But you preferred the idea of the B.M.?' Dr Burnside, I found, had drawn me up a chair and seated me in it. Several seconds passed before he judged it courteous to sit down himself. 'The B.M. must be a wonderful place to work in.'

'Yes—but yes, indeed. Only, perhaps, it wasn't quite that. I think I judged myself unfit for the rough and tumble of college life.'

'I see.' This ready communicativeness on my host's part wasn't displeasing; he seemed a very crystalline sort of man. 'And you did find there was less wear and tear in the Museum? I've heard it described as a haunt of indescribable animosities.'

'It depends on one's department, I imagine.' Burnside wasn't perturbed by my outrageous remark, which a spirit of experiment had made me concoct on the spot. 'I believe I enjoy harmonious relationships with everybody in my own part of the place. Of course people come and go. In particular, they go. *Tussis* attacks them.' Burnside laughed again and I laughed with him.

'All cough in ink,' I said. 'That's how Yeats expresses it.'

'An amusing poem. But not quite fair. No, not quite fair. How delightful to find that you younger men still know your Yeats!'

'When I was here as an undergraduate we never stopped quoting him.' It surprised me that Burnside's information ran to this poet as well as Virgil, my early acquaintance with Albert Talbert having persuaded me that the learned habitually believed literature to have stopped off a long time ago. My after-dinner call was proving a modest success. 'You seem to be concentrating a vast amount of stuff up here,' I said. 'It's almost a little B.M. in itself.'

'Ah, yes—and the Provost has been teasing me about it, let me say. Of course the archives proper are the important things, and I am glad to think they are now tolerably under control. I have been fortunate in receiving so much assistance from Wyborn, whom you doubtless are acquainted with.'

'It's an interest of his?'

'Yes, indeed. Wyborn has been going into the early history of the college a good deal. A versatile man, and one with more drive, if I may say so, than might superficially appear. As you will be aware, he has a strongly evangelical side, which is something unusual in a theologian, is it not?'

'I wouldn't know. Is Wyborn also interested in—well, the museum side of the things?' As I asked this I glanced round the vast shadowed chamber, aware that it made me faintly uneasy.

'Not in the least. One wouldn't expect it in so dedicated a man. And for my own part I can defend it only as a hobby—a foible, indeed. Not that certain significant side-lights are not thrown by it upon the former *mores* of the college. Take books, for example. Of course they are not my province. But Thomas Penwarden, your excellent librarian, has made some curious investigations there. Until recent times—for all such matters are reformed nowadays, are they not?—books, often of considerable value, would disappear from the college library to the enriching of the private collections of the resident fellows. And Penwarden has come upon instances in which these men actually had the effrontery to bequeath such volumes to the college in wills of the most pious and edifying sort. And, as with books, so often with miscellaneous chattels which were in law the property of the society. Fellows would borrow them for the adornment of their chambers, perhaps—and later they would drift around the place, with any certainty as to their true provenance having passed out of mind. What you see around you—college treasures: you will recall the old joke—may include what was private property long ago, although the only practical course is to view it as in corporate possession at the present time. Incidentally, I have been through most of the lumber-rooms around the place by now. One never can tell, after all, what may turn up.' As he said this, Burnside glanced round him with complacency. 'Do you know, Mr Pattullo? I have sometimes indulged a thought about my own will. It would beg the college to let my remains be preserved in pickle in this room. The cost of a memorial would thus, at least, be obviated. You will recall the verger's version of Wren's epitaph: *If you ask for his Monument, Sir-come-spy-see!*'

I felt that Dr Burnside had probably made this joke before, but if I was less amused by it than he was, the reason lay in my again experiencing as I looked around me more than a hint of the *déjà vu* illusion. As a consequence, the question I now asked came naturally enough.

'What about the college tower—has any of the space up there been used for lumber?'

'God bless my soul!' As he made use of this extremely violent expression the college archivist sprang to his feet. 'Would you credit it?—I never thought of that! My dear sir, shall we hasten there now?'

'I've been told it isn't very well lit at night.' This came from me with perhaps excessive promptitude. It was no time since I had paid a ghostly visit to the tower with Thomas Hardy and my former wife, and a further and corporeal ascent with Dr Burnside seemed otiose. Moreover, it was time to conclude my call, which had only been defensible if somewhat formally conceived. So I took my leave, explaining that I lived at the bottom of the staircase, and so had the hope that Dr Burnside might drop in on me one day as he went about his occasions. Burnside found some civil expression which fell short of a positive commitment to any such detour. Like Janet's husband, Ranald McKechnie, he was capable of enjoying human contact when it came at him, but unprompted to take any initiative that way.

The miraging-up of the tower during this encounter had at least put me in mind of the night's final business. There was no difficulty in getting Tony. Being out of ministerial office, he was now more frequently at home.

'Tony? It's Duncan. How are you?'

'How am I! Are you sure your call is really necessary?'

'Don't be disagreeable. How are you?'

'Fine. I believe that's what one says.'

'How is Ivo?'

'Fine. So now you can ring off.'

'Not for just a moment.' Rather surprisingly, I couldn't tell whether Tony was in a bad temper or being funny; conceivably he was both. 'Tell me a bit more.'

'Very well. Ivo's bought an Aston Martin.'

'Good Lord! On Dad?'

'You must be joking. On his grandfather, of course. The old ruffian gave him an enormous sum of money to celebrate that thoroughly poor show the brat was turned out for.'

'I see.' Tony habitually (and justly) referred to his father in opprobrious terms, although I believed him to retain some perfectly proper filial feeling also. 'Well, an Aston Martin's quite something. Give Ivo my best wishes.'

'He'll be enchanted.' There was a pause. 'He'll be rather pleased,' Tony emended on a changed note. 'So thanks. How are you?'

'Fine.'

'Oh, for God's sake! What's this in aid of, Duncan?'

'It's about another and even more enormous sum of money. The Blunderville Trust money. Is there anything doing?'

'Damn-all, so far. I thought I might get myself made an

extra trustee, but it wasn't on. I'd supposed they had power to co-opt, and I reckoned a second Mumford wouldn't be out of the way. But it seems they can collect a new chum only if one of them dies or resigns. So I can only work through the old boy.'

'Do you think he can possibly be well-disposed to the college?'

'You should have somebody look in your head, Duncan. Of course not. My father's attitude to the whole gang of you is one of settled malignity. I'm working on him.'

'Is that any good?'

'You don't understand. I'm feeding the flame in the hope that his ill will or prejudice or whatever will so plainly appear that the other trustees will feel obliged to write him off.'

'I see.' Tony as a political animal was given to oblique courses, but this one sounded like a mere flight of fancy. 'Listen,' I went on. 'There's something else. If those people did decide the college was to be a major beneficiary, could they put specific strings on the bequest or grant or whatever it is?'

'I'd suppose so. Yes—I'm pretty sure they could. What are you getting at, Duncan?'

'Well, it seems for a start that the college could urgently use a five-pound note.'

'*Urgently?* Impossible! Do you mean a sudden emergency?'

'Just that, Tony. It's supposed to be confidential.'

'Rubbish! The country at large is going to the dogs, but that's a long-term menace. The only crisis the college can conceivably face in a sudden way is some large-scale threat to the fabric. So that's it.'

'Yes, that's it.'

'Would I be right in thinking that the Provost's treating it in a hush-hush manner?'

'Yes, he is. I can't imagine why.'

'God, Dunkie, you are thick! It can't be the library,

65

because that's been coped with no time ago. It's the hall or the tower. Right?'

'It's the tower.'

'Very well. Benefactors, on the whole, want something new for their cash. If my father's confounded cronies remain unalerted they may conceivably hand over that wad of money with no strings at all—simply for the general purposes of the college. But if they get wind it might be used simply to patch up an old building at terrific expense they may well start thinking they know better. Insist on founding fellowships and scholarships for research into Wheeling and Dealing, or to promote the study of Universal Benevolence. That's what's in the head of that crafty old Edward Pococke in keeping the lid on. I give it to him.'

'What would you say the time factor is, Tony?'

'Oh, any day now. The lot will fall, the die be cast. I'll hear at once, and I'll rush you the fatal issue. I *am* trying. I took your point about that.' Tony paused on this, and I realized it wasn't a note on which he wanted to close. 'Come to dinner some time,' he said. 'Propose yourself, and I'll see what I can do. Have your secretary get in touch with my secretary, old chap.'

'Idiot,' I said. And as I put down the receiver I was wondering whether in old age Lord Marchpayne and I would still be clinging to the convention of these juvenile exchanges.

IV

IVO MUMFORD'S *Priapus*, with its wretched lubricities at the expense of Arnold Lempriere, was now a good many months behind us. It had made little stir. Those prepared to market it had been few in the first place, and of these the majority scrapped their stock hastily upon a timely word given. Thus not many people knew of the scandal other than by hearsay. A good many copies must have made their way into undergraduate possession. But undergraduates although excessively ribald are also choosy, so it was on the whole by a loud silence that the ephemeral publication had been acclaimed. In his design to achieve a stink of sulphur Ivo might thus have been judged as meeting with his customary bad luck. Still, not everybody runs to a grandfather prepared to reward such a performance with enough hard cash for an Aston Martin. And as Ivo had also got clear of Oxford (which he detested) in circumstances of reasonably diffused notoriety he hadn't done too badly on the whole. It had been Lempriere who was the chief sufferer by the affair.

But Lempriere's feelings I hadn't—as I have said—penetrated to. It was, of course, impossible for him not briefly to express a view, or at least intimate an attitude. What we had gathered of his stance was that *Priapus* had been such a *mélange* of inept and oafish indecencies from cover to cover that no special opprobrium need be attached to Ivo's photographic contributions. This was a tenable position, and admirable on Lempriere's part in that it played down the element of unforgivable personal offence in the performance.

But now—and from the opening days of this summer term —I had been aware of a question of considerable curiosity hovering ahead. Would Lempriere resume his customary visits to Parson's Pleasure? They had formed a settled part of his life at this time of year, it seemed, since that period immediately after the Kaiser's War when he was no older than any of the other youths for whom the place was primarily intended. There was nothing very singular, indeed, in his having continued to frequent it. One often observed a scattering of nude elderly men upon that innocent sward, conversing among themselves or with the striplings around them upon topics so plainly of the graver sort that it required only a little imagination to feel that here, recreated on the Cherwell's bank, was some nursery of philosophy as known among the ancient Greeks. And Lempriere, as he moved among the *ephebi*, was at once sage and gymnasiarch. In this last role, I was told, he had been known to come down heavily upon young men who had fallen to some form of skylarking that offended his sense of decency. It is true that his sense of decency was his own—strict, but with surprising contours here and there.

At the moment this business of Parson's Pleasure set me a private problem. Back in Michaelmas Term, and during a muddy walk by the Cherwell when river excursions of any sort seemed very far away, I had rashly volunteered to accompany Lempriere to the bathing place one day when summer came round. And here summer was. The undertaking was not one that Lempriere would have forgotten. Ought I to leave it to him to revive the project if he wanted to? Or would it be better to take an initiative myself, thereby implying an unembarrassed assumption that his routine was unchanged?

Meantime, and with this question unresolved, another piece of routine went forward: my weekly afternoon toddle with Lempriere around the streets of Oxford. Unless in the stillness of the night, no particular charm attaches to such a perambulation in the present age. The pavements are noisy and jostling. There is petrol vapour in the air. The university population is so outnumbered by the industrial and commercial as to be virtually an indetectable presence. There is nothing particularly distressing about this last circumstance —yet it can somehow promote the illusion that the colleges themselves are now untenanted, or have become warehouses for goods which some drift of taste has caused to be little in demand. So I'd myself have been prompted to walk further afield. But for that Lempriere's days were over, and it was incumbent on me to follow where he led. Nobody else was admitted to walk with him. It was a privilege accorded to me in virtue of the nebulous consanguinity which he had discovered to exist between us. (The only parties which Lempriere would attend were those given by Jimmy Gender's wife Anthea, and this was also a consequence of some postulated cousinship.)

The quality of Lempriere's awareness of what lay around him on these occasions became a subject for speculation with me. On our first city walk together, which had been a couple of terms ago, he had contrived to pass through a large-scale undergraduate 'demo' without betraying any consciousness of its existence—although, indeed, he had made some reference to it an hour or so later. At times I thought that his manner of moving around as if in an earlier Oxford approximated to actual hallucination, and that he was capable—it was an alarming thought—of seeing an empty street where in fact a bus was bearing down on him. At other times I believed what was in question to be, rather, a simple but sustained act of will. He refused to admit the existence of anything he sufficiently disapproved of. If this was so there were more hazards involved than that represented by an Oxford Corporation bus.

He wasn't however, abstracted or withdrawn. Our jaunts regularly began and ended with a scrutiny of the tower, and it was evident that he was keeping as sharp an eye on it as anybody. Not that there was anything to see, nor would be until—perhaps in a week, perhaps in a year—the next of the little glass plates cracked like the ominous mirror of the Lady of Shalott. I had one day said to him that the real sign of imminent danger in such a case would be not visual but aural; that whispers, sighs as of weariness, the groans of deep fatigue would make themselves heard. I had no intention of speaking mischievously, and had read somewhere of just such phenomena as I was conjuring up; I must have thought in terms of diffusing my aged companion's anxieties and rendering them less acute. But Lempriere took this new view of the affair seriously, and put in time trying to catch amid the roar of traffic this fresh intimation of advancing catastrophe. Had he appeared one afternoon for our meeting beneath the tower equipped no longer with his binoculars but with a stethoscope I should not have been surprised.

I thought of him as quintessentially the college man; indeed, on more than one occasion he had explicitly so described himself. Now I was finding that he had a finger in numerous other pies—or at least a brooding regard for how they were cooking. Almost every place he passed put him in mind of some ticklish or unsatisfactory situation within. Some of these problems—and they were all personal problems—concerned near-contemporaries of his own, and I saw that there must have been a time when Lempriere sustained a wide acquaintance throughout the university—among its historians in particular. But the typical present situation appeared to be that of one man's falling out with another man and a third man's failing to do what he could about it. To Lempriere this was a grave sin. He valued friendship even more than he valued those family relationships which he appeared only very tenuously to possess. It was apparent to him that a rift between friends should call forth eirenic effort at once—the more imperatively if the trouble lay within what he regarded as the sacred bounds of collegiate life. So one had the spectacle of this quirky and often quarrelsome old man not merely inflexibly asserting the propriety of decent manners between fellow-members of such a society but also requiring them to exhibit towards one another a positive warmth of affectionate regard.

Lempriere had a further concern. In almost every one of the colleges, it appeared, some former intimate of his now had an undergraduate grandson in residence—and these boys were all in one way or another being mishandled and mis-understood. My first conclusion here was that it couldn't be quite like that; at least some of the crowd must be getting on well. Then I realized that it *was* a crowd; I kept a tally as Lempriere talked; and it became undeniable that he was talking nonsense. It wasn't, I decided, that he was imagining things, but merely that his sense of time was turning un-reliable. Perhaps there were indeed a few such unfortunate youths in residence now; Lempriere was simply adding to their sum others who had come and gone long ago. He was holding on to them. That, indeed, was the essence of his position all round. He was firmly not reneguing on the Lempriere I had first encountered only a year before: a Lempriere, among other things, effectively combative when he wanted to be. He still represented himself as that Lempriere almost every night in common room. But now I knew that what was going on there was the grim projecting of an artificial, or at least a former, personality, and that Lempriere had in fact moved on further than one might immediately detect. Had some ingenious investigator of human behaviour fitted him up with a line of small squares of glass, these would be splintering in a succession a good deal faster than those on the college tower.

It was a disturbing conclusion to arrive at on the strength of Lempriere's comportment abroad, and I now saw it as being substantiated by what went on in college. He no longer took much part in formal business, and never seemed to be put on committees. Indeed, the college's statutes, superficially read, would have inclined one to suppose that his age debarred him from any longer being around the place at all. But such statutes exist in order to provide intellectual exercise for nicely exegetical minds, and niched in ours somebody had somewhere detected some turn of phrase interpretable as an invitation to Lempriere to stay put. Perhaps it was intended that he should do so essentially as a social presence, and it may have been by way of honouring this implicit condition that he remained for the most part silent during all official deliberations. Yet this abnegation was very partial, since Lempriere now constantly concerned himself with a shifting multiplicity of college affairs. His habit of confidential communication had grown on him. 'Tell nobody,' he would murmur, raising that conspiratorial hand to his mouth. And he would embark upon some issue the delicacy of which made it totally insusceptible—he would aver—of ventilation before so vulgar a herd as the Governing Body. Alternatively, he would take up one or another trivial matter—such as not long before he would have laughed at any man's bothering with—and urge this or that attitude to it upon anybody prepared to listen. It was activity at least showing a certain resilience or power of adaptation in the face of change. Lempriere was again holding on. But it was to something slipping as inexorably from his grasp as Penny had slipped from mine in my dream.

Cornmarket Street is an undistinguished thoroughfare. In those informed guidebooks to Oxford with which dons of literary bent every now and then seek a little to improve their fortunes it is commonly passed over in silence, and occasionally even reprobated—although the more detailed compilations will note 'a pleasantly restored sixteenth-century shop', or mention that Shakespeare regularly put up at one of its pubs which was already some four hundred years old at the time of the death of Queen Elizabeth. But in the Corn on the whole the picturesque traveller has a thin time. It will be his impulse to steer rapidly between the Scylla of Woolworth's and the Charybdis of Marks and Spencer's in order to enter the broad calm waters of St Giles'. Lempriere and I, making this perambulation regularly, proceeded at an even pace, conversing the while. It was noticeable that he had abandoned his former convention, which had required a substantial initial period of silence. I have known elderly men of settled taciturn habit who, having suffered some circulatory disaster reducing them for a time to a humiliating aphasia, turned almost embarrassingly loquacious when the power of speech was restored to them. Lempriere's condition appeared to hold some correspondence with this; he was reassuring himself that things had become normal again. Observing this further sign, I remembered the anxieties of Dr Wyborn about our colleague, and now felt that his solicitude was not un-reasonable.

'You ought to visit some Scottish schools, Dunkie.' Lempriere produced this one afternoon immediately we had left the college gate behind us. 'It's clearly your job to take them on. No fellow ought to hold himself exempt from such chores, even if he is a professor or reader or what-have-you. It's only decent to earn your keep.'

This surprising attack—the more disconcerting since I had to think for a moment before understanding what Lempriere was talking about—was at least reassuringly in his old vein of sudden and gratuitous affront. Making and fostering contacts with 'good' schools—and particularly with unassuming ones not regularly in the way of sending boys to Oxford—was an activity to which a number of my colleagues apparently gave considerable thought. It seemed an admirable concern, and one which might have astonished persons with a stereotyped notion of the exclusiveness of ancient universities. Under-lying it, no doubt, was that competitive hunt for the country's really clever children which a collegiate system nourishes. I

73

hadn't myself much instinct for this—or at least I believed that prizing individuals preponderantly in terms of their sharp wits was something to be chary about, and could even approximate to a kind of occupational disease among the academic classes. But at the talent-scouting involved I'd have been very willing, within bounds, to do as I was told. So I resented Lempriere's depicting me as a skulker on the fringes of the scrum.

'Nobody's put anything of the sort to me,' I said—and recalled even as I spoke, that Lempriere owned skill in eliciting patently inadequate replies to his remarks. 'But, of course——'

'We don't put things to people. Responsibilities emerge.'

'Arnold, you're not being reasonable. Nobody is more inclined than yourself to tick me off as a tiro—and I don't mind a bit. But the job you're talking about is for somebody who has got thoroughly hold of the ropes.'

'You have a point.' Lempriere's chuckle, although almost inaudible as we negotiated Carfax, signalled that he wasn't displeased. 'But we all have to begin.'

'Very well. Be good enough to tell Charles Atlas I'd have a go if asked—I suppose as Tutor for Admissions it's his stamping-ground. Do you visit schools yourself?'

'Now and then.' Rather to my discomfiture, Lempriere gave me, slant-wise, that glance that I thought of as new to him: the glance of a man who suspects mockery or disparagement. 'Public schools, for the most part, since I'm regarded as that sort of period piece. Damned useless places, most of them are nowadays. If I had sons I'd send them to a Board school.'

'It mightn't be easy to find them precisely that. And you're talking very great nonsense, anyway. You know perfectly well what school you'd send them to.'

By this time the greater part of the Corn was behind us, and at its intersection with Ship Street Lempriere had come to a

74

halt as if to take the measure of the traffic. It was contrary to his habit; when crossing even the busiest thoroughfare he would simply raise that arm in air much as a policeman on point duty might do. Directly in front of us now was St Michael-at-the-North-Gate, and I supposed that his pause was occasioned by a wish to compare one notable tower with another. The tower of St Michael's is not in the least architecturally splendid. It is a rectangular structure dwarfed by the surrounding buildings, and is fabricated out of something known to antiquarians as 'random rubble'. This scarcely suggests anything likely to survive the centuries, but in fact the tower was originally part of the fortifications of Saxon Oxford, and is thus far and away the most venerable building in the city; its stones must already have blackened in the vapours of the Thames valley long before some handful of scholars near-by began to regard themselves as a *studium generale* or university. The tower of St Michael-at-the-North-Gate is thus a very suitable monument for any latter-day don to take reflective notice of. But this seemed not Lempriere's intention either. His glance was directed elsewhere.

To the side of the tower, and raised a few inches above the pavements bounding it, is a small flagged area furnished with three or four wooden benches which stand in the scanty shade of a not very flourishing lime. This exiguous precinct one would somehow have supposed to constitute a haven for the elderly: for old women lugging shopping-baskets and old men in difficulty with their feet. But in fact it is the young who tend to congregate on this very ancient spot. School-children line its perimeter from time to time, out-clattering the traffic with rattled tin collecting-boxes for the relief of famine and plague in distant quarters of the globe. The benches tend to be occupied by persons only a little older but of contrastingly contemplative habit: scarcely (as might be appropriate) wandering scholars, but at least *Wandervögel* with a respectable tradition of their own. A quarter of a century before, these ragged and gentle creatures, long-haired and seemingly infrequently tubbed, would have presented an almost total contrast to Oxford's indigenous young: to that entire congregation, so various in itself as to include alike the adolescent Tony Mumford and the adolescent Cyril Bedworth. Nowadays only certain forced accents—earrings, for example, and by preference one earring rather than two— at all securely distinguished them from those junior members of the university for whom the drop-out image had its appeal. Wordsworth's vagrants, Matthew Arnold's alienated scholar or his gipsy child by the sea-shore, were their kin; their poverty, passivity, and mysterious non-attachment generated a certain awe, I believe, in those more settled of their contemporaries through whose ranks they were straying for a time. Nick Junkin, for instance, who had survived something called the First Public Examination, achieved theatrical eminence, and even acquired a three-piece suit, would stiffen at a word of disparagement directed against these apostles of a different way of life.

This was the spectacle that Arnold Lempriere had paused to contemplate. It seemed not in a sympathetic spirit. He was of a generation which resents—which even feels threatened by—inexplicable new canons of behaviour in the young. I was expecting him, therefore, to utter some words of severe distaste before this layabout or hippie scene. But then I saw that his expression was not of indignation but of something very like fear—this, and that he wasn't looking at the scattering of idle young people, but at the only person of a different age sitting among them. This was an old man—alien to the scene, and yet alike in manner and attire curiously assimilated to those around him. He was J. B. Timbermill.

Since Timbermill was, or had been, the outstanding Anglo-Saxon scholar of his time, the tower of St Michael-at-the-North-Gate was a wholly appropriate background for him. It could literally have been this had any of the several colleges of which he was an honorary fellow or the like thought to commission a portrait of him to hang on the line in hall. But nobody, it seemed, could recall a day upon which Timbermill had entered any college whatever, and the custom must have been judged, as a consequence, inappropriate to his case. Even at this late stage of his career (and how late it was, a single glance now told one) he could have prompted, indeed, a portrait very much in an Oxford academic tradition. The colleges are apt to procrastinate these commemorative activities. They may even, like the nations in Johnson's poem, to buried merit raise the tardy bust. More frequently, they go into action round about their subject's eightieth year. And as the venerable *alumnus*, consulted about a painter of his choice, often recalls some contemporary and crony of his own who is a dab hand at that sort of thing, the combined ages of sitter and painter can run well into the 160s. The image which may thus be conjured up of two aged creatures peering myopically at one another from either side of a canvas has a bizarre quality sometimes matched by the oddity of the artistic effect achieved.

I wasn't, of course, fabricating such thoughts as I stood beside Lempriere in the Corn. I was telling myself that Timbermill in his present situation was by no means to be regarded as an object of pathos. He was exceedingly unkempt —like a tramp, it might have been said, who has for some time been letting himself go. He was this to an extent much beyond the bounds of that eccentricity which in the popular mind is admissible in professors and learned persons generally. He also looked rather mad—or at least one would have hesitated to risk money on his sanity without further investigation. Yet—and even although his lips were sound-lessly moving—he could be seen to be a man who commanded himself at least to this extent: that he was where he was because he wanted to be. This was, no doubt, partly a matter

77

of the tower—about the history of which he must know as much as any man in England. But chiefly it was the young men and women around him that he had chosen. He sat among them securely, like a man amid his peers.

If the author of *The Magic Quest* had thus found and elected his final companions it looked for a moment as if he had correspondingly lost at least one from earlier on his road. I had seen him gaze at Lempriere quite unregardingly, but Lempriere might well be a man he didn't know, or at least had no reason to remember. Then he had looked at me, and again no shadow of recognition had appeared to stir in him. This shook me. A week seldom passed without my visiting Timbermill, if only briefly, and although his conversation was not without its strangeness it hadn't struck me as addressed to somebody whose identity he was prone to forget. His 'Duncan son of Lachlan' was as firmly delivered as ever. Yet now I had a sense of having floated out of his regard. And there seemed nothing to be done. Timbermill prowling Oxford bemusedly at midnight could be taken charge of and guided home. But I felt that I had no title or occasion to do anything of the sort now; felt even that, were he in need, it would be most natural for him to appeal to one or another of those young strangers among whom he sat. There was a sense, then, in which Timbermill had simply left us—'us' signifying, really, less this individual and that than the sum of his academic associations through a long and eminent working life.

I glanced again at Lempriere. He was no longer showing fear. That had been only a brief betrayal, and he was now sardonically grim. He, too, was at the end of a long working life. But he had not achieved—nor, I suspected, ever owned any strong impulse to achieve—eminence as a scholar. Collegiate life as a texture of personal relationships, alike with colleagues and with fleeting generations of young men, had made him what he was, and his only acclaim had been at those particular desks in the Foreign Office which had discovered in war-time his unexpected skill in lying abroad for the good of his country. As this old joke came back to me I saw how strange a dichotomy that interlude had represented in his life; it belonged with the same unpredictability in things as had been exemplified when Gavin Mogridge, that non-starter as a Pablo Casals, moved by way of the Mochica disaster to his mysterious career as a secret agent.

Lempriere had now looked at Timbermill quite long enough: another few seconds of such scrutiny and the effect would have been aggressive and rude. Timbermill mightn't have noticed, or in the least minded if he did, but I myself didn't take to the notion at all. I put a hand on Lempriere's shoulder—which was a temerarious act, even granted our cousinship—and propelled him forward and into Magdalen Street. He accepted this treatment in sombre silence, so that I supposed he was disinclined to offer any comment on the incident. But this wasn't so.

'Notice that poor old chap, Dunkie?' he asked suddenly and in his gruffest voice. 'Hasn't kept his form at all. Timberlake, or some such name. Spent his life digging up Anglo-Saxon shit-houses and the like. Done him no good at all.'

'J. B. Timbermill,' I said. 'He was my tutor. He got a clear alpha on the job.' In what tone I said this I don't know, but I was displeased that Lempriere should dismiss our strange encounter with so stupid a quip. 'And he wrote a very remarkable book. Not about Angles and Saxons, but about some sort of imaginary heroic age.'

'Pshaw!' Lempriere had a little quickened his toddle—with his walking-stick pointing cautiously ahead of him. I saw that he was upset. 'Fellow of Balliol,' he said, 'back in Sandy's time. Brilliant place. Never went near it. Made an honorary fellow of New College, which is where he started out. Ignored it. The same thing at Merton, I've been told. Men like that go mad. Shuffle through the streets munching apples and slobbering, so that you'd suppose they'd taken to drink. Or just been let out of gaol.'

I had no reply to this, and we walked on for some paces without speaking. Then again Lempriere halted, this time by the Martyrs' Memorial.

'A *good* tutor?' he demanded.

'Yes. He never took many pupils. But he was a very good tutor indeed.'

'I didn't know.' Lempriere produced these words in a disturbed voice which was unfamiliar to me—the voice of a humble man. And at the same time he looked around him confusedly. 'Dunkie,' he asked, 'which way would you like to go?'

'We'll go up St Giles',' I said, reflecting that he had never put such a question to me before.

Later that afternoon, as it happened, I witnessed another encounter between contemporaries—quite exact contemporaries, this time. Mark Sheldrake and I had run into each other on several occasions at the foot of our staircase, and had usually got decently further than just passing the time of day. He seemed a friendly youth in a reserved fashion, a little reminding me of a former inhabitant of Surrey Four, Martin Fish. Fish had been an Australian, and Mark Sheldrake was what I could still think of as very English; and whereas Fish had been no more than pleasantly personable this new neighbour was as he was. Their similarity consisted in their both being what I had long ago naïvely named miraculous youths—this meaning that they seemed incapable of the slightest awkwardness of adolescence and never got small things wrong. Such a gift of nature can be a liability, and off-putting if the slightest self-consciousness attends it. But those right at the top of this league table are immune even from that. Fish, becoming a close friend as a consequence of what each

80

of us regarded as deep amatory tribulation, had at times irritated me on various accounts—but never, so far as I could remember, on the score of this particular endowment. About Mark Sheldrake I couldn't as yet be sure, and I should never travel through Italy with him in dogged pursuit of aesthetic instruction. One day we'd have a glass of madeira together, and he'd tell me such things as the number of his siblings and the region of England in which he happened to live. Meanwhile we neither of us had any inclination either to sustained conversation or to hurrying shyly by.

I hadn't yet glimpsed Matthew Sheldrake. The college is a large place, so large as seldom to seem populous, and one can go here and there in it for weeks on end without running into one or another individual with whom one is perfectly familiar when one does. A peculiar grace of communal living attaches to this. We used to be astonished when ignorant persons from colleges on a different scale remarked commiseratingly that we were much too large.

But here now undoubtedly was Matthew on the east of the Great Quadrangle and Mark on the west; they were advancing upon one another each on some occasion of his own and without any hasty sign of recognition or preparation for greeting. The first thing I noticed was their clothes. One might have said that in this particular they had a common style, but within it were differences of detail, careless in seeming but perhaps not quite thoughtlessly achieved. They did their hair differently—again within a common convention of an unnoticeable sort. They weren't going to be mistaken for one another if they could help it, but at the same time they weren't taking any means to this that would suggest their attaching importance to the matter, or signal any sense that being identical twins was a very special sort of thing. But there remained, of course, the stubborn fact of their answeringly identical good looks. These would, after a fashion, remain with them all their days; but they were now of an age at which, in either sex alike, such looks take on a quality the flower-like transience of which seems set apart from sublunary things. The angels in heaven, one supposes, go on looking angelic for ever. But this can only mean that angels miss out on something and are taken for granted as comfortable permanencies in the divine regard. These mortal boys were like a bright exhalation in the evening, poignant in the evanescence of what they possessed.

Mark Sheldrake and Matthew Sheldrake met. They hadn't exactly been strolling—for strolling is, if only faintly, implicated with the offering of an effect. But they hadn't been walking briskly either, and this rendered unobtrusive the manner of their now pausing in front of one another. Hands in pockets, they exchanged what I read as trivial information, the most casual remarks. They weren't quite immobile as they did so; rather they were in faint movement, like saplings in a breeze. They took leave of each other by way of a slight backward inclination of the body and walked on. Then, with a couple of yards between them, each swung simultaneously and telepathically round, retreating backwards for a few paces so that some exchange of afterthoughts might pass between them. And then they turned again and went their ways.

Although there was nothing remarkable about this fraternal episode it was lingering in my mind when I ran into Robert Damian a few minutes later. The black medical bag he carried indicated that he was in college on a professional occasion, but since he stopped to speak I concluded that this had been discharged.

'I've just seen those twins together for the first time,' I said. 'It's taken me weeks to realize they exist, although one of them is now on my staircase. Would you say, Robert, that they interest you from a scientific point of view?'

'The Sheldrakes? Well, not really. They've so obviously been nursed upon the self-same hill. Fed the same flock, and so forth. If one of them had been snatched from his cradle by the raggle-taggle gipsies, then we'd have quite something. Bringing identical twins together for guinea-pig purposes after wholly disparate nurtures is a trick-cyclist's dream. It has been managed, I believe. But I'm not a man of science, thank God. An Empirick—that's me.'

'No doubt. A rather special condition attaches—wouldn't you say, Robert?—to those two young men.'

'Yes, indeed. *O don fatale!*, as Verdi's lady says. What obscure poet talks about the ambush of young days? I never know these things.'

'Shakespeare.'

'Ah, yes. Well, I'd suppose that at school the Sheldrakes ran into the hell of a lot of ambush. But nothing to what they'll have to put up with once the female of the species is let loose on them.'

'Perhaps so—although there are compensations, no doubt. By the way, I've had a dollop of the other end of life this afternoon, and I think you've told me that in North Oxford that's rather your territory. Embalming, you called it.'

'True enough. It's why I like this college job. I suppose the young are quite as busy just surviving as the old—only it hasn't occurred to them that the position is merely that.'

'Regardless of their doom, the little victims play.'

'Exactly. How boring, Duncan, that the whole of life can be summed up in half a dozen stupid tags like that out of anthologies.' Damian prepared to move on, and then checked himself. 'What were we talking about?'

'Only about my going for a walk with Arnold Lempriere before tea, and having a glimpse of J. B. Timbermill. My cousin Fiona Petrie believes he's a patient of yours. Is that right?'

'Yes, he is. Only he's not one for calling in the doctor. You were his pupil, weren't you?'

'I was farmed out to him for the language stuff in the

83

English School. He made me passionately interested in it.'

'Good God!'

'Yes—he's a remarkable man. Not that it became a lifetime addiction, I'm afraid. Years and years later, Fiona was his pupil in a far more substantial way. And what's happened is that we've made a pact—Fiona and I have—not to start tidying him up or away, at least as long as he has the slightest power to answer to his own helm. It may be a muddled idea, and I'm not happy about it. Timbermill doesn't seem to have a relative in the world. I thought I'd just tell you.'

Damian received this silently but with a quick nod. I judged it to be a satisfactory signal. When he did speak it was obliquely.

'I'm not Arnold Lempriere's G.P., praise the Lord. But there'll be a spot of tidying up there one day.'

'I think Arnold does have relations of a sort. An aged aunt——'

'Hardly that.'

'Well, somebody. Buried in a derelict manor-house I don't know where.'

'I see. Useful to shove in a front pew at the memorial service.'

'You have a point there.' As I made this Lempriere-style reply I thought how remarks like this from Robert Damian had an effect of giving him away. He was a compassionate man. One day a perceptive obituarist—the thought came naturally to me as a consequence of the way our minds were running—would describe him as of lively sympathies.

'Are you dining tonight?' I asked. This was a prescriptive question at the end of these brief encounters.

'Yes I am, as it happens.' Damian grinned at me. 'And I'll bring along a skull and plant it on the board.'

And Damian walked away. His emblem, the little black bag, went along with him.

V

TIMBERMILL'S HIPPIE PHASE—as I suppose it might be called—haunted my dreams, and on the following afternoon I went to talk about it with Fiona. She was out, however, and I found myself landed with her housemate Margaret Mountain instead. I don't say 'landed' as indicating that this severe young novelist and I now got on together other than well. It was merely a matter of my remembering I had been rather to blame about her. More than a week before I had read in *The Times* that *The Orrery* had won a much-publicized 'literary' award. This was quite something for a first novel; I ought to have written to Margaret at once; I did hasten to offer my congratulations now.

My performance wasn't a success. Perhaps I overdid my expressions of pleasure at this piece of nonsense, and it hadn't occurred to me that the authoress herself might feel it to be just that. She made no bones about being thoroughly upset. She hadn't 'entered' or in any way put herself in competition; she hadn't been sounded or consulted; the thing was little short of an impertinence.

Margaret's diminutive frame trembled as she came out with this. She had several times talked to me about the juvenile shortcomings of *The Orrery*, but I hadn't realized there were aspects of the book she had come actually to hate.

'But, Margaret,' I said, 'we must credit the judges with an objective view, and accord some weight to it.'

'Must we? Have you ever heard of any of them?'

'Barely, I suppose.'

'Scribblers of reviews and popular lady novelists.'

'What a supercilious and donnish remark! You ought to get out of Oxford, if you ask me. And wouldn't you like to be a popular lady novelist yourself?'

'Belt up, Duncan.' My attempt at humour had not been a success either. 'Or talk about something else.'

'Well, no. Why should I? We're *confrères*, aren't we? At least let me point out you could renounce the prize if you feel all that strongly about it.'

'Or just *de*nounce it. There was a chap did that. Pocketed the loot and then came out with a high-minded speech.'

'Perhaps he then donated the loot to some cause worthy in his own eyes.'

'I *need* the loot. I don't belong to your precious *rentier* class.'

These uncivil exchanges made us feel companionable, and Margaret produced Fiona's whisky. I had already discovered that these Second Elizabethan women had the notions of an Edwardian male society on what is meant by afternoon tea.

'Well, then,' I said, 'keep the money, keep mum, and get on with the new book. And go a bit easy on all that bed-hopping and irregular passion.'

'Oh, *that*!' Margaret was quite unoffended. 'It has to be given its place in any responsible representative fiction. But they spotlight your use of it so as to make it appear you've produced a tissue of depravities. And they love books that *are* just that, so that they can play at being no end tolerant.'

'Margaret, my dear, "they" is a notion to keep clear of. It's paranoid and dangerous.' Although the tendencies reprehended by Miss Mountain did irrefutably exist I felt that their significance could readily be overestimated by this rather brooding young woman. Remarks made about *The Orrery* had got under her skin. 'And let's face it,' I went on. 'You gave them a run for their money. There are things in that novel that it puzzles me you can ever have heard of.'

'But, Duncan, one just runs one's eye over a newspaper or two, and there they all are!' Miss Mountain appeared to have taken my further joke seriously. 'And what sort of things, anyway?'

'Well, there's the way the tables of consanguinity take a bit of a battering. And I think I'd call incest a fairly recondite theme.

86

Most people have never had occasion to give a thought to it.'

'Have you?'

'Not really—or not ever that I can remember. A Siegmund and Sieglinde would seem rather odd fowl in one of my plays, wouldn't you say?'

'I've never seen one of your plays.' Margaret paused on this, and appeared to judge it slightly bleak in effect. 'Because I never go to the theatre,' she added. 'Have some more whisky. Fiona won't mind.'

'No thank you.' I had a sense of my communion with Miss Mountain as having been checked. She was looking at me much as she had done on the occasion of our first meeting, here in this room, less than a year before: as if I were a problem of a certain abstract interest, but one not likely to reward curiosity in more immediate human terms. This was an obscure notion, and I made little of it; perhaps at the moment she was simply sensible of having shut down on some not very significant talk with a *gauche* avowal of ignorance of my professional labours. In any case I wouldn't have been disconcerted, since I was now familiar with her liability to be swayed at times by a ground swell of almost hostile feeling. She was inclined to be jealous, I supposed, of my developing relationship with Fiona—much as Timbermill, in a less controlled way, had proved jealous of the settled relationship between these two young women.

Miss Mountain seemed aware that my mind was moving in this region—or so I conjectured on the strength of her next remark.

'I suppose,' she said, 'you're hunting up Fiona to discuss that unfortunate old man with her. He seems to bulk large on your agenda.'

'Timbermill? I don't know that "unfortunate" is a particularly good word for him. He may in some way be blessed, or in a state that works both ways. Oedipus arrived at Colonus, perhaps.'

87

'Well, perhaps.' My doubtfully educated remark had gone down with Miss Mountain better than it deserved. 'I can't say I regard him with holy dread. But he may have come to know a thing or two. It doesn't alter the fact that his friends have to think about him.'

'Perfectly true. And here's Fiona. So we can have a conference.'

I had heard footsteps in the hall of the little house. But when the door of the sitting-room opened it wasn't Fiona who entered. It was Janet.

Like many impulsive people, Janet inclined to the cool and formal in her common social relationships. Our own relationship, which neither of us would have pretended had had anything common about it, had taken on an even temperature for the most part. It remained true that her appearance—and particularly an unexpected appearance like this one—affected me more than anything else on earth.

The unexpectedness was sharp. I had wondered before at Janet's having rather rapidly taken up Fiona and her friend, and now she had seemingly arrived on a footing that justified her walking straight into their house. Perhaps she found their mere youth appealing. Reckoning by the simple decades, she was as middle-aged as myself, and like myself might be subject to the charm (to the pathos, if one is feeling sentimental) of persons with so much rough country ahead of them. She might respond to the accomplished and prize-winning Miss Mountain—it now occurred to me—much as I did to Nicholas Junkin of Cokeville, or even to the still younger Peter Lusby of Bethnal Green, whose undergraduate days still lay ahead of him. Yet I might be quite astray in this. We live surrounded by mysteries—particularly if we have formed the hazardous habit of spending much time with creatures of our own invention.

'I was thinking of a river picnic,' Janet said. 'It's a purely

88

selfish idea. I do so enjoy getting Ranald into a punt. He looks as if he couldn't tell one from a motor-launch. And in fact he's as effective a performer as he is with his terrifying garden Juggernauts.'

'Is there the same sense of imminent peril?' I asked.

'Oh, yes. One is swept towards a weir, or perhaps instant decapitation. But there's a triumph of dexterity at the end. Margaret, would you and Fiona care to have a go?'

'Yes, of course.' Miss Mountain was clear on the matter, although I wouldn't have suspected her of cherishing any fondness for aquatic diversions. 'Are we to take Duncan as first mate?' she asked.

'Duncan must be in the galley. It's his special thing. He'll unpack the hamper, like the Fat Boy.'

This was the sort of remark from Janet which—such are love's intricacies—could make my heart turn over. That she could compare me to Mr Wardle's lethargic page was as wonderful as the fact that she could be relied upon never to compare me to Mr Augustus Snodgrass or Mr Tracy Tupman. Janet's indignation could be formidable. But her mockery was of the gentle sort.

'I'll work in the galley,' I said, 'provided I have the stocking of it. Lobsters, pigeon-pie, and capital cold punch.'

Amid exchanges of this sort Janet's occasion got itself fixed up. It was a routine exercise, I decided, in propelling the elusive Ranald into the society of his kind, and she probably arranged theatre-parties and stiff country walks on the same principle. She might even cherish the belief, not uncommon in devoted academic wives, that nervous benefit accrues to absorbed and brooding scholars from the propinquity of young and pretty girls. Hence—it was a new theory—her having taken up the ladies of the Woodstock Road. Both were decidedly young; Fiona was pretty; Margaret, if without obvious good looks, possessed that curious asexual quality— essentially a physical attribute—which owns a paradoxical power at times to stir the blood. As for myself, it looked as if I were being recruited only as a consequence of being around. But I wasn't confident of this. There were seldom any loose ends in Janet's designs.

She certainly had hold of me now, and I presently found that I had left a message for Fiona, and that we were walking back to college, where Janet had parked her car. This represented more of her sole society—unthreatened by anything more than a nod from an acquaintance in the street—than had come my way since our rediscovery of each other. It was a thought that silenced me, and she was the first to speak.

'How are you making do, Dunkie? Are you going to hit it off?'

'With Oxford? Well, it's my guess I'm not going to love the place quite as much as I did when a boy.'

'Which was just a little bit more than you managed to love me.'

Janet made remarks like this very seldom indeed. I had a sense—not altogether grateful—that our new relationship might be described as yet further firming up. I could have wished, somehow, for just a little more uncertainty of stance in Janet. But then that had never been a vulnerability she was noted for.

'Yes,' I said humbly.

'What about the people?'

'My colleagues? I expect I'm going to come to tolerate them too. Or admire them or something. They're quite strange to me.'

'Strange?'

'I always guess wrong. Say they have to choose between X and Y. I say to myself "Y's their dead cert". But it turns out to be X. A unanimous voice. It's almost uncanny. I must be the archetypal anti-don.'

'How fabulous! Dunkie, it's nice that you can still dramatize yourself.'

90

'Yes,' I said—and decided that once was enough for humility. 'But there's nothing surprising about my being a bit at sea with those people. A writer or artist will never be more than a guest among scholars, and that's all that's to it. But, Janet, think of you and me: how surprisingly little we know of each other.'

'Know about each other's later histories, you mean.'

'Yes, of course. You ought to be a writer. It's just being short on mere information. Do you know? I haven't even gathered when you and Ranald were married.'

'Just under three years ago. You could have found that out from *Who's Who*. It has all the professors and people.'

'Yes.' To say that I had hesitated before this means of obtaining information would have sounded like a claim to delicate feeling, so I had to let it go. 'And you didn't know Oxford at all before then?'

'I'd toured the colleges once, with a bus-load of Scottish nurses.'

'Then that's why people tend to treat you as a newcomer still.'

'Yes of course. I've hardly stopped having to sit next to all those Heads of Houses at their dinner-tables. I'm not sure it's a tactful convention to enforce, second time round. Not that it had come my way before. When Calum and I married there wasn't all that ceremony blowing about.'

'I suppose not.' This was only the second time that Janet had spoken Calum's name since the occasion of Mrs Pococke's fateful luncheon party nearly a year before. 'Janet, have I told you I saw you once—just once—in that long stretch of years?'

'Saw me, Dunkie? But you can't have.'

'It was in the National Museum in Athens.'

'I've never been to Greece.'

'How very odd.' I was shying away from what I had been about to tell. 'I'd have thought Ranald would hale you off there at once.'

'He won't go—not as long as Greece is shamefully ruled.'

Surprisingly, Janet laughed softly. 'If I were to say to him "Ranald, you *must* take me to Greece", he still wouldn't do it.'

'But he'd be terribly upset.' I managed to speak lightly, although this last small claim of Janet's had touched off a spark of feeling which I didn't care to acknowledge. 'A lot of scholars feel that way.'

'And have, from time to time, through several centuries. Poets, too. Shelley wouldn't visit a Greece prostrated beneath tyrants.'

'And his friend Peacock, I seem to remember.' I said this quickly, because the image of a Shelleyan McKechnie had almost tripped me into laughter. 'I saw you in that National Museum, all the same.'

'In your mind's eye, Dunkie.'

'If you like. I admit you'd glimpsed the Gorgon, and you'd lost the tip of your nose. But there you were. There was a fillet round your hair.'

Janet received this with a long glance, grave but carrying no reproof. I'd told her of a long-past experience among those thronging marbles—one so poignant that it had to be told. And the telling had achieved itself, blessedly, without sentimentality or constraint.

'So that's one whack of information,' I said, 'and enough to be going on with. My feelings haven't changed, Janet.'

'I wish I could be sure of that.'

I thought that Janet had never said a stranger thing—and it had come from her with a flash of feeling which seemed entirely of the past. It was as if she had suddenly become the vehement girl from whose hand I had knocked some novel of Lawrence's—*The Plumed Serpent*, it had surely been—in the hall of the Edinburgh Public Library long ago. Had she come to a sudden halt and stamped her foot on the unoffending pavement outside Somerville College it would only have completed this effect. And I was so confounded that I spoke rashly and without thinking.

'Janet, has this something to do with my long-lost cousin?'

'Fiona? I'm not being possessive, if that's what you mean.'

I was about to say 'But at least you're being maternal' when by some mercy from heaven the words died on my lips. I can only suppose, I can't really remember, that an image of Janet's drowned children had risen up before me in time to check the outrage. 'At least it's odd,' I said instead, 'that you're arranging for hock and pork pies on the Cherwell for those young women.'

'Is it? I suppose there's something to be said for all getting to know each other a bit better.'

From Janet this was a surprisingly vague and unconvincing remark. She was frowning now, aware of having got on territory she hadn't designed to tread. Were we, so to speak, to turn another corner on it we'd be confronting the awkward fact that Janet, whether instinctively or of knowledge, disapproved of Fiona. I decided we had better scramble off this ground at once.

'You think I have a rash weakness for kids,' I said. 'Fair enough. Let's go on the river, have a good look, think twice, all that. But—do you know?—there are other perils abroad. Are you acquainted with a woman called Hatty Firebrace?'

'A kind of female metaphysician? I've met her.'

'I've met her only once myself. She told me that Penny's coming to stay with her.'

'In Oxford? Oh, Dunkie—you are beset!'

'I don't think it's quite like that.' Janet's instant clear merriment had been steadying. 'But it's an awful bore.'

'That's the last thing it is. Have you and Penny kept up anything at all?'

'Nothing. Not even a Christmas card. But Mrs Firebrace finds something of the *petit bourgeois* order in the fact that, being safely divorced, we don't sleep with one another from time to time.'

'She thinks nothing of the sort. The silly woman just

thought it a with-it thing to say to a celebrated dramatist.'

'Well, yes—I did rather incline to that view of it.'

'I sometimes think, Dunkie, that Oxford tags after rubbishing metropolitan attitudes in a thoroughly demeaning way.'

'Aren't you terribly taken with Oxford, Janet?' I had been startled by this sudden uncompromising judgement from North Britain. 'Aren't *you* making do here?'

'Not all that. And, of course, Ranald is far from adoring the place either. I don't know whether that makes it easier or harder.'

'Good Lord! Ranald's been here all his days. I'd suppose him steeped in Oxford.'

'You'd be quite wrong. He doesn't feel it's him at all.'

'How extraordinary!' This unexpected new theme came to me for a moment with a certain relief.

'You know how we live in the country, and how he comes in as little as may be.'

'He could go somewhere else. He could find a Chair anywhere in the world at a term's notice. In the United States, for example.'

'Dunkie! Are you seeking to banish my disturbing presence from the Oxford of your dreams?'

'Of course not.' My heart had absurdly jumped at this harmless joke, which again wasn't of a kind that Janet had any facile recourse to. 'But eminent scholars do go off to America. And it seems to be not just that the money's good. They like it. I don't know why. I'm constantly meeting men who hop over there for a bit whenever they can, and return making enthusiastic noises. Presumably they move in anglophil circles, and are much admired.'

'Ranald wouldn't notice whether he was being admired or not. As a matter of fact we're going quite soon, but only for three or four months. But there's no question of his taking a permanent job there, praise the Lord. It still wouldn't be promotion—not even Harvard or Princeton.

Oxford's the top of my learned husband's little tree.'

'But surely Ranald isn't the sort of man who——?'

'Of course he isn't. Status means nothing to him in itself. But he'd think that removing himself to some less esteemed job would be read as a disparagement of his present colleagues, or as indicating disapproval of the standard of Classical scholarship at Oxford, or something of that sort. So he wouldn't dream of it.'

'I think your Ranald's an extremely high-minded man.'

'Yes, isn't he? It can be quite too awful.' Janet laughed happily. 'You like him, don't you, Dunkie?'

'I like him very much.'

'Then that's most satisfactory. Which is more than can be said of your present hunted condition, Duncan Pattullo. So let's go back to that.'

'To this business of Penny turning up? I dare say it will pass off quite well. Did I ever tell you about my Uncle Norman's wife?'

'It's improbable that you didn't—but I'm afraid I don't remember. I do remember about Norman. He was very dismal. And the just gods punished him with some physical affliction which gave him the appearance of shedding tears non-stop.'

'That's right.' I was now talking, as Janet could very well see, almost at random. In that fleeting passage about Fiona something had remained unexpressed between us, something much clearer to Janet than it was to me. I didn't want to go back to it, although again I didn't know why. 'Well,' I went on rapidly, 'Uncle Norman's wife was more dismal still, as well as excessively devoted to the practice of her religion. She used to send my father postcards saying things like *Maranatha* and *Prepare to meet thy Doom.*'

'What did your father do?'

'He'd draw her a little scene illustrating some incident in Christ's Ministry, and send it to her with the words *God is Love.* He wasn't a believer, so I don't know that it was quite

95

fair. But he adored his brother, and hoped to bring my aunt to gentler courses.'

'And did he?'

'Oh, no. Lugubrious resignation was as much as she ever rose to.'

'I see. But why are you telling me this?'

'I can't think. Yes, I can. It was because, speaking of this visit of Penny's, I said "I dare say it will pass off quite well". That was the summit of the wretched woman's expectations about anything whatever—and the most favourable verdict she could manage on any family occasion. It didn't matter whether it was a wedding or a funeral or a visit from some relations in the next parish. Her benediction on it would be that it had passed off quite well.'

'Dunkie, you were never very fond of that side of your family, were you?'

'No, I wasn't. And my brother Ninian wasn't, either.'

'You resented these simple people.'

'You mean I was a snob?'

'Of course you were a snob.' Janet, a crofter's granddaughter and fisher-lad's widow, had fired up. 'Not always. But you were quite insufferable at times. All that about being the wee laird's wee nephew. It made the cat sick!'

So here was a wonderful moment—almost a sacramental moment, in a topsyturvy way. I replied hotly; Penny and Fiona were alike clean forgotten; we marched down Oxford's Cornmarket furiously arguing—as two children had long ago marched down Princes Street or the Royal Mile in just such an absurd dispute. The hazards of Carfax were confronting us before we pulled out, laughing and perhaps a little abashed. Janet's colour had heightened, and I am afraid I felt a moment's dangerous triumph at this further signal from the past. She got into her car rather quickly—she was late, she said, and there was the dinner to cook—and vanished in the direction of the Berkshire Downs.

VI

JUNKIN'S PLAN FOR producing *Tamburlaine the Great* was now taking on urgency. He had extracted from me the information that the Governing Body (of which up to that moment he had never heard) would feel bound to endorse any view which Talbert (of whom he hadn't heard either) put forward, and vigorous questioning had obliged me further to reveal that this obscure old gentleman had been my tutor—'back in that Hitler's time' Junkin almost accurately concluded after doing sums on the matter. It at once became clear to him that a felicitous start to negotiations would be secured were I personally to introduce him into Talbert's presence.

'Quite like the Turkish court,' he said to me lucidly. 'Amurath an Amurath succeeds—or rather not Amurath but Harry. There is an Amurath in *Tamburlaine*, isn't there?'

'Bajazeth. But they were both Turkish emperors.'

'That's it. But what I mean is, a tutor introduces his pupil to *his* tutor. That's going to produce a good impression at once.'

'Perhaps so. But Talbert may find it perplexing that I have a pupil reading Modern History. He's an old-fashioned type, Nick.'

'That will be absolutely okay, Duncan. I can explain about my being interested in drama from the historical point of view.'

'So you can. But I think I'd better be "Mr Pattullo" for the purpose of the interview. Those antique ways again.'

'I get. Where can I do some prep?'

'About Talbert?' I was impressed by the speed with which Junkin's mind was working. 'Well, they offered him a little *Festschrift* for his sixty-fifth birthday——'

'Threw a party for him? Jolly d.'

'No, not a party. A collection of learned essays on the Elizabethan dramatists—by various hands, as they say. There's a memoir of him at the beginning. You could read up about him in that. But I wouldn't——'

'Have no fear. You just promote the scrap and I'll manage the K.O.'

I can hardly have regarded this metaphor as promising, but I undertook to take Junkin to call on Talbert on the following day. In an eight-week term, it will be recalled, everything has to happen in a hurry.

'Then it's in the bag.' Junkin drained the beer with which I had lubricated our conference, and scrambled out of the depths of my sofa. 'By the way, the college garden's no good. All those trees and so on. Too pastoral.'

'But Tamburlaine's a shepherd, Nick.'

'Not once he gets storming towns and things. It will have to be in the Great Quad.'

'My dear man! You can't turn the Great Quadrangle into a bear garden for the better part of a week.'

'All those battlements—absolutely the ideal set-up for big scenes. The tower, too. That's where we'll hang the Governor of Babylon in chains and shoot at him.'

'The Governor of Babylon comes in the second part of *Tamburlaine*, not the first.'

'Oh, didn't I tell you? We've decided to do both parts, but in an abridged form. I've got an egg-head English Scholar working like mad on that now. We reckon we can play it in just under four hours.'

'That will be gorgeous,' I said. And I pushed Junkin out of the room.

Talbert received us with gravity—his manner suggesting that of a judge in chambers when about to rule upon a matter to which he has accorded several hours of private cogitation.

His behaviour, however, almost immediately became perplexing. Seating himself at one side of his small square table, he motioned Junkin to the small round chair opposite. It was what my Aunt Charlotte would have called a kitchen chair, meaning one the design of which wholesomely excludes the menial classes from any possibility of seductive ease. I remembered it perfectly well; it had a brutally protrusive ridge in quite the wrong place, and further embodied a slight but effective declivity the surface of which was so shiny (even shinier now, it was to be supposed, than when I had myself been accustomed to occupy it) that a constant pressure of the toes on the uncarpeted floor was required to maintain one's backside in any sort of stability. The third chair in the room was of the same sort. But as it was at present mysteriously occupied by a sack of potatoes I was constrained to perch myself on a stumpy yet shaky column of bound volumes of *The Journal of English and Germanic Philology*. This accession to Talbert's learned resources was the only innovation I could see in the room, which was still destitute of any other books. There continued to remain in evidence, however, that small empty bookcase in which it was his design eventually to accommodate what he called 'a succinct reference library'.

The situation was now clear. Talbert was taking Junkin (on whom he had never set eyes before) quite for granted as one of his pupils, and was waiting for the essay to begin. What he made of my presence I can't think; he had confined his awareness of it to a brief glance of mild surprise; conceivably he supposed me to have come about the electricity or the gas and to be respectfully waiting for permission to prosecute my craft. There succeeded a meditative silence, perfectly familiar to me but liable (I conjectured) to disconcert the unknowing Nick.

'Shelley?' Talbert said, huskily and on an interrogative note.

'Marlowe,' Junkin said promptly.

'Ah, Marlowe! A very interesting man.'

It was at least promising that Talbert hadn't said 'A very noisy man'. The wild thought came to me that Bedworth was mistaken in his recollection of that long-past lecture, or even —as was very possible—that he had been unappreciative of one of Talbert's fleeting strokes of elfin humour. And although Talbert said 'A very interesting man' whenever one announced the subject of one's essay (and occasionally said nothing else, indeed, throughout what he would have called one's private hour) it seemed to me now that an unexpected spark of genuine interest had glinted behind his spectacles.

'Marlowe,' Talbert said, weightily and communicatively, 'must be judged the father of English dramatic versification. Well did Ben Jonson speak of Marlowe's mighty line.'

'Yes, sir.' Junkin received this flight into an empyrean of literary criticism very well. 'And we want to produce *Tamburlaine* in the Great Quadrangle.'

'Yes, of course.' Talbert now gave me a significant and familiar glance. It was evident that the actual occasion of our conference (which I had outlined to him on the telephone the evening before) had swum back into his consciousness and that he was taking it quite in his stride. 'An excellent proposal, Mr Junkin.' He paused, and added unexpectedly, 'My wife will be extremely interested.'

'Thank you, sir.' Mark Sheldrake himself could not have been more prompt than Junkin with this proper response.

'Only we must arrange for the presence of the Fire Brigade.'

'Sir?'

'You will recall, no doubt, that it was upon the occasion of a production of *Tamburlaine* that one of the Elizabethan playhouses was unhappily burnt to the ground.'

'Yes, sir. Mr Pattullo has told me about that. He knows I'm interested in the drama from the historical point of view.'

Junkin, having got this in, clearly felt established. He signalized the fact by standing up, rotating his chair through 180 degrees, and sitting down again with his arms disposed comfortably on its back. The ridge must now have come in an anatomically appropriate place. It was chastening to reflect that I had endured three years of Talbert's tutorial attentions (or inattentions) without hitting upon this simple solution of a fundamental difficulty.

'But the Fire Brigade, Mr Junkin, is always most co-operative. There will be no difficulty there. I shall make the arrangement myself—speaking, if necessary, to an appropriate member of the City Council. You must be careful to secure gunpowder of good quality.'

'I've been thinking about that, sir.' Junkin made this mendacious statement unblushingly. In face of these surprising developments he was keeping his end up well.

'And naphtha flares. As we shall be playing far into darkness they will be most effective, if provided in sufficient quantity. We shall be presenting, Junkin, vile outrageous men who live by rapine and by lawless spoil—razing cities, and so on. Blood, too. Vinegar suitably tinted is better than red ink. It comes off more easily afterwards. "A small bladder of vinegar prickt"—you will recall the stage-direction. Yes, indeed. "Blood the God of War's rich livery." And we must have an abundance of martial music, barbaric in suggestion. "The thunder of the trumpets of the night." All that sort of thing.'

Talbert was now on his feet. He had lit one of his little cigarettes and was pacing up and down his minute room, puffing so furiously that it was hard to distinguish between wreaths of smoke and his abundant white moustache. Behind both, his rosy complexion suggested a distant view of some Persian metropolis given over to devouring flame. Even when he knocked over the sack of potatoes he disregarded the fact. He might have been a prophet new-inspired.

'But costume is the most urgent thing,' he said. 'There is not a moment to lose. Have you consulted Dr Seashore at the Ashmolean?'

'I'm afraid not, sir.' Junkin had certainly never heard of Dr Seashore—nor, probably, of the Ashmolean Museum either. 'But, of course, he'd be our man.'

'Precisely. He is the author of a most distinguished monograph on Inigo Jones's *Designs for Masques and Plays at Court*. I shall discuss the problem with him tomorrow.'

'Sir, we don't know if the Governing Body——'

'There will be no difficulty, my dear Junkin.' Talbert had raised a magistral hand. 'I shall make the necessary representations to the Provost tonight. Our project is, after all, to be of a thoroughly scholarly sort. The college must put up with any minor inconvenience there may be. And I am confident of success. It is true that it is a long time since I have produced a play. But I have a modest confidence of success. And it is proper to say, my dear Junkin, that I am most sensible of the compliment your Dramatic Society is paying me. One other thing. I keep early hours, and am commonly in college by ten past eight. If you and I meet regularly in this room at that time there will be scope for substantial discussion daily before tutorial work begins.'

'I'll be here, sir.' Junkin, who regarded ten o'clock as the civilized hour for coming awake, gave this desperate undertaking at once. 'And thank you very much.'

This concluded our interview, and we were out in the quad before a dazed Junkin spoke.

'But you never *told* me!' he said.

'Nick, I simply didn't know. I swear I didn't know. It's a revelation. A new and unsuspected Talbert.'

'He's taking it for granted he's going to *produce* the thing?'

'It bears that appearance. And he said something rather significant about his wife.'

'Oh, Lord!' We walked on for some paces, and then

Junkin squared himself. 'But at least it's coming off.' We walked in a further silence. 'Gunpowder,' he said. 'He doesn't know about cassettes.'

'Cassettes don't *smell*, Nick. No smoke, either. Much better have the real thing. As to what he does and doesn't know about, I'm not at all sure.'

'I saw a funny look in his eye.'

'Yes. It's there. Not often—but it's there.'

'And that about the Fire Brigade. I ask you!'

'A very wise precaution, all things considered.'

'Well, I'm grateful to you.' Junkin said this stoutly, and looked at his watch. 'Opening time. Come over to the Bear and have a pint.' Having made this generous proposal quite urgently, he added thoughtfully, 'It can be on the Dramatic Society, I'd say.'

Tamburlaine, thus launched, went forward in a big way, occasioning throughout the rest of the term a good deal of vexation and annoyance in almost everybody over the age of twenty-two or thereabouts. This I expected, since I remembered perfectly well the high nuisance value which these outbreaks of Thespian enthusiasm can achieve. What hadn't occurred to me was that I'd be blamed for the whole thing. It wasn't, I felt, altogether fair that such censure should be visited upon one now expected to earn his keep by fostering interest in Modern European Drama. Moreover, the fact of the matter was plain: the real blame, if blame there had to be, lay less with my complaisance than with Junkin's guile—and less again with that than with the unexpected enthusiasm of Albert Talbert. It was Talbert, certainly, who put the project in funds through the instrumentality of a speech of overwhelming *gravitas* delivered at the next meeting of the General Purposes Committee. It voted a substantial sum for the project—enough to buy sufficient gunpowder to blow up the college. Yet Junkin's was the originating spirit. Had the eventual production been (as it was not) an overwhelming artistic success the credit would have been properly his. As it was—although the chain of events here was as devious as it was unexpected—Junkin's zeal proved productive of a great deal more than torrents of Elizabethan huff-snuff and rim-ram-ruff. Later it was to be curious to reflect that had he not been edged through that First Public Examination by Lempriere, and thus—much against his expectation—been spared the penalty of rustication, the major fortunes of the college would have been much affected.

It is scarcely possible at Oxford to look forward apprehensively to what is elsewhere called a long hot summer. Before the end of June the place has folded up. Such undergraduates as continue occasionally to be glimpsed are around only for the melancholy purpose of *viva voce* examination—which means that, granted a little luck, they will presently be undergraduates no longer. It is not unreasonable, however, that a short life should seek to be a merry one; and as it is in the summer term that the ephemeral character of a student's career is borne in upon many, the summer term can be lively while it lasts. Those of too lofty a spirit much to concern themselves with academic laurels, and more particularly those whose political persuasions are of the activist order, thus own a disposition to kick around from time to time, making a shambles or two while the sun shines. Not that the sun is always their ally. In nice weather even a well-organized sit-in, adequately serviced with hamburgers, cokes, top pop groups, and instructive allocutions by visiting persons understood to be in the forefront of insurgence in distant places, tends to become rather dreary when it has to be conducted in the near-dungeons in which key university personnel prove resigned to labour. Open-air affairs are more agreeable. But on a very hot day even these appear to evoke dusty answers. One marches and gestures and shouts in a manner indistinguishable from that to be observed in television records of 'confrontations' of the most authentic sort. But there are no riot police at the other end of the street, and from beneath the level eyebrows of their straight-headed Tudor windows the dim and ancient buildings, discouragingly domestic and forbearing and benevolent, survey the shindy with an air of inexpugnable repose. It must be excessively frustrating. As our Provost was accustomed suavely to remark, it stood much to the credit of the good sense of British youth that arson was not rife among us, and that reprehensible and ill-judged jokes with fireworks represented the nearest Oxford got to being a fashionably bomby place.

Not that the Provost offered to these signs of the time an attitude of careless disregard. Senior common rooms are full of aged ostriches; their voices, muffled in the sand, can be heard muttering that such inconveniences and absurdities will quickly pass. Edward Pococke was too intelligent not to remain alert to them, and this alertness governed (I imagine) his approach to *Tamburlaine*. In my own time his attitude to college theatricals had been courteously obstructive. Although he would turn out manfully even to productions *en plein air*, swathed in rugs and armed with insect repellants provided by his wife, and would move among the players in an interval, amiably recalling his own involvement in such activities when young, it would nevertheless have been only under pressure that he had sanctioned so profitless an activity in the first place. Nowadays, it was plain that he regarded the Dramatic Society as purveying a useful sort of bread and circuses. Young men absorbed in rehearsing scenes of rapine and lawless spoil, and young women competing for the part of the divine Zenocrate, were distracted from more grievous forms of nuisance. He invited Junkin to luncheon—an ordeal to which Junkin, as it happened, had been subjected on a previous diplomatic occasion connected with the fate of

Ivo Mumford. And he remembered that Dr Seashore of the Ashmolean, having several times assisted the college by providing gratuitous expertises on some of our pictures, rated for similar polite attention at a more august level. (It was here that lay the fateful link between Junkin's project and the graver fortunes of the college.)

The attitude of many of my colleagues to the forthcoming theatrical explosion was the more edgy, I believe, because of their anxieties about the tower. It was impossible for sensitive and cultivated men to pass daily beneath this magnificent assertion of the college's consequence, and to reflect that at any time it might be tumbling about their ears, without uneasiness of a highly creditable sort. There were even those who judged the state of the tower's fabric to render additionally inexpedient the dramatic jamboree looming ahead in the Great Quadrangle. Might not the mere din—including salvos and fanfares and heaven knew what—fatally upset some delicate balance of forces deep within the stonework? Again, it was rumoured that a wretched undergraduate, abjectly eager for fame, was to allow himself to be suspended in manacles high above the quad, and there indecently to simulate a hideous death agony. This would involve all sorts of scramblings on the very surface of the tower itself— and what greater madness could there be than to permit that? The Provost proved to have consulted unimpeachable authority. There was, it appeared, no rational ground for anxiety. The dangling body of the unfortunate Governor of Babylon would be as innocuous to the fabric of the tower as the depending therefrom of a spider by its thread.

VII

THE LUNCHEON FOR Dr Seashore took place in the
senior common room dining-room. Mrs Pococke had
established a rule that, at least in term-time, only undergraduates were to be invited to lunch in the Lodging: an
ordinance making it possible to be fairly lavish with favourites
while allowing everybody at least one glimpse of this particular aspect of academic high-life. It was also remarked,
however, that the favourites were increasingly selected on
other than common social criteria, since Mrs Pococke's
sense of purpose in the matter was much governed by what
she judged to be the needs of odd and awkward young men.
These she often entertained in batches, but with an old-
fashioned regard to the propriety of laying on an answering
bevy of young women from St Anne's or St Hilda's who
were neither awkward nor odd in any way. Whether the
regime achieved much therapeutic success I don't know. The
attempt, at least, had to be admired. As for the male guests,
they may or may not have conscientiously got up pastoral
staves and flat ornament out of regard for what were tradition-
ally understood to be the ruling passions of their hostess.
Probably not—the laxity of the times scarcely conducing to
laboriousness of that sort. This note on Mrs Pococke's
progress is by the by; it was quite a change from the time
when Tony Mumford and I enjoyed the *entrée* to the Lodging
for no better reason than that we brushed our hair and could
be lively without impudence. One result of her missionary
zeal was that the Provost, when disposed to entertain senior
male persons, was constrained to turn out of doors for the
purpose.

On this occasion, in addition to Seashore and myself, the

guests were Albert Talbert, our librarian Tommy Penwarden, and the elusive Dr Burnside—of whom I hadn't had a glimpse since my bold call on him earlier in the term. In mere point of cognomen Burnside and Seashore went felicitously together; I was reminded of the distant time when my friend Martin Fish enjoyed as his nearest neighbour on Surrey Four a pious man called Clive Kettle; it even occurred to me that mere gamesomeness here had dictated the Provost's choice. But this last was a frivolous thought. The luncheon, which clearly wasn't to be particularly oriented to the Dramatic Society's affairs, seemed rather arranged with a certain sense of learned dustiness as its keynote. I had simply to hope that I could keep my end up.

Seashore wasn't precisely dusty, his surfaces being too polished to make this suggestion apposite. He might have been said, rather, to have acquired a patina, or even to exist slightly obscured behind a varnish that had browned with age. As he was by profession the university's Keeper of Paintings some symbiotic process may have been responsible; and he also owned the gentleness, the mild sadness that the severer forms of connoisseurship seem liable to induce. He was certainly not a bustling sort of person, and one wouldn't have supposed him to be a promising wardrobe mistress to a pack of impatient undergraduates. (But Talbert's judgement here proved not to be at fault; Seashore was to produce appropriate sketches with admirable expedition, and to possess a good sense of what was practicable within the customary scurrying conditions of the venture.)

When the Provost introduced me Seashore was delivering a sustained if rather fatigued monologue to Talbert and Penwarden, and this he continued without the interruption of doing more than shake hands—although with an air of discerning at once that I was a man equipped instantly to pick up the thread of his discourse. It concerned Bernard Berenson and the enchantments of the Villa i Tatti. Most art historians,

I reflected, possess a routine they can go into on this. They like to tell one of their own past possession of the *entrée* there, and Seashore wasn't an exception.

'Did you learn a great deal?' I asked when the moment came for me to chip in respectfully.

'I learnt an *enormous* amount. To have the run of the whole queer set-up was an artistic education in itself. And Mr Berenson, although tricky and mildly comical in so many ways, was extremely kind.'

I was impressed. 'Mr Berenson', I knew, represented the very mark and acme of propriety; mere pretenders to intimacy invariably referred to the eminent *Kunstgeschichtler* as B.B.

'Berenson's work,' Talbert interposed, 'was in a field which is unfamiliar to me. Yet analogies suggest themselves. When I was myself a young man, Seashore, just entering upon Elizabethan scholarship, there was a sanguine belief that much could be achieved through scientific methods in the task of attributing texts, or portions of texts, to specific authors. The comparative philologists were an example to us. They had achieved much by rigorous analysis.' Talbert paused, evidently the better to marshal a good deal more that was to come. I wondered whether everybody would have to deliver himself similarly before we got anything to eat. 'Vocabulary tests,' Talbert pursued, 'metrical tests, rhyme tests, recurrent imagery: we believed that great things could be done with them.'

'Most fascinating!' Seashore said, in a tone balancing weariness or dejection with an intent courtesy. 'Yes, I recall reading about that sort of thing.'

'Unfortunately it was largely eggs in moonshine.' As he made use of this archaic figure Talbert's mysteriously internalized laughter was faintly heard.

'In fact,' Penwarden said a shade impatiently, 'you neglected to consider that two men who have never passed the time of day may develop the same taste for rhyming hot with pot or ham with jam. Whether it be so with painting, I wouldn't know.'

'Extremely interesting!' Seashore murmured. 'There is a real analogy. Yes, indeed.' He was inclining his head now towards Penwarden and now towards Talbert as if in doubt as to which were the more likely to place him agreeably under instruction. 'It is true that one man may pick up from another man's canvas the flick of a brush on a fingernail or on the lobe of an ear. However, it must be said for the Sage of Settignano that he refined upon the Morellian criteria in various ways. I don't know that his method was strictly scientific. I wouldn't presume to say. But he was an assiduous man, particularly when young.'

'At least there were tangible rewards,' Penwarden said. It didn't seem to me that Penwarden was in a good temper. 'The young Talbert didn't build up a fortune by swearing that one piece of rubbish was by Robert Greene whereas the piece next to it was by Thomas Lodge.'

'Young Talbert was wasting his time,' Talbert said—and produced what was now an overt chuckle, so that I felt I had never before known him approach so near to levity. 'But at least he did no harm. Nobody was the worse off in his pocket.'

'No. No. Indeed, no. That is so.' Seashore was relieved that at this moment the common-room butler announced luncheon as served. The monetary consideration upon which my colleagues had ventured had distressed him, and he now edged away from them, so that he and I found ourselves walking across a corner of the Great Quadrangle towards the dining-room together. 'Your Provost,' he murmured to me surprisingly, 'always strikes me as a very *stately* man. Sometimes, indeed, when I attend your college chapel—itself so very beautiful a building—his processional appearance—if that be a proper term—transports me to the Cappella Brancacci itself.'

'It's a most august comparison,' I said, doing my best, and wondering whether I should find myself still neighbouring this cultivated person at table.

'Masaccio's *St Peter*, my dear Dr Pattullo. Almost the first unchallengeably sublime thing in Italian painting. He has been a simple fisherman. But he will hold the Keys. He knows his place—almost as Piero's Madonnas are to know their place. He walks through the little street at an unutterable remove. And the *storpi* are healed as his mere unregarding shadow falls on them.'

'Yes,' I said, startled to find my mildly-mannered companion capable of this impropriety. We didn't ourselves much run to facetious remarks about the Provost, and it was wicked in a guest to do so. But, after all, is it facetious to compare a member of the Anglican higher clergy with St Peter—the top man, one might say, in the whole profession? I found myself rather taking to my deceptively masked companion, who might be genuinely sad but certainly wasn't dull. When we did sit down, and I discovered myself on his right hand as he was on the Provost's, I reflected that I was at least better off than I should have been with Penwarden in his present frame of mind.

'Dr Pattullo and I,' Seashore said blandly, 'have been talking, Provost, about aspects of ecclesiastical portraiture. May I venture to mention the pleasure which—in common, I am sure, with all your friends—I received from your notably successful portrait at the Royal Academy last year?'

'My dear Seashore, you are very kind.' The Provost made a graceful gesture which lightened the formality of this response. 'The artist was a delightful fellow, and we had several absorbing talks. I don't know that I have so enjoyed meeting a painter since I had the privilege of entertaining a great one in the person of Pattullo's father. And that was rather a long time ago.'

'How very *pleasing*!' Seashore's tone acknowledged the

respect he felt for a man who seldom missed this sort of conversational trick. 'Unhappily I never got to know your father well'—he had turned to me—'but I am sure those were right who judged him the best talker since Whistler. And he was certainly a much nicer man.'

'We must not discuss in what aspect Duncan a little inherits from him,' the Provost said. 'Duncan is something of an unknown quantity with us as yet—old member though he undoubtedly be.'

Seeing no means of contributing to this jocosity—which didn't perhaps represent the Provost at his best—I glanced round the company. Talbert was on my right, and devoting himself with a serious mien to such pleasures of the table as the occasion afforded him. Mrs Talbert, I imagine, was little given to fine cuisine; and her husband, although so dedicated to austere intellectual pursuits, was not inattentive to meat and wine when placed freely before him. This absorption—for it came to that—had for the moment left Penwarden and Burnside to entertain each other: something of which they seemed to be making heavy going. A college librarian and an archivist must in some measure patrol common ground, and I wondered whether these two a little bumped up against one another from time to time. But it was hard to believe that Burnside, who had the same gentleness of manner as Seashore but gave no sign of Seashore's ability to bite, could get seriously across anybody. I remembered that I must ask him if he had yet explored the tower as a potential lumber-room.

'It occurred to me the other day, Provost,' Seashore was now saying, 'that an interesting monograph in the field of academic iconography might be framed in terms of your praepositorial predecessors. If that is a correct expression. I fear I wouldn't know.'

'It has been used,' Penwarden said from across the table.

'Ah, thank you!' Seashore allowed himself faint surprise at

this interposition. 'I always try, when I can, to enter your college by way of Surrey. Because of the statue—perhaps "effigy" would be more correct—of that old Provost. I forget his name——'

'John Harbage, 1647–1710,' Penwarden said. 'I believe it to be tolerably well-known that he designed Surrey Quadrangle. And that his, indeed, was the first conception of our New Library.'

'How very forgetful of me—I do apologize. And then there is that earlier Provost in the niche over Howard gate. Blagden, would he have been called?'

'Antony Pagden, 1509–1573. Educated at Westminster School. Matriculated 1524. Provost 1555–1561, and afterwards Bishop of Salisbury. He is best known by his *Alphabetum theologicum ex opusculis Roberti Grosseteste collectum*.'

'Thank you, my dear sir. A most *amusing* statue in that delightfully chunky Tudor style. Is anything known about the sculptor? The statuary, as he would have been called.'

'The carver, more probably,' Penwarden said.

'The carver, no doubt. I am sadly ignorant, I fear.'

'I can find out nothing about him.' Burnside spoke for the first time, and unwontedly briskly. He judged, no doubt, that our librarian had already been as informative as civility allowed. I myself felt rather on Penwarden's side, there being something of affectation in Seashore's air of being a mere man of taste among the learned. I had read his books, and knew him to be sufficiently erudite in his own line. So, probably, did Penwarden.

'It would be *nice* to find out,' Seashore said. 'My own only thought would be Gerard Christmas—or Garrett Christmas, as I have sometimes found him called. But it is clear that your Provost Pagden was too early for him by several decades.'

'It would appear that the college also owned a painting of Pagden at one time,' Burnside said. 'I came on the record of it only the other day, and have been eager to tell you about it,

Seashore. That it may still be extant is a most exciting thought.' Burnside was certainly excited; he had suddenly become boyish and absorbed.

'Yes, indeed! Particularly if it is a *Holbein*. That would put the good *Christmas* in the shade.' Seashore didn't fail to enunciate this on his fatigued note, but his interest had been kindled. 'And here the dates *could* be right.'

'Unfortunately it can't be so. The name of the painter—the limner, as the document has it—is recorded, and is what I want to ask you about. I have been quite unable to identify the man. But I am sure, Seashore, that it will afford you no difficulty.'

'Here is an event!' the Provost said with pronounced enthusiasm. A conversation of the kind developing appealed to him as very much the proper thing at his table. 'What is the name, my dear Christian?'

'Not only can I not identify it, Edward. I quite fail in the ability to pronounce it either. I must positively have recourse to pencil and paper. If people will bear with me so far, that is to say.'

The Provost indicated our forbearance by picking up the menu in front of him and presenting it face-downwards to our archivist. Penwarden brought out a pencil—but not without remarking, in a tone of some injury, that this was the first that he had heard of the thing. Burnside held the instrument for a moment poised almost suspensefully in air.

'Hans,' he said, and wrote. 'But *Holbein*, alas, is not what follows. Let me be sure that I get it right.' He wrote again with deliberation, and handed the card to the Provost—who was too courteous to glance at it before handing it at once to Seashore. It then went round the table. We read:

Hans Eenvouwts

'You will appreciate my difficulty,' Burnside said with humour.

'Yes. Indeed, yes. But how very intriguing!' The card had

114

gone back to Seashore. 'Hans Eworth, to be sure. The name crops up in a dozen forms. The Tudors were very little disposed to standardize in such matters. Does your document, Burnside, give any further information?'

'Very little. It is a mere entry in an inventory. But, even so, it is not without some curiosity.'

'No doubt,' Penwarden said, 'you can reproduce that for us verbatim too?'

'Literatim, I do believe.' Burnside was delighted by the challenge. 'Provost, may I have back that card?' This time he wrote currently, but then paused to check the result with care. 'Yes,' he said happily. 'I believe I am fairly confident I've got it right.'

Once more the card went round—a little more slowly. It read:

> Item one tabil ful wele depeynting
> Ant. Pagden S.T.P. Praepositus
> aetatis 46 with satyres and quaynte
> devices the limner Hans Eeuwouwts

There was a moment's silence. Then Talbert, who in addition to being much occupied with his knife and fork had appeared a little eclipsed during these exchanges, suddenly unmasked a surprising battery.

'Hans Eworth,' he announced in his huskiest and weightiest voice, 'is, of course, well known as having worked for the Office of the Revels from 1572 to 1574. It is remarkable that in Seashore we should happen to have with us the prime authority in that field. I have myself naturally—but in a more modest way—inquired into his career. Note the date of the lost Pagden portrait as it may be inferred from Pagden's then age as given in the inventory. 1555 or thereabouts—hard upon Pagden's election. Am I right, Seashore, in believing that the mid-fifties marked something of a turning-point in Eworth's career?'

'Perfectly right, Talbert. It so happens——'

'Precisely!' Talbert interrupted in his most pregnant manner, plainly intending that a further salvo or two should not be filched from him. 'His appointment by the Master of the Revels shows that he retained throughout his period of working in England a fondness for allegorical painting of a kind which I understand to have been in vogue in Antwerp, where he had his training. It was a bourgeois taste, delighting in a proliferation of incident. But in England he rapidly became a court painter, adopting in the main a style of aristocratic restraint—and along with it something of the manner of Moro, perhaps, and indeed of Holbein, whom we have been mentioning. Hence the probable extreme interest of a portrait embodying, as we are told, satyrs and quaint devices, since not much of his work in that earlier style is extant.' Talbert paused—his pink complexion, already flushed by wine, rendered yet more rubescent by this triumph of learning on the mere periphery of his own subject. 'Seashore, am I wildly astray?'

'Far from it.' Only a slight additional weariness in Seashore's voice betrayed that he was perhaps a little piqued at having his thunder stolen in this fashion. 'It sounds much as if Eworth's portrait of Pagden resembled his portrait of Sir John Luttrell—still in the possession of that family, and to be viewed at Dunster Castle. I don't recall Sir John as being companioned by satyrs, but the canvas is an amazing gallimaufry of allegorical references. Sir John was a species of corsair or military adventurer, and his life no doubt abounded in incidents giving scope to the imagination.'

'It all sounds,' I said, 'as if a hunt for Eworth's Pagden might be well worth while. Burnside, what about the secret of the tower? You will remember we talked about that.'

'Yes, indeed! And I assure you I was not wholly neglectful of your advice.' Burnside turned to the Provost. 'Pattullo and I had an amusing conversation about my foible for rooting among the college treasures. You have made fun of it—very delightfully—yourself.'

'My dear Christian, far be it from me to be a mocker. I leave that to Duncan, who will doubtless make us all dance on the boards one day. But pray proceed.'

'Pattullo mentioned the tower as possibly a fruitful hunting-ground. There are several large chambers there in addition to that housing the great bell. I took heed, and approached the head porter. He was dissuasive, and had a good deal to say about cobwebs and dust. I felt him to judge me not entitled to the key, and I didn't press the matter. But I made a resolve to appeal to higher authority. I do so now.'

This was a dramatic moment, which I would scarcely have suspected our archivist capable of contriving. Coffee having been served at table, the luncheon was over and the Provost free to stand up—as he promptly did.

'Authority is to be stretched to its limit,' he said. 'Ullage shall surrender the key. And when we descend from our quest he shall be on hand to brush us down.'

We all produced supporting murmurs in face of this fiat, although perhaps with varying degrees of conviction. It was with a certain sense of achievement that, minutes later, I found myself accompanying five senior persons on a wild goose chase which one might have supposed only undergraduate *élan* could have achieved. It might have been held, indeed, that the spiritual form of Nicolas Junkin accompanied us. In the chain of events concatenating itself he, as I have said, had forged the first link.

VIII

As we ascended a surprisingly ample staircase within one of the bastions of the tower there not unnaturally recurred to me the memory of my dream encounter with Penny and the deceased Thomas Hardy. The Hardy-figure was elusive, but Penny remained vivid as a visual image—at least in the moment in which she had plunged, a female Icarus, into a wine-dark sea. For some seconds this renewed vision entirely absorbed me, and it was with a start that I returned to an awareness of my companions.

'At least I've thought to collect some dusters,' Penwarden was saying with gloomy satisfaction. 'What's the time?'

'Five to three,' I said, glancing at my watch.

'It just occurs to me to wonder what happens when the bell tolls. A major dust storm, I imagine.'

'The bell tolls,' Talbert said—reproachfully and a little breathlessly—'only upon the occasion of the death of the sovereign. Then alone is it swung. At other times it is merely struck by a clapper, which is operated by a mechanical contrivance. We may properly say simply that the bell rings.'

'Nonsense, Albert. A door-bell rings. It would be absurd to describe a bell of this size as ringing.'

'Whether it rings or tolls,' the Provost said, 'it may prove disconcertingly resonant. Ah, here we are!'

We had emerged in a large rectangular chamber. It seemed very lofty: virtually a cube, in fact, but with its four walls canted or chamfered (neither of these, perhaps, is the correct architectural term) where they met as if with some aspiration to the octagonal. East and west—as one knew it to be—the walls were pierced by large Perpendicular windows. This was all there was to look at; apart from what felt like half an inch of dust on the floor, the place was utterly void. The vacancy, as well as being disconcerting to treasure seekers, somehow produced a deeper unease. It was as if, having nothing visible with which to occupy itself, the mind began inexpertly fumbling with notions of mass and weight and balance, stress and counterstress, and was vividly aware—but with a helpless ignorance—that the tower was unceasingly at work upon itself, and had so been for something just short of three centuries. Such certainly was my own state of mind when the bell invisibly above us banged out three. The dust at once fulfilled Penwarden's prediction, rising around us to an effect of momentary suffocation. And if the whole tower didn't tremble, it did at least vibrate. I wondered for a second what the college could be thinking of to permit this hideous additional hazard to the fabric twice in the twenty-four hours in twelve differing degrees. Then my faith in Edward Pococke (which had been curiously building itself up by imperceptible increments during the period of my renewed acquaintance with him) quenched this apprehension at once. He had doubtless obtained from the highest authority—once again—an assurance that these periodic mild shakedowns were harmless to the health of our threatened architectural splendour.

'At least we now have an undisturbed hour before us,' Seashore said—politely if with no marked enthusiasm. 'But it would be idle to expend a minute of it upon this somewhat disillusioning vacancy. Is there anything above us except that gargantuan bell?'

'Certainly there is. A moment's calculation would assure one of the fact.' This came from Penwarden, whose command of *bienséance* was scarcely on the mend. 'There is another chamber precisely like this. A little less lofty, perhaps, but otherwise identical.'

'In that case,' the Provost said, *'excelsior!'* He uttered this exhortation with surprising fire, and I was reminded that there lay behind him not only his Wimbledon triumphs but a notable career as a member of the Alpine Club; at the same time he shook himself vigorously in the manner of a spaniel emerging from a ducking—so that the dust, caught in a shaft of sunlight, floated around him like a nimbus.

We climbed again. The second staircase, although narrower than the first, was still sufficiently broad to have admitted the passage of, say, a grand piano without difficulty; ascending it, one became aware of the tower as larger and more massive than the elegance of its proportions suggested from the ground. Tinkering with it in a big way would be a very sizeable job indeed. I believe we were all a little short of breath, and that this conduced to a growth of self-consciousness among us, as if we now did feel ourselves to be engaged in a juvenile escapade. It might, of course, end in triumph which would banish anything of the kind.

At least we were not, on our second emergence, greeted by a void. On the contrary, the entire space was an impenetrable jungle of mahogany and cedar and oak and pine, all brutally hewn and sawn and carpentered and varnished into one or another article of domestic furniture. The range wasn't wide: chairs and tables, wardrobes and chests of drawers. Nor was the chronological span; practically everything belonged distinguishably to Victoria's middle time. Here was a comical antithesis to that Aladdin's cave of proliferating wonders with which I had crammed the tower in my dream.

'An unexpected confrontation,' Seashore murmured. And he added admiringly, 'And how exquisitely hideous!'

'What the removal people call a repository,' I said.

'Or depository, Duncan.' It was Talbert who thus addressed me—with an incisiveness calling up those lexical diversions with which he, his family, and his captive pupils had been accustomed to refresh themselves in Old Road. 'An interesting instance of true synonyms that are virtually homophonous as well.'

'Like Harbage and garbage,' Penwarden said—not too politely and wholly without accuracy. 'A mass of junk which won't tempt even Burnside, I imagine.'

120

'A curious spectacle,' the Provost said, promptly and smoothly. 'Is it evidence of a revolution in taste—even of a successful revolt—on the part of junior members long departed? And why lug it up here rather than despatch it to the sale-room? But labour was plentiful, and conceivably some old-fashioned bursar judged it demeaning to auction off college chattels. Those were spacious times.' The Provost offered us a restrained mock-helpless gesture. 'Whatever are we to do with the stuff?'

'As an old rowing man,' Burnside said suddenly and un-expectedly, 'let me make a suggestion, Edward. When the college next goes head of the river, have the undergraduates build a bonfire of it. As Seashore says, it is all extremely hideous. *That*, one may discern at a glance. One would feel guilty even in dispersing it among the poor.'

'Not if they were also blind,' Penwarden said. 'Unsightly objects of practical utility might find grateful recipients among them. And there may be some charitable organization that deals with such things.'

Nobody responded to this—perhaps because it was impossible to be sure whether it was intended as a sarcastic comment upon Burnside's aesthetic nicety or as a prosaically practical suggestion.

'Yet we must do nothing rash,' Burnside said to the Provost. He had opened a wardrobe door and was peering hopefully inside. 'For here is something on which I really am an authority, my dear Edward. I can lay it down, pretty well *ex cathedra*, that anything may lurk within anything else. And not merely do little things conceal themselves in big things. Irrational though it may seem, the converse is possible. Or so I have come to persuade myself. Moreover, the wildest incongruities frequently attend the sort of search to which we have applied ourselves. The portrait of Provost Pagden may have been rolled up and thrust unregardingly into an umbrella stand.'

121

'Or a golf bag,' Penwarden said.

'Precisely. Or a golf bag. We must by no means pass such an object over, should we happen upon it.'

'It would appear to be a task,' the Provost said, 'to occupy a long vacation. Either that, or have the entire college turn to on the job. A species of *levée en masse*. But can we have neglected, I wonder, any less unpromising Tom Tiddler's ground?'

'Assuredly we have.' Talbert, who had been silent for some minutes, spoke in the manner of a man who, having bided his time, breaks pregnantly in upon idle talk. '*Flectere si nequeo superos*—my dear Provost—*Acheronta movebo!*' Achieving this arcane *sortes Vergilianae*, Talbert predictably rumbled. 'The heavens have proved unpromising. We may yet attempt the nether regions.'

'Good heavens!' Burnside exclaimed. 'The original gate towers——'

'Precisely, Burnside. The flanking turrets were by no means demolished. I believe that two small vaulted chambers remain. It may well be possible to enter them to this day. We have only to descend and investigate.'

I was beginning to regret any initial impetus I had given to the wild goose chase; even to feel (like undergraduates at a demo) that it was time to call it a day and go home to tea. But there was no help for it. Talbert's inspiration had to be followed up. There was even a specious logic in the idea that Provost Pagden's most likely lurking place would be within some part of the college already extant in his time. So we retraced our steps—climbing down through the decades and centuries, as it were, but without shedding much of the dust acquired during our upward progress. By the time that we arrived at ground-level we were prepared, I think, for disillusion—and with disillusion the first of Talbert's postulated chambers almost immediately confronted us. A short tunnel-like passage, low and damp, brought us to a narrow archway where a door had once been—although of this the only surviving evidence was a pair of rusty iron stumps recessed in blackened stone: on these, it was to be supposed, massive hinges had at one time swung. The door itself had been replaced by a stone wall, and this had the appearance of having been built very long ago. Perhaps we were not the first generation to have been confronted by the need to strengthen the fabric of the tower.

'It is probable,' the Provost said, 'that the other turret will have suffered the same fate. We had better have a look at it, all the same. And that means going through the porter's lodge. It is to be feared that Ullage will be further discomposed.'

Ullage, standing by with a clothes brush, certainly wasn't pleased. But his providing the Provost with a large electric torch seemed to give a hint that, this time, we were not to be confronted with a blank wall a few yards on. There was a general revival of spirits—most marked in Burnside, who must be supposed to have a nose for this sort of thing. We passed through a door—a commonplace door which nevertheless opened with difficulty, as if nothing had disturbed it within anybody's lifetime. There was again a narrow passage, distinguished from the first only by a faint new smell. 'Musty' would be the unassuming word for this. But when I glanced at the Burnside nose I persuaded myself that it was actually twitching—much as the nose of an oenophilist may do at the whiff of a particularly appealing claret. And now there really was another door in front of us: small, massive, and of the most undoubted antiquity. It beckoned us from behind a curtain of cobweb, rather to the effect of an odalisque (it was possible to feel) who has cast off all veils but one. And then as the beam of the Provost's torch steadied, we saw that there was a very large lock, and in it a very large and rusty key.

'If that key is turned,' Penwarden said, 'we're not likely to get any further without the services of a locksmith.'

This was discouraging, and seemed only too likely to

prove true. We had come to a halt, and in uncomfortable conditions—being crammed together as tightly as a group of politically unfortunate persons suffering deportation in a cattle-truck. Burnside, however, managed to edge forward enough to put a trembling hand on the key. He wrestled with it, and nothing happened.

'My dear Christian, will you allow me?' the Provost asked mildly, and stretched out a long arm. There was a harsh grating sound (such as gaolers contrive in grand opera) and the key turned in its wards. Then, to a great effect of drama, the door swung open by a couple of inches of its own accord. There it stuck. The Provost, edging past Burnside, gave a shove, but to no effect. He shoved harder, although still with caution—being perhaps apprehensive that Provost Pagden himself might receive damage. Something did, in fact, slither or tumble, and now the door swung fully open upon near-darkness. There was thick dust in the air again; it danced in the beam of the torch; the beam circled and was suddenly still. We were peering—one man over the shoulders of another—at a large wooden crucifix: ancient, worm-eaten, yet with much paint surviving on it. Still strongly realistic, it might have been Flemish, German, Spanish—I couldn't tell. It was canted against what appeared to be a pile of rubble or plaster. There was something shocking, even ghastly, about it, and this effect was enhanced by its being upside-down, as if it were temporarily standing in for a martyrdom of St Peter.

We found ourselves hanging back, and then encouraging Seashore to enter the chamber first, since a further glance had revealed that its contents—which were abundant—seemed very much his sort of thing. My eye fell on a stone image of the Virgin and Child, with both the heads knocked off, and behind this was a splintered wooden affair—still perhaps utilizable as firewood—which looked as if it might have been a small triptych from an altar.

'We seem to be confronted,' the Provost said with careful

want of emotion, 'with certain evidences of the Reformation in England. Or perhaps of a zealous afternoon's work in Commonwealth times. Some of these ruined things were probably very beautiful. But they were condemned as what were called objects of false devotion. This is a dark day for us, I sadly fear. Seashore, I wonder whether I am right about those slabs of plaster against which the crucifix is leaning.'

'Yes, indeed. Yes, I fear you are.' Very gently Seashore had picked up a fragment of the rubble and examined it. 'A fresco—or wall-painting of one sort or another—bashed to bits and chucked into this beastly hole. Oh dear, oh dear!'

'Something may be recoverable,' Burnside said. His voice was shaking. 'Restoration may not be impossible here and there.'

'We had better make a quick survey,' the Provost said with authority. 'Or rather, Seashore, we will leave it entirely to you. Please take this torch.'

We stood in our huddled group, and Seashore poked around. The air was close but dry, and we were conscious that from somewhere a faint daylight filtered through the place. Only the torch, however, lit anything securely, and as Seashore worked his way to the far end of the chamber he became himself a mere silhouette.

'*Interesting,*' he said. 'Interesting but sad.' His weary manner was returning to him. 'Dear me—here at the back are some paintings, I do believe! A small stack of them. Panels mostly, but one or two canvases as well.' He was silent for some moments, and I shifted ground in an attempt to see what was going on. Seashore was tipping over and examining a number of rectangular shadowy objects one by one—not very enthusiastically, but rather with a kind of polite diffidence, as if here, tilted against a studio wall, were the accumulated labours of some not too successful artist, awaiting purchasers who didn't come. I glimpsed him reaching the last, and pausing over it fractionally longer than over the others. 'I fear,' he said—as he set each of the dim appearances to rest

125

again one upon the other—'that we have uncovered stuff of no more than curious interest. And the good Provost Pagden has eluded us to the last. Provost, I think we had best withdraw. Later, an inventory must no doubt be attempted. But there is nothing more to do now.'

We edged out of the place—subdued, and more than physically uncomfortable. I myself had the fleeting thought—but it was certainly unjustified—that our expedition had been an irresponsible buffoonery occasioned by the Provost's not particularly abundant wine. From the mouldered cross the thorn-crowned head regarded us wrong way up. We pushed through the door. Seashore closed it, managed to turn the key and extract it from the lock. He handed it silently to the Provost, who accepted it without a word. We filed back through the farther door and into the lodge. Ullage, clothes-brush in hand, received us as if we had been up to no good.

We parted in the Great Quadrangle, without saying much, but Seashore accompanied the Provost towards the Lodging. As I made my way to Surrey I saw them come to a halt by Bernini's fountain. Perhaps, I thought, Seashore had some appropriate word to say about it, as he had about Pagden's chunky effigy earlier. But it didn't look quite like that; there was something intent in the brief conference I was witnessing. Then the Provost made his customary stately bow—it was scarcely to be distinguished from the one he would have made had Seashore been an altar—and the two men parted. I myself walked on, and before reaching my rooms encountered Dr Wyborn. He passed me with no more than his elusive sidelong smile. It occurred to me that he might well have made one at the Provost's luncheon party, since it had appeared he was accustomed to assist Burnside in his archival labours. Then I recalled that, according to Burnside, Wyborn wasn't interested in 'the museum side of the thing'. Moreover he walked by himself. The communal rummaging upon which we had been engaged would not have appealed to him.

IX

THAT EVENING I was rung up by Tony. Or rather I was rung up by Tony's secretary and told to hold the line since Lord Marchpayne proposed to speak to me. This uncivil manner of initiating a private conversation used to annoy me precisely, I suppose, as it would have annoyed my Uncle Rory. (Uncle Rory might have taken it from his solicitor or his dentist without much noticing, but from a former cabinet minister would have regarded it as unspeakable insolence.) On this occasion I submitted to the ritual patiently, since I rather expected Tony to use me as a channel of communication with the Provost when any hard news about the Blunderville money came through. This, again, wouldn't have been Lord Marchpayne's politest course. But as a politician he had trained himself in expressing shades of relationship through such devices. And he would never now fail a little to distance Edward Pococke—and this for the bad reason that Edward Pococke was one of those to whom Ivo had behaved with peculiar outrageousness. Politicians are an inveterately unforgiving race: a proclivity only less distressing than the chumminess one may remark in them as they prowl the corridors and haunt the bars of the Palace of Westminster. (The Provost, although—as Tony now acknowledged—something of a professional politician himself, has to be recorded as decently immune from this frailty.)

'Is that you?' Tony's voice demanded.

'Yes, it is. My secretary's on the other line to the Secretary of the Cabinet's secretary.'

'Don't be a fool, Dunkie. Can you lunch with me tomorrow at my club?'

'Perhaps I can. Are you going to have anything useful to say?'

'About propping up your tottering pinnacles? Yes, of

course. With a bit of luck, that is. Just another part of the Mumford service. Trust your childhood's friend.'

'Then I'll come.' I could tell that Tony was jubilant. He was always at his most insufferable when in high spirits.

'Capital! You know my usual dump. One o'clock. Goodbye.'

'Hold hard, Tony. I want a hint or two now, please. How does the matter stand?'

'Look—I'm fearfully busy. But I'll tell you this: I've got the old maniac where I wanted him. He's a pro-college man. Just in time. They have their decisive meeting tomorrow morning.'

'He's backing the college after all?' I didn't need telling who the 'old maniac' was. 'I thought you said our best chance was to have him on the other side. Put his fellow-trustees' backs up.'

'Joke, joke, joke. Not that it isn't a little complicated. There may be a condition or two.'

'What the devil do you mean?' There came to me an obscure sense that in this last remark of Tony's there again lurked joke, joke, joke. 'Who's going to make conditions?'

'You'll see, old boy.'

'Tony, there are limits. One of them is being called "old boy". I won't stand for it.'

'Fearfully vulgar, isn't it? Wouldn't do in your common room. Comes of my plebeian ancestry and coarse associations. But you'll see, as I say. All quite harmless. One o'clock.'

And Tony rang off.

The Provost proved to be dining, and I wondered whether I ought to tell him what was in the wind. He was, I felt sure, counting the days until the position came clear. There had still been no public disclosure of the state of the tower, and for this reticence he had been responsible. I had little doubt that there was substance in his persuasion that the Blunderville trustees might be scared off by the notion that their money, if it came to us, would be tumbled straight into stone and mortar—or at least that they might stipulate for its being used in other ways. It was even possible that some leak had occurred, and that Tony's cryptic talk about conditions hitched on to this. What seemed to me material was the fact that the college's keeping mum over any extended period of time about danger to anything so famous as its tower might become liable to very adverse comment. So I ought not, even for twenty-four hours, to keep mum about anything relevant myself.

But then I thought of Cedric Mumford—the old maniac. He really was just that. And so consistently was he on record as hostile to the college and all its ways that it seemed extraordinary he should have come round to favouring it. I had no doubt that Tony had played fair, accepting the view that Ivo's disasters made firm support for the college the only decent family attitude. We had even agreed to call this the Mumfords' Reply. But I knew little about the degree of influence that Tony might exert over his father. On the occasion of my first encounter with Cedric, Cedric had done as he was told. But so, for that matter, had Tony; both had been knocked over by the circumstances of the moment, which had included the possibility that Ivo was booked for gaol. Since then, I had formed the impression that Cedric Mumford would be a singularly unpersuadable old person. Yet beneath his posturing as a brutal eighteenth-century squire there lay a commonplace Establishment character—a City of London man, more at home with Bulls and Bears than with pheasants and partridges. It was possible that he stood rather in awe of a son who had been an important Minister of the Crown.

My problem was solved for me when the Provost walked straight out of hall after dinner, which was the custom if a man had some engagement precluding his going into common room for dessert. There, I presently found myself sitting be-tween Bedworth and James Gender, who struck me as suitable people with whom to share my anxieties. But first—and as in honour bound at this convivial hour—I offered them as lively an account as I could manage of the afternoon's treasure hunt. Since it hadn't been without its aspects of comedy, this wasn't difficult.

'But how strange,' Gender murmured as he pushed a decanter at me, 'that the place should have been unremarked for so long! One can imagine its not being peered into for years on end. But you would seem to have been breaking in upon the solitude of centuries. That really is a most remarkable thing.'

'It can't have been that,' Bedworth said. 'The surveyor's people can't have neglected it. Not conceivably, Duncan! It was their business to sound every inch of the old structure.'

'But not to report the presence of a pile or two of old lumber, Cyril.' Gender had said this after a pause, as if there had here been a legal point which had to taken (as my brother would have said from his bench) *ad avizandum*. 'But there is the Domus Visitation. There has certainly been a slip up there.'

'What on earth's that?' I asked.

'But, Duncan, it's in the Statutes—the Domus Visitation is.' Bedworth had answered me, and been unable to suppress a tone of reproach before such culpable ignorance. 'Stat. XXII, iv, I think. The Governing Body is required to under-take a decennial survey of the whole college. And not by proxy. The Provost and Fellows as a body. They're directed to peer into everything—including the houses of office, which means the loos.'

'And that makes it not unnatural,' Gender said, 'that this aspect of our duties has fallen into desuetude. Do you think, Duncan, that anything of great value has been mouldering away?'

'I wouldn't know. I didn't see everything, for one thing. This chap Seashore did most of the poking around. He was suitably distressed, but didn't seem particularly excited about it all. Burnside was much more agog. I suppose he smelt documents.'

'But didn't find any?'

'Well, not there and then. Clearly the whole mess must be hunted through.'

We were silent for a moment, the subject of the debris in the old gate-house having exhausted itself. Gender sipped port, I sipped Sauterne, and Bedworth—abstemious not on principle but from honourable economic considerations connected with school fees to come—munched a walnut. So I turned to my other topic—although I wasn't confident I ought to do so. Bedworth knew all about the Provost's hopes of a rich endowment from the trustees of the late Lord Mountclandon, but I was far from clear that Gender did. He was a most senior man, and in an affair likely to have its legal aspects if it came off at all it would be natural to suppose that he had already been consulted. Yet the college was full of strange pockets of secrecy, and the Provost had certainly not been broadcasting his intelligence. But it looked as if there might well be some public announcement on the following day, and I decided to go ahead.

'Jimmy,' I asked, 'do you know all about the Mountclandon or Blunderville millions?'

'I know they must exist.'

'Nothing more?'

'Certain suspicions have visited me. Murmurs among Chancery men.' Gender was himself murmuring in his most diffident fashion. 'Cyril, you are no doubt well ahead of me?'

'Well, yes—perhaps I am.' Our Senior Tutor was uncomfortable. 'It so happened——'

'Yes, of course. How convenient that Edward should wear two hats—and both capacious, as befits that massive head. So much can be kept under them. A veritable hive of bees, like the helmet in the poem. A buzz of high policies! Sometimes one imagines one can hear the hum.'

Bedworth suspended the cracking of a second walnut the better to utter one of his rare laughs. Like many earnest men, he could be delighted by deft nonsense.

'Duncan's in on this,' he said, 'because it's mixed up with Tony Mumford—and with Tony's father, that rather difficult old man.'

'Difficult,' I said, 'is an uncommonly temperate word.'

'So I'd suppose.' Gender passed a decanter again. 'I hope it's not also mixed up with the young Mumford who had to be sent down?'

'I can't be quite confident as to that.' I was surprised to hear myself say this, since it wasn't an aspect of the matter that had been consciously in my mind. 'But now Cyril will tell you how a group of gentlemen know as the Blunderville trustees are going to rebuild our tower—or hopefully, at least, as people now say.'

Thus challenged—and not without a cautious glance round common room—Bedworth explained the situation. He did so with admirable clarity. Gender listened in silence, now and then gently rotating the remaining wine in his glass.

'Fairy gold,' he murmured, when Bedworth had done.

'You think so?' I asked sharply.

'Well, the crock is really there at the end of the rainbow from time to time, I suppose. But all money is pretty scarce these days, wouldn't you say?'

This expression might have come from Tony Mumford himself. It spoke of the Gender who went abroad among men of affairs. For those were days in which all such people subscribed to gloom and doom. The Establishment had not been so frightened, I told myself, since the railings went down in Hyde Park and Matthew Arnold, that prince among dons, had gone round crying woe.

'Tomorrow,' I said, 'much may be revealed.' And I explained about my lunching with Tony.

'We'll wait most anxiously,' Bedworth said. And he cracked his second walnut with care.

Gender and I left common room together. We walked across the quad and paused by the fountain. The great chub had not yet gone to bed. Against a still luminous night sky—always its best backdrop—the tower stood, austerely beautiful.

'Quite a different thing,' Gender said suddenly. 'It came into my head as I mentioned that young man.'

'Ivo Mumford?'

'Yes, indeed. It's about the dead boy's brother.'

'Peter Lusby?' I was afraid that, for Gender, Peter Lusby was always going to be 'the dead boy's brother'. Paul Lusby's fate was to continue formidable for him. 'I hope,' I added gently, 'that when Peter comes up it won't be too much as that that he continues thinking of himself.'

'Duncan, you're perfectly right. He could too easily be burdened by his sense of mission. I'll be very careful, I promise you.'

This was humbly said, and I hadn't the smallest doubt that in Jimmy Gender the younger Lusby was going to be fortunate in his tutor.

'How has Peter cropped up?' I asked.

'He's a boy—it was you who discovered it—with a strong religious sense.'

'It's in the family. His mother is a devout woman.'

'Yes. Well, Peter Lusby has been inquiring about the devotional life of the college. It's not a common thing. They're usually anxious to know whether they should bring up sheets and pillow-cases.'

'Mrs Lusby might write in about that.'

'Yes. Well, Peter Lusby has written to Wyborn.'

'How on earth should he know about Wyborn?'

'He may have got hold of a university calendar, seen Wyborn described as our Pastoral Fellow, and decided he was the right man. But I have a notion there may be some other connection.'

'How very odd! I suppose he ought to have written to that young chaplain—who would be pleased, no doubt.'

'Yes, of course. We're most of us so damned secular, aren't we? A nest of unbelievers, including myself. You, too, Duncan—if I'm not being impertinent.'

'I'm afraid so.'

'It makes me feel uneasy, which I'm sure is wrong. But religious enthusiasm—to put it crudely—can be a hazard in a place like this. Distracting. More so, even, than girl-trouble, or your confounded theatricals.'

'Yes, I know.' I hope that I, in my turn, spoke with due humility. 'Was Paul inclined to religious fervour?'

'I don't know. If he was, it never appeared.'

'Never reared its ugly head.'

'Oh, God!' Thus exclaiming, Gender glanced at me, unoffended. 'It's odd, isn't it, how we go on invocating the dead deity?'

'The whole history of a place like this is bound up with institutional religion.'

'And we go on trooping into chapel from time to time. Yet we are—most of us—as we are. What do you think Edward makes of it all?'

'I don't recall his ever discussing it. Jimmy, do you think any action is called for about this pious boy?'

'No, no—I just thought I'd tell you. Keep you in the picture. You served him well.'

'He may do marvellously.'

'Or decently, anyway.'

We looked at each other for a moment discontentedly, but with understanding. And then we said good-night, and went our ways.

134

X

PARKED CARS CANNOT have been welcome in St James's, since at just that time anything of the kind was liable to harbour an infernal machine designed to incommode the class of society supposed to frequent the thoroughfare—Tony Mumford's class, one might fairly say. Nevertheless there was an empty car casually drawn up by the kerb outside Tony's club. For some reason I glanced back at it as I climbed the steps, and it may be that it conveyed an obscure message to me. If so, the message had nothing to do with what the police were still circumspectly describing as incendiary devices.

It was already one o'clock. But Tony—not uncharacteristically, it must be said—hadn't yet turned up. Even out of office he was of course a much occupied man. I resigned myself to that kind of wait under semi-surveillance by a porter in a small glass box which is the fate of those who arrive in clubs before their host. There was a deep narrow hall, comfortably furnished with leathery sofas and easy chairs, but it seemed to me that these lay beyond an invisible line past which it would be presuming to advance. Feeling rather like a mesmerized hen confined within its circle of chalk, I studied my more immediate environment. There was at least a wooden bench. I was moving over to this when I saw that it was already in part occupied by a young man, and that the young man was Ivo Mumford.

The car, then, had been an Aston Martin, and it was this and its possible significance that I had vaguely registered. Ivo jumped to his feet, and I remembered that in matters of minor comportment the manners of the tiresome boy were seldom to be faulted. They could scarcely have been picked up from his grandfather. Perhaps drastic measures had been taken to inculcate them at school.

'Hullo, Ivo,' I said. 'Are you lunching with your father too?'

'Well, yes, sir. I am.' Ivo's 'sir' hadn't been, as it could be, insolent and distancing. Rather it had been sheepish—and he was looking sheepish as well. 'As a matter of fact, I've never been in here before.'

'No doubt you'll be a member one day.' I was determined not to treat Ivo as a pariah, and I exercised my seniority by at once shaking hands with him. But I was angry with Tony. Had I allowed my mind to dwell on the obscene prominence accorded to Arnold Lempriere in *Priapus* I'd have been very angry indeed. It was no doubt proper that Tony should be concerned to rehabilitate his son, who shouldn't be thought of as cast out for all time from decent society. But this encounter bore the stamp of Mumford humour in one of its less appealing aspects—and Tony was quite capable of having made himself late for his appointment in order to contrive its happening in just this way. Not for the first time, I reflected that there was something freakish about the Mumford mind. The fact was to receive further exemplification quite soon.

I was meeting Tony in order to discuss a matter with which his son had nothing to do. It seemed likely, therefore, that it wouldn't be broached at table, and that Ivo would be packed off before we got down to it. I took another look at the boy before resigning myself to the wooden bench, and had to decide that he was exactly a boy no longer. All undergraduates suffer mysterious and immediate change as soon as they leave Oxford—whether in discreditable circumstances or not. Ivo had changed, and I was without reason to suppose it was for the worse. Indeed, I felt him to have matured, or at least to have got on better terms with himself. Perhaps he had found an environment more congenial than Surrey Four. His mere attire suggested settling down; he wore the kind of dark suit which had lately superseded the black above and stripes below effect previously prescriptive in the City of London. Presumably he had somewhere hung up a bowler hat and furled umbrella.

'What are you doing now, Ivo?' I asked.

'Doing? Oh, I'm in a Discount House. It seems to be one of my grandfather's concerns.'

'I'm sure it is. What happens in a Discount House?'

'I don't really know. We advance the value of bills before they're due. There seems to be a lot of money in it, although I can't think why. Not that much of it comes to me. I'd say I'm a kind of remittance man who stays put. And they don't bother to explain anything to me. What's a bill, for example? It seems a pretty central point. But I just don't know.'

I felt willing to credit Ivo Mumford with a glimmer of divine discontent. Incongruously, moreover, his former neighbour Nicolas Junkin came into my head. Ivo's mind seemed to be taking on something of the groping quality which distinguished Junkin's intellectual progress.

'Is there anything you'd rather do,' I asked, 'than discount bills?'

'Well, I have thought a bit. You see——' Ivo broke off, startled at finding himself on the verge of confidence. 'But I don't know. Everybody's very nice, of course. A lot of little men with one foot in the grave, and quite prepared to accept me as in the nature of things. Not that *that* isn't rather uncomfortable. There are girls too. Most of them just think I'm good for a meal at Le Gavroche or Le Grand Véfour. They couldn't get it wronger than that, could they? But not all of them. One or two are quite game for a lay, if you ask me.'

This interesting approach to Ivo's social life was cut short by the arrival of his father. Tony made no apologies, his note being one of hurrying hospitality. Ivo and I might alike have been badly in need of a square meal, which was an improbable supposition in either case.

'Take your time, of course,' he said to me as I was handed an unsurprising bill of fare. 'Don't think I have to hurry off.' He must have judged he had overdone the bustle. 'The turbot's reckoned the thing, you'll remember; they bring the whole of it on a lordly dish. It's just that my father may be dropping in round about coffee time.' It struck me as a point of grace that, in his son's presence, Tony refrained from referring to Cedric Mumford by an unfilial periphrasis. 'I think he'll be able to tell us he has the whole thing tied up. Some say he's past it—but you damn-well have to give it to him. He has those chaps right under his thumb.'

'Have they told you so?' I asked.

'I expect my grandfather has,' Ivo said, speaking for the first time. His father's arrival had produced something of a regressive effect; he was again the wary and defensive youth who had once come to lunch with me in college.

'He naturally keeps me informed,' Tony said comfortably. 'Mind you, I admit that his idea may seem a little odd. It invites the trustees to go a shade out of their way, without a doubt. But, you see, there was a connection between the Mumfords and the Blundervilles——'

'A family connection?' Ivo asked. 'It's the first I've heard of it—and all balls at that. In the Blunderville heyday the Mumfords were the next thing to proles.'

This was a rude speech, but somehow I didn't altogether dislike it. And Tony seemed unoffended.

'No, no,' he said. 'Of course not a family connection. But a good deal of political association, which the trustees may perfectly properly recognize.'

'Are you talking about the conditions you mentioned on the telephone?' I asked. It seemed that our business was to be discussed in Ivo's presence.

'Yes, I am. And it turns on something that I'm sure will gratify the college very much—and particuarly that pompous old donkey Pococke.'

'He may be pompous,' Ivo said. 'And I didn't like him a bit—not any more than I did the rest of the silly crowd. But I wouldn't call him a donkey.'

'Quite right,' I said. And I reflected that Ivo, although he would never be clever, might well hold his own in a board-room one day. 'But let your father go on. Tony, just what is going to delight the college?'

'My father has decided to make it a substantial gift on his own account.' Tony was looking at me wickedly and with extreme enjoyment. 'Not a legacy or a bequest, mark you. Hard cash now.'

'I simply don't believe it. It's difficult enough to believe that you've persuaded him to back the college's interest with those confounded trustees. But that he wants to give us money off his own bat just doesn't make sense. He detests the place.'

'Yes, he does,' Ivo said. 'Do you know? I think he detests it a lot more than I do. I had some quite good times, really. And I got into the Uffington earlier than he did.'

'So you did,' Tony said humorously. 'Well, as I was saying, my father proposes to found a scholarship.'

'A scholarship!' It is probable that I stared at Tony blankly. 'Your father—*found a scholarship?*'

'On condition that the trustees stipulate that a small part of their benefaction be allocated to founding another one. The two things are to be tied up.'

'Do you mean that the trustees giving the college money is to be made conditional upon its accepting your father's money too?'

'It might be put that way, I suppose.' I thought that for a moment Tony's confidence had faltered. 'Yes, that's about it.'

'What absolute nonsense!' Whether my incredulity was wavering or not, I don't know. At least I fell back upon rather feeble sarcasm. 'Does your father propose to favour some branch of learning especially near his heart?'

'Oh, no—nothing of the kind. The scholar will be free to

read any School the college approves. But the scholarship will have a name. It will be the Ivo Mumford Memorial Scholarship.'

'I see.' I realized that I wasn't listening to Tony Mumford cooking up an impromptu fantasy. For here was something authentic, at least. An Ivo Mumford Memorial Scholarship was a conception which could have been minted only in Cedric Mumford's brain. I glanced at Ivo—from whom I believe I expected an explosive laugh. To my surprise, he had gone very pale.

'I say!' he said. 'It's damned funny, of course. But I don't think it's really on. Name in vain. That's impertinent—even if he is my grandfather. Have to live with it. Like Christopher Robin.'

'My dear Ivo, don't get it wrong.' I believe Tony was more surprised than I was by his son's discomposure, but he managed to speak easily enough. 'Your great-grandfather was an Ivo, you know, and quite an ornament of the college. Anybody who likes to think it's his scholarship is free to do so.'

'Ivo? He was nothing of the kind. My great-grandfather was Richard something-or-other—I don't know what, but it wasn't Ivo.' Ivo was now furious. 'You're planning to make a fool of me.'

'It was a pet name,' Tony said hastily. He now appeared astonished and at sea before his son's reaction. 'Everybody had a pet name in those days. It was used by a man's friends as well as by his family.'

'Where's the loo?' Ivo had jumped to his feet, knocking over a wine-glass. 'Where's the loo?' he repeated. 'I want a shit.'

'Off the hall, to the left of the staircase.' Tony had gone very pale too. I was abruptly in the middle of a first-rate parent and child row.

'Mr Pattullo's coming as well,' Ivo said. This time he almost shouted, so that several of Tony's fellow-members glanced discreetly round at us. 'He's going to be sick.'

With this unveracious announcement, Ivo stormed out of the room. I glanced at Tony, from whom it seemed reasonable to take instructions in his family contretemps.

'Yes, do go,' he muttered. 'And wring his neck.'

I found Ivo standing in the middle of a large marble-sheathed wash-place. He didn't seem to be proposing any further retreat.

'I won't have it!' he burst out as soon as he saw me. 'It's quite beastly of my grandfather. It's a stupid, stupid gaga joke.'

'It's certainly that.' I think I was more interested in the oddity of Ivo's mind and the manner in which his uneasy self-regard had been pricked than I was indignant about his bad behaviour. It was his bad behaviour that I had to tackle, all the same. 'It's certainly that. It's also, I think, a piece of very great nonsense you'll soon be able to forget about. But remember this: you and your grandfather aided and abetted each other in getting out your disgusting rag. And that was designed as a piece of stupid insult and insolence to people you were indebted to. Now you've come very near to making a most improper scene while a guest in your father's club. You'll return to the dining-room at once, Ivo, and apologize to him.'

I was surprising myself; I must have sounded like an adjutant telling off a subaltern for some near-impertinence to his commanding officer. The trade of playwright, after all, although hazardous, does endow one at times with something of the actor's assurance. And I must have played my role quite well, since Ivo, although sullen, was instantly subdued. The sullenness prevented my feeling bad. I suppose I was less out of sympathy with Ivo than with his seniors. I was particularly indignant with Tony, who had promised genuine good-offices in the wretched business of the Blunderville money and then let a sadly misplaced sense of mischief lead him into joining in an atrocious charade. At the same time I wasn't wholly insensible of its allure. There was something undeniably funny in the vision of the Provost being offered—as it were on a plate—an Ivo Mumford Memorial Scholarship.

I was struggling with this unregenerate stirring as we returned to the dining-room. Ivo got out his apology as we sat down. This time, our neighbours were careful not to give us a glance. A waiter had already laid a table-napkin over the mess; now he impassively poured Ivo a fresh glass of wine. Tony said something about the choice of puddings. Like his son he was subdued. I began to feel sorry for him. We concluded our meal.

We went into a smoking room for coffee. Elderly men were reading newspapers and journals, but there was a certain amount of low-toned talk. I wondered what was going to happen next.

What happened was the voice of the oldest of the extant Mumfords. About it there was nothing low-toned at all. Cedric, as he marched into the room, might have been described as screaming and gibbering. He was accompanied—and it seemed very necessary—by that moderating influence known to me as Jiffy Todd. Jiffy, on this occasion not attired as for the stable, contrived to look as if nothing in particular were going on. In fact I don't suppose there had been such a scene in this particular club since it had been London's most fashionable gaming place in Regency times.

'For heaven's sake!' Tony exclaimed. He had sprung to his feet, and now shoved his father into a chair. He turned to Jiffy. 'Is the old ruffian drunk?'

I saw Ivo's eyes widen. Like Nicolas Junkin in relation to another chain of events, he was in a sense the original architect of what was now going on. Probably nothing of the sort occurred to him. For the moment he was simply aghast in a very conventional way. It was true that he had himself nearly created a scene. But he had inherited conventional feelings about exclusive clubs in St James's and thereabouts.

'Cedric is a little upset,' Jiffy said pleasantly. 'Off his balance, in fact. Very understandably. Brandy—wouldn't you say, Marchpayne?' Addressing Tony in this rather formal way, he sat down too. 'Afternoon, Pattullo. Afternoon, Ivo. Some time since we met.'

This *sang-froid*—insouciance, indeed—worked. Cedric Mumford fell to a mere mumbling, and brandy was obtained.

'They've cheated me!' Cedric presently managed to articulate in a cracked voice. 'Made a fool of me—curse my arse!' Achieving this extraordinary imprecation seemed to steady him. 'Not playing at all. Laughing at me behind their bloody mugs. That was it!'

Glancing at this phrenetic old man, I had no doubt it was indeed that. Who his fellow-trustees were, I had no idea. Some of them may well have shared his brutality of approach to things in general. But I had been right in suspecting that they couldn't conceivably have thought of backing his eccentric and unseemly plan. If Tony had thought they could, Tony's customary acumen had deserted him.

'It's settled,' Cedric said. 'They've settled it on a vote, and instructed the solicitors. God damn their eyes!'

'So may we ask,' I said, 'where the money's to go?'

'Half to Eton, and half to the Royal Society.' Cedric glowered at me. 'Whatever that may be!'

I caught the next train from Paddington—having had enough, for the time, of the historic Blundervilles, the unhistoric Mumfords, and all their kind. I didn't quite succeed, however, in turning my mind to other things. I thought of Ivo, idling in his incomprehensible Discount House, and wondered what smothered ambition he had almost disclosed to me. It was probably something exceedingly commonplace: owning a gun-shop, training race horses, becoming a top motor driver on the international circuits. It might, on the other hand, be something quite surprising. I was unlikely ever to know. I did know that he had suddenly broken adrift from what had been the least insecure of his moorings. He had been very much his grandfather's child. The attachment hadn't been likely to do him much good—but it had been there, and that was something. Tony had always been too busy forging himself a political career much to concern himself with a son who showed small promise in that or any other rat race: and when Tony had attempted anything with the boy it had been ineptly and on a basis of too little knowledge. Ivo and Cedric, on the other hand, had been in some sort of rapport. Now Cedric had blotted his copy-book. His absurd plan to embarrass or humiliate the college hadn't been nearly as culpable as his encouraging his grandson to publish *Priapus*, but it had happened in some curious way to offend Ivo's vanity. Yet perhaps this conclusion wasn't wholly just to Ivo. He was maturing after a fashion—I had sensed this—and his grandfather had been revealed to him in his last escapade in a disenchanting light.

Back in college, I rang up the Lodging at once—to be told by Mrs Pococke that the Provost, too, had been in London, and was expected to return only by a late train. I might have run into him, his wife added briskly, had I visited the National Gallery. This information was unsurprising, Edward Pococke's artistic interests being what they were. Was it not true that I might never have entered the college had he not once discussed Dürer with a Scottish painter wandering Oxford in quest of a place of education for his son? I told Mrs Pococke that I'd hope to catch the Provost immediately after breakfast, and rang off.

For a bearer of bad news—I found the following morning —I was very complacently received. Whether it would have been so had I embarked on the story of the Ivo Mumford Memorial Scholarship, I don't know. It was something I judged might keep for another occasion, and I confined myself to stating where the Blunderville money was now definitively to go. The Provost offered no comment on the merits of the two institutions involved, but it was clear that he didn't regard them with any ill-will. Remembering how he had gone out of his way to cultivate the atrocious Cedric, and how irritating it must be to see him now exposed as a broken reed, I judged that Edward Pococke was comporting himself pretty well. At one point, indeed, I had a sense of his exhibiting an almost exaggerated unconcern. He was not a man who could ever conceivably betray that his attention was wandering from you. But as I got up to leave I did have the impression conveyed to me that we both had other matters to attend to, more significant than the Blunderville fairy gold.

XI

It was as I left the Lodging that I saw Penny. There she was, my sometime wife, crossing the Great Quadrangle in the direction of the entrance to Surrey. So definitely I *had* a matter to attend to remote from the lost Blunderville benefaction. If I was more startled than I need have been, it was perhaps owing to a sense that the philosophic Mrs Firebrace had failed me. I had come to think of her rather as if she were one of those enormous globular devices, to be glimpsed here and there around our coast-line, which are understood to provide early warning of the approach of missiles of a particularly undesirable kind. I can scarcely have thought of Penny, even in the most fancifully metaphorical way, as an atomic bomb; in any image of the sort she would have come to me as a menace long since defused and buried in the sand. Nevertheless I had been relying upon Mrs Firebrace.

Then I realized that I was perhaps being unjust to Mrs Firebrace. A few days earlier I had become aware of her across the breadth of the High Street as about to enter a provision shop near Carfax. Her circumstances could be discerned at once as harassing. She was accompanied by Jacob Firebrace and by both of Jacob's younger brothers. Each child carried a basket and each child appeared to be in a bad temper—so that I was reminded, inconsequently, of Mrs Pardiggle in *Bleak House*, impelling her five recalcitrant infants forward on the hard road of charitable endeavour. Jacob Firebrace, indeed, appeared quite furious—perhaps because, in addition to the basket, he was charged with the haulage of a large golden retriever, and was in consequence without a free finger to minister to his nose.

Mrs Firebrace, thus employed and companioned, had spied

me in the same moment that I spied her. She had nodded to me, hesitated, nodded much more vigorously, and disappeared into the shop. I now conjectured that what I had been offered was not a reiterated salutation but a salutation followed by a piece of news. Yes, indeed—Mrs Firebrace had been signalling—Penny had arrived.

And here she was. I quickened my pace in order to overtake her, being certain there was nobody she could be seeking in the college other than myself. What I made of the situation, I can't be certain: not even whether I wanted, or didn't want, some casual renewal of contact. But if Penny wanted it I mustn't automatically conclude that it was in a frivolous or idle spirit. We had stood before an altar—an object which the most hardened agnostic cannot quite equate with a cocktail bar or a kitchen table—and taken extravagant vows. That had proved an error. Yet vows they were. Obscurely at the end of this train of thought was the persuasion that it wouldn't do to dodge, duck, or defer Penny when she had decided to look for me.

The persuasion didn't last—and for the most trivial of reasons. Penny was moving rapidly, and I was too far behind to arrest her by anything less than a shout. And 'Penny!' bawled across the Great Quadrangle would have been some way from quite right. So I simply continued to follow. Then, entering Surrey, Penny paused for a moment, felt in a hand-bag, and brought out an envelope. Holding this, she glanced round as if to distinguish between the staircases, and made her way towards Surrey Four.

I found that I had halted in the shadow of the library. I hardly knew why. The probability was that Penny had provided herself with a note to leave for me if I proved to be out: a precaution which people take commonly enough. But now I thought of another explanation. Penny wasn't proposing to contact me in person; she wanted—perhaps as a preliminary feeler, or perhaps because she had only some impersonal matter in mind—merely to make me a written communication. That envelope was simply to be left in my letter rack. There would be an element of the intrusive, therefore, in my catching up with Penny.

So sophistical an argument scarcely requires analysis. I was skulking from Penny precisely as I had laughed at Mrs Firebrace for hinting I might be prompted to do. It is true that this craven behaviour didn't last long, and that within the space of a minute I was moving forward again. The delay was crucial, all the same. For Penny, having reached Surrey Four, disappeared only for seconds within its portal. Emerging, she turned away without observing me, vanished for a moment behind the statue of Provost Harbage, and left the college by Surrey gate. I might still have hurried after her. But it seemed evident that she had made no attempt at a call; had simply left the note and gone away. So I walked on to my rooms instead.

My section of the staircase's letter-rack was empty. The college messenger (a tortoise-like old creature who took all morning on his round) not having arrived with the day's mail, there seemed nothing waiting for anybody. Perplexed, I went into my room. Penny might have had time to knock, listen, and then slip in and leave her letter on a table. But when I looked round there was no letter in evidence. I went outside again, and had another look at the rack. There was one envelope just visible, after all. It was in the section of the rack immediately above my own: Ivo's once, now Mark Sheldrake's. Although it wasn't a proper thing to do, I picked out the envelope and looked at it—thinking that Penny had dropped it into the wrong space. But it was addressed to *Mark Sheldrake Esq.* And the writing was Penny's.

I was extremely surprised—and conscious, too, of another emotion which I hadn't leisure to identify. There had been a step on the stair, and Mark Sheldrake was beside me. It was a moment the awkwardness of which was all of my making. The lie of things was such that the young man could not have been conscious of my misbehaviour; I had only to slip the letter back in Sheldrake's space as if I had just found it erroneously delivered in my own. What inhibited me from such a small and prudent deceit was—I soberly believe—Mark Sheldrake's edifyingly god-like appearance. Purged of any power to deceive, I had to go ahead as I might.

'I'm so sorry, Sheldrake,' I said, and handed him the letter. 'I had a notion this had been put in your part of the thing by mistake.'

'Thank you very much.' Sheldrake took the envelope, glanced at it unconcernedly, and at once faintly blushed. There were two inescapable conclusions: he knew Penny's handwriting, and he knew what our relationship had been. The letter he was holding, if it wasn't signed simply 'Penny', was signed 'Penny Pattullo'. Perhaps at our first meeting in Junkin's company Sheldrake had realized that here was the former husband of a lady known to him. There was nothing embarrassing, or even remarkable, in these facts in themselves; what did hold an awkwardness was my being found intercepting—for it looked like that—a letter which was no concern of mine. Or rather which *was* just that—in a dream-like or nightmarish way. I might have been an injured husband—something of that kind.

'What happened was,' I said, 'that I saw Penny coming in here with a letter, and rather rushed to the conclusion it was meant for me. I do apologize.'

'Not a bit, sir.' Sheldrake was now self-possessed again, and he didn't faintly obtrude a forgiving note. 'My brother and I don't know Mrs Pattullo well. But we met her at a party, and she said she'd try to look us up if she came to Oxford.'

'Ah, yes,' I said. 'You'll find her charming, and very entertaining.' It struck me that if Sheldrake's account of the matter represented the whole truth he would have been unlikely to know Penny's hand. But he was entitled to a little reserve, and it was now my business to retreat in as good order as I could manage. The young man, however, appeared to feel that it would be tactful to leave me in possession of the field of my disarray; murmuring something about a lecture, he departed into the quad.

Back in my room, I didn't find it difficult to sort out Penny. If leopardesses have spots—as I suppose they have—they don't change them any more readily than leopards do. I wondered whether Penny had amused herself by hinting to her friend Mrs Firebrace of predatory intentions relating to myself when she had quite other prey in view. Robert Damian had remarked to me that the Sheldrake brothers would have a stiff time when the female of the species was let loose on them. It was my bet that this was about to happen now.

I found myself disliking the idea. Mark Sheldrake impressed me—as Matthew Sheldrake would probably do—as having the bearing of a distinctly chaste youth. My conviction was strong that these were not a kind of young men whom Penny might at all harmlessly initiate or advance in her particular sexual lores. This was very right-thinking in me, and as a feeling I believe it was genuine enough. But I had to ask myself—when at length I came to confront it—whether the obscure stirring of which I had been conscious as I looked at Mark Sheldrake's name on an envelope where I had expected my own hadn't bobbed up from some jealous hiding-place many years deep. I had often enough been aware of Penny as in more or less clandestine correspondence with admirers.

Meanwhile, I was conscious of the curious fact that I hadn't really *seen* Penny. I had recognized her at once. Although feminine fashions—and therefore silhouettes—must have changed over the preceding dozen or so years, the mere back view of her had said 'Penny' instantly. Then, when she had turned to leave the college, her profile had been presented to me at only a moderate remove, so in a sense I must have seen her clearly enough. Perhaps, had she greatly changed, I would have become sharply aware of the fact. But in middle life most people don't, in a decade, change much: least of all a woman who is giving thought to not doing so. The page being unarresting, I had succumbed to an impulse not to read what I saw. And thus the Penny most vivid to me in the hours succeeding this near-miss in Surrey was again the Penny of our dream encounter on the college tower. That Penny in turn had been the Penny of our first encounter of all, when—at a dinner-party in my freshman year—the Provost's butler had announced 'Mrs Triplett and Miss Triplett' and thereby opened up a new stretch of my unremarkable destiny.

I now regretted that I hadn't spoken to Penny. Had I done so, it is true, it would almost certainly have been to reveal my persuasion that she was looking for me—in which case it might, or might not, have amused her to make the error clear. It was uncertain whether she knew that my rooms were on Surrey Four. I doubted whether Mrs Firebrace did, although the quad itself I had happened to mention to her. Penny might have noticed my name in the moment of dropping her note into the letter rack. That would have amused her— as a small and unexpected echo from the past as she engaged in her habitual pursuit of picking up very young men: 'baby snatching' as I had more than once denounced it to her during my earlier and unhabituated encounters with the predilection.

So Penny was now in my head, and showing some reluctance to clear out of it. This was a state of affairs contrasting with that which had obtained hard upon Mrs Firebrace's announcing the likelihood of her arrival in Oxford: then, I had almost been troubled by my indisposition to think about the matter at all.

Thus caught up as by a distant sensual music, I found

myself forgetful of other matters—for example, what was going to happen about the college tower now that the Blunderville gold had sunk below the horizon. Janet's water picnic was looming ahead in an opposing quarter, the more compellingly because of the hint of the enigmatical in its purpose. Janet wanted to have something more clearly under her regard, and this was going to be achieved within the confined theatre of a punt. I wasn't sure that I liked the Cherwell. That muddy and makeshift Arcadian stream was associated in my mind with some not very pleasing occasions: my first glimpse of my friend Martin Fish's involvement with the deplorable girl called Martine, and Arnold Lempriere's nostalgic fixation upon the juvenile splashings of Parson's Pleasure. At this time of year the Cherwell would be populous, and floating over it would be plenty of music more or less sensual—much more of it than in Fish's time, which was before a transistor radio was humped around by every amorous swain.

The day came, and brought a minor change of plan. In my own college, were a tutor sick, he would simply pin a notice to his door intimating that he was unable to meet pupils that day. Women are more conscientious—as a consequence of which Fiona had to stand in for a senior colleague during a couple of morning hours. So it was arranged that I should pick her up when she was free, and drive her to a rendezvous some way up the river. I was pleased by this arrangement.

'One thing about you'—Fiona spoke as she settled into my car, and as if taking up a familiar theme—'is that you insist on being even older than your years. Or perhaps it isn't a matter of insisting. Perhaps it's constitutional and comes naturally. It's evident in your plays. Margaret, who hasn't seen any of them, says it appears in your speech.'

'The devil she does? Confound Margaret!'

'There it is. "The devil she does" and "Confound

Margaret". It's positively Edwardian.'

'So it is.' One has to respect the penetrations of the young—particularly the very clever young, who publish novels or gain college fellowships when their perambulators are not far behind them. 'But perhaps it's only a mannerism. Perhaps I'm young at heart.'

'Nothing of the kind.'

'Then what about yourself?' I was annoyed by Fiona's pragmatical note. 'I say nothing about the movement of your mind, or of your idiom either. But you have a very dry way with you, Fiona my dear. Perhaps it's all those cigars. One might be listening to an emeritus professor.'

'You see me as assimilated already to my faded academic sisterhood?'

'Don't be silly.' I felt that, having elected collegiate life, Fiona ought not to offer that sort of gibe about her colleagues. But it would be equally silly to assume the privilege of my years and set about correcting my cousin's manners. 'Let's talk of something else.'

'Very well. I've met your wife.'

'She isn't my wife. She resigned.'

'Did she resign, or did you resign?'

'I see no reason to go into the details. But I'm very willing to hear what you think of her in a general way. There was a time when I thought I knew all about Penny. But now, when I look back, I see or imagine areas of perplexity.'

'Do you do a lot of looking back, Duncan?'

'No, I don't. But perhaps I shall when I'm really as old as you think I am. How did you come to meet Penny?'

'Oh, it was just at a party the other day. I caught her name when we were introduced, and the penny dropped.'

'What an idiotic pun!'

'So it is. I hadn't intended it. We were both taught—weren't we?—that it's ill-bred to make jokes about people's names. Some Scottish names are distinctly rum. Yours is.'

'Yes. And Colkitto and Galasp would make Quintilian stare and gasp. One of the poets says so.'

'You're quite as pedantic as I shall ever be. But about your wife—or Mrs Pattullo, rather.'

'Call her Penny, for heavens sake!'

'Very well. Of course she didn't know about our peculiar relationship, Duncan, so you weren't referred to.'

'What do you mean—our peculiar relationship?'

'Don't you feel it to be funny?' Fiona seemed mildly amused. 'Have you met her yet, by the way?'

'Only glimpsed her. I don't know that we'll meet. She certainly hasn't come to Oxford for the purpose. What did you think of her?'

'She struck me as an old hand at her sort of thing.'

'Yes.' I considered Fiona's brisk appraisal in silence for a moment. 'Yes, I suppose she would.'

'I talked to her for quite a time. She wasn't remotely interested in me, of course. But not a flicker betrayed the fact.'

'No, it wouldn't.'

'Naturally I was interested in her. I managed to hover while she was talking to some other people.'

'Did you, indeed.'

'And I came away with a question to ask. Only I don't know which way round to put it. It's either Why did you marry her or Why did she marry you.'

'More simply, Why did we marry each other. It's a question that has been asked about many faithful couples, and about many faithless ones as well.'

'I suppose you were already capable of that sort of sage remark, but it's not an endowment that would make you exactly glamorous.' Fiona glanced at me wickedly. 'However, you were probably very good-looking in those days—and in an intriguingly boyish way. Young Pattullo, wasn't it?'

'Yes, it was.' I didn't know how Fiona could have come by

this forgotten manner of naming me. 'But I was twenty-eight, as a matter of fact, at the time of my marriage.'

'The virgin bloom remained, Duncan. You were very rapable still, and that must have fetched her. What else was there—on that side of the bargain, I mean?'

'I'd just had my first and only big success.'

'*The Bear-Garden*?'

'Yes.'

'*The Bear-Garden* isn't a patch on *The Accomplices*. Your plays get steadily better. Not spectacularly. But consistently.'

'I'm very pleased indeed you think so.' This was true, but I was also amused by the complete confidence of Fiona's verdict. It was something I had come to remark as character-istic of the academic mind when prompted to assess literary or artistic productions. 'As a matter of fact, I believe that *The Bear-Garden* enjoyed the run it did simply because people wanted to see a dazzlingly pretty young actress called June Trevivian. On such adventitious aids do dramatists depend. Anyway, there I was, fancying myself no end, and actually quite a figure in the metropolitan scene. It may have counted with Penny, I suppose.'

'And you were also—behind that pink and white boyish disguise—a swift and ruthless lover, weren't you? You must have been.'

'I was nothing of the kind!' Taking my eyes from the road for a moment, I stared at Fiona in surprise and—I believe—indignation. It is natural for a man to be gratified at being credited with violent sexual propensities, but not by a girl cousin who is making fun of him. And for a moment Fiona had the decency to appear embarrassed; it had been only uncertainly that her glance met mine. 'Look,' I said. 'If you'll be serious I'll tell you why I married Penny. As clearly as I can, that is. These things tend to retain a certain mystery.'

'I'd like to know,' Fiona said, with unusual simplicity. We were now on the Northern by-pass and near our destination on the riverside. There would be no time for a tedious exposition of my marital history—which, I suppose, was why I chose to embark on it now. I was coming to feel that Fiona was entitled to hear it if she wanted to, although I had no reason to think she devoted to me the ration of serious thought that I devoted to her. It wouldn't be that sort of tumbling out of oneself to another that commonly—although not, I imagine, always—happens between two people avowedly in love. It wouldn't be like that at all. But between Fiona and myself some sort of intimacy, not clearly defined, had established itself. It was reasonable that we should a little advance in reciprocal communicativeness from time to time.

'You see,' I said, 'with Penny I began by missing out, when I was still little more than the boy you keep on talking about. And missing out was something I'd done already with another girl—and when really a boy. In fact a schoolboy still.'

'So that was in Scotland?'

'Yes, it was.' Fiona's comment had been weighted with some meaning, and this was natural enough. She knew, at least in its bare outline, that Janet McKechnie—now to be our hostess in some ten minutes' time—had been my first declared love. 'It's not to be spoken of too grandly,' I went on. 'I was a kid and I muffed it: call it that. But it left its mark.'

'And your first fancy for Penny was one of those rebound affairs?'

'It wasn't quite so simple. Penny burst into the situation a little too early for it to be called that. So there was an element of infidelity to it.'

'But infidelity was rather in the air?'

'Not on the other girl's part. Definitely not. We weren't engaged or anything. And suddenly she was in waters much too deep for me. It's difficult to be lucid about.'

'Apparently so.'

'The relevant point is that the Penny thing—the first Penny thing—was equally sudden with me. It was when I was an undergraduate. I used to go to tea in North Oxford with an old lady called Mrs Triplett. Penny came to stay with her—was sent to stay with her, in fact, to keep her out of mischief elsewhere. Her relationship to Mrs Triplett seems to have been quite nebulous—more so, say, than mine or yours to Arnold Lempriere—but the old lady had a masterful way with her, and had Penny more or less under control. She turfed out one undesirable admirer in the most expert and ruthless manner bang under my own nose at a tennis party. But that's another story. What's relevant is that I was overwhelmed by Penny in what I suppose was the most absurd fashion. And then, equally absurdly, as a feasible proposition it was all over and blown sky-high within a matter of days. And I got it mixed up, incidentally, with another man's misfortunes in the same line. That very much added to the muddle. Then this man and I—he was an Australian called Fish—made the best of things. We wandered about Italy for the better part of a long vac, licking our wounds. Eventually we voted them licked. But it wasn't quite so—or not with me. And that's the end of Act One.'

'Is this a three-act drama?'

'It's at least that—only I'm not going beyond Act Two now. And between them, as the programmes say, eight years elapse. Wholly uneventful, the years between Acts One and Two.'

'Sexually uneventful?'

'Say non-significant.'

'Then I needn't hear about them.' Fiona was clear on this. 'Our turn's the next on the left.'

'I know it is. Well, *The Bear-Garden* has been produced—and there I am, convinced that all London is ringing with the young genius's triumph. I go to a party. And there is Penny.

'Quite unchanged.'

'In eight years? She can't have been—nor I myself, either.

157

But that was the effect. The identical qualities that had bowled me over once did so again.'

'Are they mentionable with decency, Duncan?'

'Penny was a very attractive young woman whom I immediately and clamantly wanted to possess. And I wasn't going to muff it again. I went for her! There's nothing unmentionable about that. But the sheer force of the impulse takes some explaining. Everything about her was small and delicate and—you might say—manipulable in a fashion enormously appealing to the tactile imagination. But I'm not going to offer you an inventory of her charms.'

'No need to. We'll just say that Penny's attractiveness didn't consist primarily in the possession of a well-stocked mind.'

'Of course it didn't. She had plenty of culture-patter and some brains as well. But she was without an idea in her head.'

'Did you realize that, Duncan, even while the first enamourment was upon you?'

'I rather think I must have done. Still, the thing wasn't—my side of the thing wasn't—a simply sensual affair. What I called Penny's qualities included facts of personality and disposition. I found *them* bowling me over. Yet to this day I can't get their appeal quite clear in my head. It sounds idiotic.'

'There's our boat house, straight ahead. And of course what drew you to Penny wasn't the way her arms and legs were stuck on. That's all nonsense.' Fiona was as confident about this as she had been about the relative merits of *The Bear-Garden* and *The Accomplices*. 'It was the way she ticked. You instinctively knew that her character made her just your cup of tea.'

'Absolute nonsense! Penny's character turned out——'

'Yes, I can guess. Perverse and promiscuous. You see, Duncan, it was a matter of how you were brought up.'

'And how do you know about how I was brought up?'

'By using *my* brains—and by reflecting on your behaviour and inclinations in middle age.' Fiona offered this strange remark with a curious flash of fire. 'Take your childhood. Lachlan Pattullo was a great painter—and had a Bohemian slant to him, no doubt. But on that side of your family you had a background in a sort of peasant Calvinism. The sinfulness of this and the wickedness of that. I'm quite sure you hated that whole bag of tricks. But its stock-in-trade—damnation and reprobation and heaven knows what—had its fascination. If mere naughtiness was mortally dangerous, then mere naughtiness was additionally fun. Penny's pull—certainly that second time round—came from your sensing that she might be very naughty indeed.'

'Rubbish, Fiona!' Having said this rather heatedly, I had in honesty to add: 'Not that she didn't turn out rather that way'.

'So there is Duncan Pattullo for you—subject to that insistent little prompting to sup with the Devil. And being careful always to carry a sufficiently long spoon in his pocket.'

'Fiona, of all the——'

'They've arrived before us,' Fiona said. 'We can get moving. And I'm quite hungry. Your company, Duncan, gives me an appetite.'

'I'm glad to hear it—that's fine.'

'For strange viands.' Fiona looked at me mockingly. 'Unknown to my days of innocence.'

Fiona's anatomy of Duncan Pattullo had failed to enchant me, but I didn't feel this was because it had come uncomfortably near the bone. She had got me wrong, and perhaps it was the very fact of our kinship that prevented her getting me right. It is notorious that our wives and husbands, our children, our most intimate friends all exist to the end behind veils of our own devising. Mere acquaintances are the people we see most clearly, undistorted by solicitudes and desires. This paradox must not be pushed too far: in the interest, for instance, of gloomy fictions asserting that the closer we try to come the lonelier do we find ourselves to be. I didn't want to be a gloomy fiction in Fiona's regard. Thinking of myself (as most healthy people think of themselves) as a fairly decent fellow, I was only anxious—perhaps naïvely—that she should arrive at a perfectly accurate view of me. This gratifying state of affairs didn't seem to be coming about.

Penny had become a liability. Fiona's absurdly attributing to me a kind of milk-and-water Satanism seemed to arise from the notion that there must be something positively kinky about a man who could fall for a little bitch like that. Long ago, I might myself have come to such a conclusion about Fish in relation to his awful Martine. But I hadn't. There are some ways in which women are undeniably more tiresome than men. As we walked the last few yards to the river-bank I thanked the Lord that Penny need at least be no longer in the picture that day.

We found that our party had been augmented in an unexpected fashion. In addition to the McKechnies and Miss Mountain the Bedworth children were awaiting us. Mabel Bedworth had been called away to cope with some brief exigency in her parents' home; Cyril Bedworth was up to his manful shoulders in college business not to be put by; Janet, having happened on this situation, had taken charge of Johnnie and Virginia. This made rather a crowd for a single punt, but I saw at once that the occasion had been a success so far. Johnnie was provided with the sort of diminutive butterfly net in which tadpoles—even minnows with luck—may be ensnared, and Virginia had brought something like Albert Talbert's succinct library in her father's rucksack. It was true that the children now inspected Fiona and myself with some hostility; our late arrival made us intruders upon the established order of the day, and it became our business suitably to ingratiate ourselves in that quarter.

It seemed to me, however, that it was my own first business to take over the punt pole, which was something I could do without unreasonable misgiving. But my offer was brushed aside by McKechnie with unusual robustness. He was dressed for the part in a sports-shirt—wontedly subfusc, indeed, and with a small armoury of writing implements clipped in the breast pocket—and in trousers dating from an era in which the term 'flannel trousers' accurately described such garments. It became apparent at once that he had a powerful if erratic command of our craft, which he treated (as Janet had forecast) much as if it were one of the alarming mechanical monsters with which he controlled the extensive grounds of his Victorian vicarage. Johnnie had formed a high regard for his performance. In fact these two—the other male members of our party—were getting on notably well. And it was to McKechnie that Virginia, clambering the length of the punt for the purpose, appealed for the elucidation of the occasional hard word encountered in the course of her studious pursuits. That one of years so tender could read at all was sufficiently phenomenal. But she was clearly her father's child—and had announced, hard upon our getting under way again, that she would read 'until the scenery became more interesting'.

The scenery was unlikely to become particularly that. But it was agreeable enough, and on this upper reach of the river not much animated by pleasure craft. The Cherwell is on the whole the possession of the young, and the spectacle of a boat-load of mature persons is faintly anomalous on its waters. But here it was possible to feel that the presence of the Bedworth progeny redressed a balance, or struck an average of a saving order.

I didn't know how Janet regarded children, and I discovered in myself a certain reluctance to attempt observations in the matter. Death by water must be unusual on the Cherwell (although it had nearly befallen Fish and Martine) but was something that happened around the Western Isles, which was where Janet's own children had perished. I found myself rather crudely trying to assess Ranald McKechnie—now viewed in so physically vigorous an aspect—as a potentially procreative person. The years—his wife's years—were running out. It was up to him to get on with it.

Almost as if these were indecent reflections (which they were not) I switched my attention to the ladies from the Woodstock Road. It wasn't easy to associate Fiona with children: somehow the whisky and the little cigars and the emeritus professor's articulation got in the way. Yet these were surely the flimsy props of a hastily run-up persona— almost a hang-over from what Robert Damian would call an identity crisis of adolescence. I had ceased to attach much weight to them, and it didn't surprise me that Fiona had an observing eye for Johnnie and Virginia. Miss Mountain, on the other hand, quite excluded them from her brooding regard. Novelists can cope with children a little better than playwrights can—but not all that well, all the same. Jane Austen didn't try, and even George Eliot had an uncertain touch; Dickens, although miles better, got bogged down now in sentimentality and now in the grotesque; in English fiction, at least, the best children are the achievement of writers of the second rank.

We gained the proposed picnic place quite soon, and pitched camp at a point on the river bank where it was flanked by meadowland cheerfully sprinkled with flowers appropriate to the May. It *was* May, for we were in the fourth week of the summer term, and the weather was of the unusual English sort that makes *al fresco* feasting entirely rational. I remarked on this to Miss Mountain, reminding her that Miss Austen's Mr Knightly (for Miss Austen had been in my head) had judged 'the nature and simplicity of gentlemen and ladies' —as I remembered the phrase—to be 'best observed by meals within doors'. But Miss Mountain was not in a conversable mood, or was at least not disposed to converse with me. She and Janet exchanged remarks now and then. These were entirely commonplace. But I listened as one lately become irrationally wary before women in general.

The picnic being in the main of my providing, I did the unpacking of it. McKechnie proposed to help, but as his exertions had already been so considerable I began by opening a bottle of wine, pouring him a glass, and ordering him to sit down and recruit himself. He obeyed at once. We were now entirely unconstrained in each other's company. Those occasions—the last of them less than a year old—on which we had scurried unacknowledgingly by in the street had become memories (with both of us, I imagine) no longer embarrassing but merely comical. Now he sat in silence for a short time, eyeing me with the mildly interested and favourable regard which he might have cast upon a ponderable but not exactly exciting quiddity in the text of Aeschylus.

'I suppose,' he asked presently, 'that Janet has told you we go off to America in about a fortnight's time?' It was now McKechnie's habit to assume that I saw much more of Janet than I did of him, and that she was thus a constant channel for the transmission of such McKechnie family intelligence as there was. This wasn't so, but as the misapprehension appeared to afford him pleasure there was no particular reason to correct it. It might have been maintained that the persuasion cast him in something like the role of a complacent husband. But that would have been nonsense. In any company, I believe, Ranald McKechnie's would have been regarded as a commanding or at least incisive intellect. As a result he inevitably carried a certain severity around with him, together with an emphasis on getting the measure of things exactly right. These qualities got in the way of one's describing him as notably diffident. But he was undeniably modest and unassuming—and in consequence quite capable of deciding that I was a person of livelier conversational resource than he commanded, with whom it was thus agreeable to think of his wife as recreating herself. This was far from meaning that McKechnie thought all that of me. Rather he remembered me from our schooldays as a harmless entertainer, and had himself in maturity come to a judicious view of the legitimate if minor place of such persons in the scheme of things. And this state of the case, curiously enough, didn't seem to have militated against our becoming rather fond of each other.

'Yes,' I said, 'I've heard about your going to America, but I didn't know it was to be quite so soon. Shall you be lecturing?'

'I hardly think so. There is no such obligation, certainly. And the semester will, of course, be over. So, no—it's a straight think-tank arrangement.'

This expression (which McKechnie uttered with a slightly awesome whimsicality, presumably elicited by the American language) had by now come to enjoy English currency; I had first heard it, however, on a visit to Princeton, and an image which had then come into my head now recurred to me.

'Do you all swim about together?' I asked.

'Distinctly not. There's even, you know, an acknowledgement that anything other than a civil minimum of hospitality is a distraction. That must come hard to the American mind. Its instinct is to be magnificently hospitable.'

'So it is.' It hadn't sounded as if McKechnie had been offering a wholly commendatory remark. 'So just how are you accommodated?'

'We have a villa—a substantially isolated villa. Or say retired. A retired villa, with absolutely everything laid on. And everybody things twice before coming near us.'

'And *you* think all the time?' I just saved myself from going on 'And Janet thinks all the time too?' The easiness between McKechnie and myself, I had to reflect, was a stream which, like the Cherwell, occasionally threatened sudden snags.

There were no snags about the picnic; whatever its original inspiration, it went forward blamelessly and agreeably. The presence of the Bedworth children lent it, if delusively, something of the air of a family outing. It was the McKechnies

who chiefly occupied themselves with Johnnie and Virginia:
Janet in seeing that they were suitably fed, and Ranald in
amusing them through a variety of surprising small accom-
plishments such as making flat stones hop across the river and
producing unnerving noises by blowing through blades of
grass. These activities, I had to tell myself, represented yet
another unsuspected facet of his personality exposing
itself.

'Ranald,' I said to Janet as I went round with the wine,
'would have been a much more useful man than I was at
Johnnie's birthday party—which I went to some weeks ago.
Look what he's up to now.' What McKechnie was up to was
bringing into being a bow and arrows. The bow was quite a
stout affair, and for a bow-string he had boldly filched from
the punt a length of nylon cord designed for mooring it.

'It looks like the real thing,' Janet said, a shade apprehensively. 'And what's he doing with that penknife?'

'He's making arrows—notching them at one end and
getting them distinctly pointed at the other.'

'Oh, dear!' Janet was as perturbed as if anything that her
husband put his hand to were liable to turn distinctly lethal—
as, indeed, I knew that mechanical contrivances, at least, were
apt to do. But at once she laughed at her own anxiety.
'Dunkie, I can rely on you to restrain him if he decides to play
at William Tell, or something like that. But why aren't you
useful at a birthday party? You like children, don't you?'

'I'd like to—but it doesn't always seem to come off. The
young appeal to me—I've been becoming increasingly aware
of that—but my interest seems to stop short of juveniles.'

'I'm glad you like younger people,' Janet said gravely—and
I thought that for the first time her glance went meaningfully
to Fiona and paused there for a moment. 'There are people
who seem only to be irritated by their juniors, and jealous
of them. That would be a horrid fate.'

'Yes, I agree.' I wanted to say 'But nobody appeals to me

like you'. Only that was a kind of speech I made sparingly to Janet. So I left the next remark to her.

'Of course one needn't be undiscriminating,' she said. 'One needn't adore absolutely everybody in an age bracket. Or even like them. When Ranald was a college tutor and his pupils came around, I liked nearly all of them very much. But there were one or two who just wouldn't do. I definitely had an instinct that way. And there are times when one has to be quite positive—don't you think, Dunkie?—on the strength of instinct alone.'

'*Bang!*'

This had been a shout from Johnnie, and its effect was to disrupt our conversation. We both glanced up, and as we did so there came a second shout—this time a warning one from McKechnie. McKechnie had fired his first arrow; Johnnie, being a modern child unable to conceive of propulsion without explosion, had offered his familiar bomb-noise; and in the same moment McKechnie had become aware of the unfortunate circumstance that his arrow, although travelling well, was doing so in the direction of somebody who had suddenly appeared on the field path bordering the river. McKechnie's shout brought this person abruptly to a halt—but not before he had been conscious of the arrow as passing uncomfortably close to his ear.

The person thus menaced was our Pastoral Fellow, Dr Wyborn. His bobbing up here was not without surprise. But he was very much the man, when one thought of it, to indulge himself in old-fashioned solitary rambles in Oxfordshire. His identity had become plain to McKechnie as soon as to myself, and McKechnie had now dropped his bow and was running forward in a somewhat ungainly fashion and with a very proper apologetic intent. As I watched this I was comically reminded of a not dissimilar spectacle many years before. But that had been on a golf course, and Cyril Bedworth had actually winged the Provost.

McKechnie's shot had fortunately produced only a near miss.

It wasn't socially possible for Wyborn, thus happily spared, simply to walk on. He had to pass the time of day with us, and be introduced to Fiona and Miss Mountain; indeed, to have the junior Bedworths presented to him as well. He was an ascetic-looking man—more likely, I supposed, to consent to being comforted with apples than stayed with flagons. I offered him some of our wine, nevertheless. He accepted it, and even consented to sit down on a rug—perhaps judging it indecorous to consume such refreshment standing, as if in an invisible public bar. He was probably more alarmed at suddenly finding himself in predominantly female company than he had been by his equally abrupt encounter with the arrow that flieth by day. But he was a formally courteous person (when not denouncing the darkened state of men's minds) who felt obliged to stay put until adequate civilities had been exchanged. These were participated in by Miss Mountain to the extent of her advancing upon him and proffering a slice of what had been generally voted an uncommonly good cold pie. She appeared to take an interest in Wyborn—as if he were himself an out-of-the-way pie affording something promising to bite on. Although, as she had once asserted, the untoward situations in her fiction might be gleaned from newspapers, it was to be presumed that her sense of human character came to her in the main unmediated from real life. So she had perhaps discerned something promising in Wyborn. (I had no feeling that she had ever done so in me.)

Wyborn declined pie; he had, he explained, consumed a sandwich shortly before. As he gave us this information he surveyed the remains of our picnic with what appeared to be a censorious eye. This was uncomfortable. Partly because I was unused to purveying such things, and partly because I had facetiously borne in mind the standards obtaining at the Fat Boy's Dingley Dell, my arrangements had been on the lavish side. Wyborn now intimated his consciousness of this clearly enough.

'Had the day not been so enticing,' he said, 'it was my intention to attend the Starvation Lunch.'

'What is that, Dr Wyborn?' Janet asked.

'A misnomer, I fear. It consists of soup and bread—and I am uncertain whether there may not be cheese as well. But the dramatic terminology no doubt appeals to under-graduates, and the root idea is meritorious. They pay so many pence for what they think of as a frugal meal, and give what they might have paid in excess of that for the relief of famine in Bangladesh.'

'One has to hope,' McKechnie said, 'that what the money buys gets to those it is intended for. A great deal of corruption thrives, I have been told, on these good intentions.'

'We must not let that daunt us, my dear Professor.'

'No, indeed!' McKechnie was horrified at being thus charged with introducing a Laodicean note into the discussion. 'One can barely think of a meaner form of theft.'

'Quite so. And there can seldom have been an age'—Wyborn was now addressing the company at large—'in which the works of corporal mercy were more urgently required of Christians. All seven of them. Feeding the hungry. Giving drink to the thirsty. Clothing the naked. Visiting and ransoming the captives. Harbouring the harbourless. Visiting the sick. Burying the dead. Yes, even that last—and in more regions of the earth than one.'

This stiff homily, although perhaps unseasonable, was undeniably impressive. The Bedworth children were round-eyed, and I suppose the rest of us wondered who was going to speak first. Wyborn came to our rescue by continuing to speak himself.

'How to give of our superfluities,' he said, 'is a large question, indeed. And I have been minded to speak to you both'—he clearly meant McKechnie and myself—'about what may be an urgent issue of the kind. It is being said—although only, it may be, as rumour—that the college may receive some very large benefaction in the immediate future. Do you know anything of that?'

McKechnie looked blank, and for the moment I decided to look blank too. News of the Blunderville gold had, after all, got abroad—but belatedly, and when it was already water under the bridge. Seeing that neither of us had anything to say, and disregarding the fact that the ladies were being relegated to the role of a passive auditory, Wyborn pursued his theme.

'If it be indeed so, I see a grave danger that wealth for which some pious and fruitful application might be found will be squandered upon the repair—almost the re-edification, it would seem—of the college tower. To me—and you will recall that I have addressed the Governing Body on this—it is far from self-apparent that a tower, and a merely secular tower at that, should enjoy the sort of priority that some would appear to propose. I most earnestly beg you both to give serious thought to this.'

'It certainly deserves it,' I said. It seemed to me that Wyborn's appeal was not of a sort to snub, and that McKechnie would agree with me if he had more than a hazy notion of what was being talked about. 'But I do know a little, as it happens, about the possible benefaction you mentioned. Unfortunately it's now entirely off the cards. There isn't a hope of it. So, as far as I know, the problem of the tower remains exactly where it was.'

'And so does the tower itself,' Wyborn got to his feet, with the air of a man who has said his say. 'The whole thing may well be a foolish scare.'

'I don't think so,' I said. 'The danger is real enough—whatever we're to do about it.'

'It may be so.' Suddenly Wyborn had produced a handkerchief, and dabbed his nose with it as appeared to be his habit in moments of perturbation. 'But towers may be opprobrious things, Pattullo. Not infrequently have they been associated with idolatry and overweening pride. *Proud towers to swift destruction doomed*. A powerful line, which lingers in the mind.'

With these words, followed by correct but abrupt farewells, Wyborn went on his way. Fiona began pouring coffee from a thermos, and after a minute it was Janet who spoke.

'Oxford colleges really are rather odd places,' she said. 'I didn't know what to make of that at all. Except that he's somebody who means what he says. And that he's not mad.'

'That last bit was north-north-west mad.' Fiona produced sugar. 'But I'd agree, not more than that. And Oxford's full of madmen when the wind's in that quarter.'

Milton from Wyborn, I thought, and Shakespeare from Fiona. Oxford was also full of persons whose minds inclined to slip into literary grooves. But it was Virginia Bedworth who, for the moment, had the last word on our untoward visitor.

'Angry man,' Virginia said.

I took the punt down-stream without mishap, although it was an exercise demanding care. The afternoon remained sunny, and as we drew nearer to Oxford it became apparent that this had drawn numerous pleasure seekers to the river. Many of those handling one sort of craft or another were a good deal less expert than I was. With elderly disapproval I marked what appeared to be an increased incidence, as compared with former years, of young people disposed to regard these aquatic exercises as a lark rather than a modest display of athletic prowess. This sentiment made me all the more anxious not to tumble into the Cherwell. I steered—as well as shoved—with care.

I still contrived some awareness, however, of the natural scene, and even of what, in the muted fashion possible upon so unremarkable a voyage, might be called landmarks. The momentary glimpse of a distant spire, small boat houses and abandoned landing-stages, narrow rills and dubiously navigable backwaters: all these were capable of making a call upon the memory. Was it here that Tony had stripped and dived for what he declared would be pearl oysters—or it might have been dead men's bones? Was it there that Johnnie's father had most inadvertently played Leda to a swan? There had been names, facetiously concocted, for unremarkable inlets and sluggish little tributaries. Was it, for example, Fornication Creek that we were now approaching? Did people still call it that? And hadn't we, more familiarly, said Fornicaggers? Did such weird locutions any longer obtain?

These questionings may have made me briefly inattentive to my business. From behind a tiny islet another punt had suddenly appeared, powerfully propelled by a tall and fair youth in its stern. On the minute decked prow (as Oxford, but not Cambridge, regards it) sat just such another youth, idly dabbling a hand in water. These were the Sheldrake brothers, Mark and Matthew. Between them, amply cushioned in the middle of the craft, Penny reclined. She was a striking figure—and not all that more mature, after all, than Cleopatra when she sailed down Cydnus.

My mind had paused to achieve all these identifications before registering the fact that we were on a collision course. But I knew how to use my pole as a rudder, heaving it in a wide arc through the sluggishly resistant stream. Mark (for it was he who was the handsome Palinurus of the other vessel) did the same, more swiftly and to more saving effect. As a result the two punts glided harmlessly past each other, although with only inches between them. Matthew didn't know me; Mark had time for a brief and perhaps embarrassed grin; Penny looked at me unsmilingly but with slightly parted lips. And then an impact of sorts did take place—although not of a physical kind. It was a near-hallucination, indeed: a species of false recognition so instantaneous and momentary as to be hard to describe. Mark had glanced backwards to assure himself that all was well, and I had done the same. Our eyes met. It was a point at which the river was overhung by trees in their first abundant leaf, and in the brilliant sunshine odd touches of chiaroscuro were at play. Now it was as if, in quest of some clever dramatic effect, for a photographic image on a flickering screen there had abruptly been substituted its negative. And dramatic this present effect was—although the drama was entirely confined within my own head. For an instant the fair Mark Sheldrake vanished and in his place stood another young demi-god in the person of a dark-skinned Italian boy. Frediano was his name, and he had been quite as much in Penny's picture as either or both of the Sheldrakes was ever likely to be. And between Mark's extreme good looks and Frediano's there was surely a real resemblance—masked, it might be said, by pigmentation only.

So now did I know why, at that first encounter with the English youth outside my rooms in Surrey—rooms once tenanted by Henry Tindale, the White Rabbit—I had been visited by an unease I had largely failed to identify? The moment, and this strange question, passed even as I shoved my punt pole once more into the opaque and torpid Cherwell. But it was not before I had seemed to hear an Italian voice.

'*Come son' crudele, le donne!*' Frediano had said, cynically yet sadly, winding up his sense of the affair.

XII

THIRTY OR THEREABOUTS seems to be the age at which most men conclude themselves to have outlived the phase of absolute youth. Women, although they are to cling much longer to the idea of being short of 'middle age', already have misgivings at twenty-five. The men start doing exercises even although they still play games, and on the women's dressing-tables familiar cosmetics designed for the immediate enhancement of beauty are supplemented by others supposed to own some preservative virtue. These are objective signs but the whole business is entirely subjective, no doubt. At eighteen, and during my first year at Oxford, youths senior to me by no more than three or four years seemed to have attained a phase of adulthood entirely remote from my own. I never questioned this. My friend Martin Fish, standing as he did at about that chronological remove from me, appeared grown-up as I was not—and this even although his misadventure in love (of which chance had made me so close an observer) was of a kind belonging still with the hazards of immaturity. And in my final year in college I shared with nearly all my con-temporaries a sense that the freshmen were so absurdly childish that it was embarrassing merely to be in the same pub with them. Yet we hadn't, at that period, developed any uneasy sense that age was creeping up on us: or, if we did, it was only within the narrow context of looming jobs and careers. Milton, indeed, on his twenty-second birthday saw Time as a subtle thief already at work on him. But life was shorter and men more precocious in the early seventeenth century.

Intellectually, I counted as moderately precocious myself. In a merely public way, that is, and on the strength of delusive early success in the theatre. This persuaded me that I had matured all round, yet I still felt wholly young. I married Penny feeling that way—the persuasion not being at all impaired by a sense that I had achieved this union at a dogged long last. It was a sense supported by the calendar, almost a decade having passed since our first meeting at Mrs Pococke's dinner-party. Yet the man who married Penny was still the boy whose muddled head had then cast her in the role of life-line for the shipwrecked Fish. The calendar again shows only three years as passing between our marriage and my turning thirty. The period has a much longer feel—being subject to the law that, in retrospections, the decades and the lustres here stretch and there contract in the manner of a telescope or a lazy-tongs. Certainly at the end of it I was no longer blissfully young. Thirty was to stand out for me as the 'grim promontory' that I seem to recall forty as somewhere so named by Henry James.

Penny owned a liking for places which nobody had ever been to. By this she didn't mean the remoter stretches of the Sahara or the Gobi or the Tarim Basin—localities familiarly known only to intrepid explorers like my contemporary Gavin Mogridge. The entire Australian continent would have come within the terms of her description as certainly as the Victoria Desert or the Nullarbor Plain. 'Nobody' meant 'nobody one is likely to meet at a party'. For there was an element of what had lately been dubbed one-upmanship in Penny's notions of travel, and it was what took us to Calabria for our honeymoon. Nobody had ever been to Calabria—except, of course, Norman Douglas. It might be possible, Penny thought, to contact this legendary figure in the guise of pilgrims seeking guidance on the region. Unfortunately he proved recently dead.

It is hard, I see, to put Penny—the still quite young Penny—faithfully on the page while at the same time seeking to suggest the complex way in which I was in love with her. Did I see her much less clearly then than I do now? I doubt it. Time hasn't to be called in to unveil Penny, much less to unmask her. At times she was to surprise me, but it was the residual surprise of the sculptor at what his chisel frees: a form known to him in its essentials from a first moment in the studio or the quarry. Penny was all there from the start; and at least at the start her absurdities and perversenesses (a necessary if clumsy word) were part of her enchantment.

It has become fashionable to put in the forefront of one's description of a woman—be she fictitious, or alive and resident still in the next street—that she was this or that in bed. I suppose I could go about Penny in such a way. Certainly I was much occupied with her in bed—there being times, indeed, when this seemed self-evidently the whole thing. But here detailed exposition, whether to be regarded as decorous or not, wouldn't be easy. If I were to say that Penny was at once enterprising to a point of astonishment, taking in her little stride measures of which I had only read in books, and at the same time undeviatingly detached and cool like one participating in the mildest social rituals; if I were to say this, and elaborate upon it, I should arrive at a needlessly unsympathetic picture of my wife upon these intimate occasions. Penny's coolness wasn't cold. The elusiveness whereby she would suddenly be occupying herself less with the affair in hand than with a disarranged *coiffure* was attractive in itself. I'd have felt cheated had she made away with it.

I puzzled less about Penny than about myself—about myself, that is, in relation to her. At the time of my marriage I had drifted into that casual and carnal view of sex which possesses young men with some element of bafflement and frustration behind them in adolescence. It might be held that I did so the more readily because of assumptions and norms of conduct current among the sort of people with whom I was beginning to make my way. One can always blame a lot on the theatre, as on literary and artistic society in general. But in fact to almost any sort of artist seriously inclined the sirens' unsupported song becomes boring after a time, seems to turn to mere Fescennine piping, so that he will listen to it only in those phases of fatigue and *desœuvrement* which are likely to plague him intermittently throughout his career. Alert, he wants his sensual music interwoven with other themes. And if one seeks to know how other people are compounded a simplistic view of sex is of little utility. There were a good many purely social filaments in the web spun for me by Penny Triplett.

There was the strand of upbringing, for a start. I think I have recorded that the Triplett ancestry lay in that odd aristocracy of intellect, curiously bound together as much by marriage and thickening consanguinity as by vocation and intelligence, which had so strikingly predominated in England throughout the Victorian Ages and the Edwardian Age. This alone had for a time commanded my imagination a good deal. Behind young Pattullo had lain on the one hand a father who was an isolated and splendid phenomenon sprung up amid the folk, and on the other hand the little lairdly people of Glencorry, confident in their immemorial station but innocent of anything that a restless boy could think of as a movement of mind. From Penny herself, indeed, inherited intellectual habit appeared to have almost entirely fined away, so that mere upper-classness was her predominant note. But not quite. She held a confident belief that large subjects were amenable to small talk, and that there was nothing on which she couldn't adequately have her word. She knew the names; she could catch the tone; and she was, for that matter, quite far from being an uneducated girl.

When I first encountered her, therefore, Penny stood out in dazzling contrast to my Glencorry cousins. Anna and Ruth—relieving their boredom with cheap romances, walking their slavering dogs, glumly counting the slaughtered grouse

176

in the rain—would have been dumb, resentful, outraged in the presence of Penny's widely-ranging prattle. (So, for that matter, would their parents.) Yet between these lumpish girls and Penny there was a link. They all had an unfaltering certainty about their place in the world.

In my earlier visits to Corry Hall I must have stood a good deal in awe of my cousins. While still in shorts, indeed, I had recognized them as extremely stupid. But there I was, sufficiently scruffy to feel very much *filius terrae* in an oppressively ancestral abode; and there were they—discontented, it is true, but at the same time inexpugnably assured of their own consequence. And I could make no impression on them (or only on Anna as being for certain purposes less chancy in the heather than some gillie's son). Year after year as I went back to the place I must have been better-informed, more in command of rapid speech and even a kind of wit, eager to argue, entertain, and (no doubt) show off. But nothing of all this made me of any use to my cousins. I can't have been pleased.

Penny's upbringing, in the nursery and schoolroom sense, may have been very much the same as that of the Glencorry girls. Put all three in a room, stop your ears to anything except social cadence, and it might be some time before you much distinguished between them. But Penny had been trained to believe that conversation was not merely a duty but a pleasure as well. My Aunt Charlotte frowned only on awkward silences; old Mrs Triplett—Penny's hostess and chaperon when we first met—would view with disfavour any remark lacking at least some positive quality: incisiveness, perhaps; or lively interest; or reach of information; or simple elegance of phrase. Penny had been taught to be alert, receptive, responsive—preconditions to which, when achieved, she was free to add any nonsense or prettiness she chose. I suppose she was the first girl in whom I ever encountered this remunerative social discipline. It even included, although

177

sparely and to an effect of irony or fun, an element of old-fashioned deference to the brute fact of one's masculinity. This was something new to me as a boy; such persiflage would have been impossible from Janet; the charm of it in Penny must have lingered with me long after I had become familiar with a wide variety of feminine batteries.

These have been thoughts prompted by my wedding journey to Calabria. We drove there in a car a good deal more impressive, if less businesslike, than that in which Fish and I, during my first long vacation, had effected our extensive survey of the 'art cities' of Italy. Penny had got up this more restricted project to her customary standard of drawing-room research. It was to be Salvator Rosa terrain (*What savage Rosa dashed*, she quoted from some poem) and there were to be abundant hints of Mrs Radcliffe, whose romances were enjoying a vogue at that time. In particular there were to be *banditti*, and Penny was not without hope that these might endeavour to capture us and hold us to ransom—in which case she would gain a useful measure of my manhood right from the start. I said that in such an event it might be the brigands' manhood that she would be more immediately made aware of, and we entertained ourselves with lurid fantasies based upon this supposition. I can see this nonsense now as not unconnected with a certain tug which the perverse could exercise over Penny's sexual imagination, and possibly communicate to my own.

An hour out from Naples, and fatefully as it was to transpire, I had the idea of making the short detour which would take us to Ravello, being prompted to show Penny a place that lingered in my memory—and in which, indeed, I had stumbled unwittingly upon a sexual episode again not of the most straightforward sort, although no *banditti* had been involved in it. I had told Penny the story of Colonel Morrison and Alec Mountjoy. I suppose I told her everything within my experience that came into my mind. Or almost everything. For I think I never mentioned any matters concerning the girl who, many years ahead, was to become the wife of Ranald McKechnie.

Ravello hadn't much changed in the nine or ten years since I had been there. *Turismo* hadn't gained its hoped-for grip, although it proliferated on the coast below: there, entire monasteries were being transmogrified into hotels, including one reputed to have been founded by St Francis himself. Ravello remained a slumbering little town, only less un-prosperous than Scala perched on the opposite hill. Penny professed herself at once as having fallen in love with it—an instance of a kind of obligingness in which she had considerable facility. She had decided, a shade extravagantly, that I owned a strong sentimental regard for the place; and she felt that enthusiasm, which costs nothing, would con-tribute to the general niceness which she was at that time genuinely predicating for our marriage. As a consequence, we decided on a stay of several nights—not in the hotel where Fish and I (and possibly D. H. Lawrence before us) had put up, but in one, declared by the guide-book to be rather grander, at the other end of the town. We had hardly settled in, however, before Penny discovered from the same source of information or misinformation that Ibsen had written *A Doll's House* in a hotel at Amalfi a few miles away. She was all for moving there at once, being as excited at the thought of dining, so to speak, with Nora Helmer as Fish and I had been intrigued at sleeping in a room haunted by the ghosts of Connie Chatterley and her lover. It would certainly have been a splendid talking-point for a party. But fortunately Ravello had Wagner on its side, to say nothing of E. M. Forster—a figure as legendary as Norman Douglas but indubitably alive, with whom Ravello might be discussed at an encounter to be engineered one day. So Penny returned to being in love with our present surroundings, and we ate our dinner in amity. Yet, if we had transferred to Amalfi, various things could have fallen out differently and various destinies been altered. Henry Tindale, the White Rabbit of Surrey Four, had vacated his fellowship and now lived there permanently. I may well have been unaware of this, since news from Oxford came to me scantily at that time; certainly he never entered my head during those days at Ravello, although I had known long before of his owning a retreat in the neighbourhood. We might have run into him, however, and the immediate course of events might have been changed as a result. In which case we'd never have seen the Villa d'Orso, nor would Frediano (*'Come son' crudele, le donne!'*) have been known to us at a not distant future time.

This is conjecture, and conjecture of a trite sort. The Villa d'Orso was a fact—an attractive fact, even although (and initially partly because) only to be peered at through a small iron grille. It took its name as commanding, in common with its neighbour the Palazzo Rufolo, the sweep of coast-line closed by Capo d'Orso to the west. It wasn't itself commanded, since it owned that sort of ingenious seclusion amid a huddle of other dwellings which only Italian architecture can contrive. It was small and unassuming, but hinted a respectable antiquity. Its English equivalent would have been an affair of thatch and what house-agents term exposed beams. Penny, a very urban character, approved that sort of thing. She similarly approved the small garden of which a glimpse was also afforded us. It was untended and had been invaded by everything that grows in spring in the valleys of the Dragone and the Raginna. A knowledge of wild flowers was part of Penny's correct education, and she fell to enumerating them rapidly: wood anemone, periwinkle minor, green hellebore, rock cress, euphorbia. I was thinking again of Penny's party manner—for it was just thus that she would efficiently tick off current books or plays—when she suddenly cried out to me.

'Oh, Duncan,' she said, '—the deep, *deep* cyclamen! And the lizards—starting again!'

The cyclamen were indeed deep in hue—glowing in shadowed moist places almost with the fire of gentians in snow. The lizards, darting from crevice to crevice on a crumbling wall, were in process of shedding tetterous skins to reveal a summer green.

'And dung beetles,' I said. 'Dung beetles among the asphodels. It's emblematical. Mortality and immortality.' I produced this deep thought at random, and while reflecting on the significance of the fact that I could be arrested by any impulse of spontaneity on Penny's part. For her exclamations hadn't represented her assuming for the moment a charming role; it was a real Penny who had swiftly responded to the little creatures at once so slumberous and so electrically alive; to the flowers so magically uttering the mystery of earth. I suddenly knew that I much wanted to have children by Penny, and that at the end of our twenties we had no time to waste. But what I went on to say was prosaic enough. 'It's not exactly *ben mantenuto*, is it? The house must have been untenanted for ages.'

'Duncan, you must climb in!' Penny cried. Her mood had changed to that of a slightly factitious urgency. 'You must climb in and get me some corms. Half-a-dozen will do.'

'Corms?'

'The cyclamen bulbs, of course. I'll plant them in one of our little terra-cotta troughs—the ones with *putti* from Impruneta. As a *giardino di finestra*. They'll look absolutely marvellous.'

'Yes. But if you want cyclamen bulbs we can dig up any number in the woods. I've an idea they're surprisingly large and go quite deep down.'

'The barbed wire *is* rather rusty. But I think you can wriggle through.'

'I don't intend to do anything of the sort.'

'And—darling—see if you can get into the house. Perhaps you can unbolt something and let me in as well.'

'Why not do the wriggling yourself?' I asked. 'You're smaller than I am—even round the bottom.' I knew very well that Penny would do no wriggling through wire, since she had old-fashioned views (or so I thought of them) on the physical activities appropriate in women—or appropriate in circumstances attended by any possibility of publicity. (There was to be an exception to this—but at present it lies some way ahead.)

'Or there may be an easier way on the other side—and I'd hate you to scratch yourself, darling.' Penny was expressing this rational solicitude because she knew that when I'd said I wouldn't wriggle I'd meant it. She was very quick in assessing these minute situations. 'Round the corner,' she urged gaily. 'Come on!'

The Villa d'Orso was surrounded on all sides by narrow *scale* running between high, blind walls. There was no yard of its perimeter, that is to say, that was level ground; everywhere you were treading one of those rocky and irregular staircases which in that part of Campania not only abound in the little towns or link *podere* with *podere* but think nothing of running up to mountain-tops as well. Being proportioned for the convenience of mules rather than men, these peculiar thoroughfares are irritating even on short stretches and distinctly fatiguing on longer ones. They are, of course, picturesque, and were part of what Penny was busily falling in love with.

'There!' Penny had halted triumphantly before a mouldering wooden door set in the garden wall, and secured by no more than a chain, one link of which was hitched over a rusty nail. 'And, Duncan.' she breathed, 'look—just *look*!' She pointed to an almost obliterated sign-board hanging askew above the door. The flaking paint read *Casa in vendita*. And below this announcement there had been scrawled, apparently at a somewhat later date, the encouraging addendum:

a buon prezzo

'That's what we'll call it,' Penny said. '*Il villino a buon prezzo*. Won't it be a splendid address? I can see it on our letter-head. Can't you? Is there a harbour?'

'A harbour?' I repeated—and with a feeling that my bride had perhaps gone out of her mind quite in Mrs Radcliffe's manner. 'Do you mean a garage? There's probably stabling of a sort.'

'Stupid!' Penny impatiently stamped a foot. 'Down below, of course. In the place where the duchess lived before they strangled her.'

'There's a harbour of sorts at Amalfi—yes. Nothing much.'

'Then that's where we'll keep our yacht. Darling, we'll be free of the entire Tyrrhenian Sea. And we'll get round the corner to the Ionian Sea as well. Like Gissing.'

'Like Gissing.' I wondered whether, for Penny, George Gissing—at a revival of whose reputation publishers were then labouring—was still as much in the land of the living as Mr Forster, and to be cultivated on what I was coming to recognize as her peculiar geographical plan. The Strait of Messina seemed rather a roundabout way to this particular lion hunt. That Penny cherished a dream of lions—a Pattullo *salon*—was another fact I was getting a grasp of. Of course she wasn't wholly serious. She was too sophisticated to be that. All this was an ironical sort of fun, and I was still sufficiently in love to be amused by it. Only Penny didn't securely distinguish between fact and fantasy, and was capable of taking steps to actualize her imaginings in an impracticable and alarming manner.

We entered the wild garden, and then the villa itself through a broken window. I bought it that afternoon, and at once had to resist Penny's suggestion that we immediately follow this up by scouring the Costiera Amalfitana for a suitable yacht.

Penny would scarcely have known one end of such a craft from the other, and I'd have been little better myself. Money seemed at that time not much of a consideration. My success with *The Bear-Garden* had persuaded me that I was going to earn more than later proved to be the case, and I was already aware of the effect which my father's final ascent from eminence to fame was to have for Ninian and myself in that department of life. As for Penny, she had come into a lot of money on marriage under the will of a wealthy aunt.

There was thus nothing rash in our sudden action, but I can see it now as evidence of my being no longer sure that youth goes on for ever. Calculation was beginning to touch my vision of our future married state. Penny, I felt, was too fond of a social life—metropolitan and modishly 'with it' in a nebulously artistic way—which I knew would irk me in more than moderate doses. (This, paradoxically, was only the more true because just such a society provided the background for much that I wrote.) But Penny was also fond of Italy, as I was. Her Italian was better than mine—and although it was doubtless very politely Tuscan she was clever at finding it intelligible when mutated into one or another outlandish dialect. She'd get no end of fun, I felt, out of superintending the virtual rebuilding of the semi-ruinous but potentially commodious little house, and fitting it out in a manner appropriate to cultivated persons well-seen in Italian antiquities. In a minuscule way we'd take on between us the role of that Lord Grimthorpe who had dolled up the neighbouring Villa Cimbrone in a highly mediaeval and Decameron-like fashion. Ravello, as I have somewhere chronicled, finds mention in the *Decameron*, and although Boccaccio was by many centuries even less available for a *salon* than Norman Douglas the circumstance was gratifying in itself.

With some preliminary dispositions made, we drove south to Calabria. It was my guess that, *banditti* being little in evidence, so out-of-the-way a region would not please Penny for long, and that our first venture there would be our last. In this I proved to be in error. If there weren't bandits there were fisherfolk—commonly lounging around tiny harbours as if the fish could wait. There were fishermen old and young, gnarled and twisted, or flawless in a first manhood, sun-tinted to copper or gold, their naked torsos like ancient bronzes dredged from the sea, and the rest of their persons scantily clothed in insolently paraded rags. Some of them, even the youngest, bore evidence that fishing really did go on—this as lacking a finger or two on one or another hand. Swordfish are a hazardous catch. Penny was fascinated by this latter macabre phenomenon. On several occasions when we went rowing or sailing—dutiful tourists not venturing to neglect some commended grotto or cave—she contrived to chose from among those eager to crew for us handsome youths thus strangely mutilated. I didn't in the least object to their good looks, and would have picked them that way myself. But I think I'd equally instinctively have preferred four fingers to three. It would be easy to evolve a Freudian commentary on this small point of fascination in Penny.

XIII

THE VILLA D'ORSO became habitable, and then in numerous ways rather more than merely that, with remarkable speed. Behind the curious system of straw screens which festoon Italian scaffolding the *muratori* worked furiously. Penny, superintending their labours, was charmed by their singing and unoffended when she caught the sense of the libidinous remarks they exchanged at her expense. In the interior she was particularly concerned with the appointments of the *gabinetto* in which my masterpieces were to be written; they were certainly much in excess of anything Ibsen had enjoyed in his Amalfi hotel. The books were to live behind expanses of glass as if they were hot-house plants, and when I got tired of the view (which was tremendous) I could refresh myself by studying a large collage by Rauschenberg, at that time very much *le dernier cri* in advanced artistic circles. A certain restlessness attended the achieving of all this and much else, and as Penny was apt to remember that the next necessary object was presently located in London or Paris we spent a surprising amount of time suspended in air above the Alps. This was exhilarating in its way, and even conduced in snatches to a good deal of dramatic composition. In fact I achieved under these conditions what turned out to be my worst play to date.

Eventually we did in a fashion settle down, and Penny had leisure to take stock of our social situation. It wasn't promising. Of her established acquaintances the nearest lived in Rome, and if any of them owned house or land in territory getting on for the *Mezzogiorno* they had no disposition to put in time there. Ravello itself was not well provided with persons of cultivation, or even of substance. Lemon-groves bring nobody a fortune, or even shoes to the feet. Vineyards are another matter, and the two principal families of the place lived in a style attesting the fact. These showed us proper attention. Indeed, since they lived in a bitter rivalry which had subsisted for generations, they were ready to vie with one another in providing entertainment. But Penny judged them stodgy and bourgeois, and was shocked that they displayed little brass plates on their front doors intimating their status as oenologists. Beyond these people was a mere darkness until one reached the *contadini*, with whom she professed to be enchanted. But rustics don't drop in for cocktails, and have never heard of Rauschenberg; they were thus only a limited resource. Moreover, these peasant neighbours of ours were for the most part either children, whose only interest lay in exchanging oranges for cigarettes, or seniors whom the advancing years were already contorting into a semblance of the olive trees surrounding them. Here and there one came across a young woman, but hardly ever a young man. Campania is a region from which the able-bodied depart when they can. *Fare San Michele, sloggiare, sgombrare*: one learns that there are many terms for thus packing up and clearing out. What I hadn't yet quite taken the measure of was the extent to which this state of affairs deprived Penny of a major interest in life.

We were left with the White Rabbit. Henry Tindale wasn't young, nor was he the kind of invert who is receptive and responsive in the company of women. Women simply alarmed him—and I believe it was for this reason, and not sheerly through lack of other society, that Penny took to him, or at least took him up. She enjoyed having him back away from her, or substitute for a simple exchange of glances a fixed glare over her shoulder. I don't mean that she tormented him; on the contrary, she behaved very nicely. It is probable that Tindale felt she liked him, and was ashamed of

187

the uneasiness he couldn't shed in her presence. He wasn't easy with me either—any more than he had been on that first evening of our acquaintance, when he had taken me into his bedroom and explained how undergraduates climbed into college through one of his windows. He had retired early from his fellowship, but not (as I was to discover some averred) in consequence of any impending scandal. From a family business of an unassuming sort he had come into a modest private fortune, and had used it to withdraw from a way of life that obscurely frightened him. He had managed to conclude his dealings with Pope Zosimus, some twenty years of unremitting study having enabled him to say of this obscure and fractious prelate all that fell to be said. I am not aware of ever having met anyone who had read Tindale's book.

Amalfi, like many towns on that coast, is in part ingeniously crammed into mere fissures in the rock. Tindale's house lay at the stony heart of the place, and very much within sound of the duomo's campanile. The great bell there may have reminded him of college days, but it was much more loquacious than anything Oxford would put up with. Although nothing much happens in Amalfi the inhabitants have a highly developed sense of time, and require a tintinnabulary performance every fifteen minutes throughout the day and night. The racket would have been insupportable but for the extraordinary construction of this crowded quarter. The narrow lanes consist of twisting *scale* which are for the most part roofed over; the wanderer in them may be said to be in open air, but his impression is of having penetrated to a troglodytic or catacombish manner of living. There is plenty of internal din, the denizens being seldom without matter to talk or shout or sing or whistle about from dawn until a very late hour. But the reverberations or shrill clangour and loud alarms from the belfry are muted by much intervening stone.

Dwellings disposed within such a complex remain private

188

even although populous, and it was as if the White Rabbit had secured a secluded retreat in the very middle of what was essentially a warren. He had established himself there on a vacation basis some years before retirement; in fact this was the house which he had once regretted being unable to lend to Fish and myself because it was already promised to sojourners who later proved to be Colonel Morrison and his boy-friend Alec Mountjoy. Now, at this later time, he shared the place for much of the year with a middle-aged friend of his own called Ulric Anderman. They were an oddly-assorted couple. Anderman was a baronet and his family of some antiquity, an ancestor of his having been in the first flight of those coaxed into that money-spinning order by James I. As a young man he had been a notable athlete. Then, when still young, he had become abruptly expatriate, spending the greater part of his time cruising idly round the Mediterranean basin. He and Tindale shared a powerful common interest, but it was of a kind which almost necessarily precluded their taking any such interest in one another. Penny, although inquisitive and learning all the time, was not yet well-seen in such situations. She imagined that two homosexuals sharing an establishment must as a matter of course be on the most intimate terms, and she expressed an extreme distaste at the thought of these two 'ugly old men' making love. But this was not at all the state of the case. Sexual deviations are almost always extremely specific, and Tindale and Anderman, because alike tied to the image of youth, were in a relationship untinged by erotic feeling. Indeed, there must at times have been jealousies and a mutual antagonism between them. Proust comments on the distrust and suspicion of one another which inverts of identical disposition commonly feel. It was to the credit of these elderly Englishmen that they got along as they did.

Penny's distaste was far from taking us out of this couple's society. On the contrary, she put in much time alertly watching for what wasn't there, but which would no doubt have proved scabrously amusing if it had been; and I myself, as a consequence, found myself attending to them more than I might otherwise have done. It was my conclusion that, if their interests coincided, their achievements did not. They were temperamentally wide apart, and in a manner not unconnected, perhaps, with their social origins. For some three hundred years the Andermans had been accustomed to grab or inflict what they chose, whereas it was probable that the Tindales had commonly been at the receiving end of the stick. Tindale was thus much the more conscious of the pressures of society; he was inhibited and unconfident where his friend was ruthless and untroubled. But there was more than this to the difference between them: something that went deeper than any social conditioning, and that inclined me to a more sympathetic attitude towards one man than the other. Anderman's were all compassable goals; he knew the limits of what he was going to get; out of a certain monotony of event he extracted contentedly what variety he could. Tindale hadn't thus come to terms with himself. He hoped for absurdities, and hesitated or halted before the cheated expectation his intelligence told him lay ahead. As undergraduates we hadn't been quite wrong in writing him off as ineffective in the quest of what his nature prompted him to. I didn't write him off now. I only wished him luck—or rather the rare miracle of a complete relationship which does sometimes come, like a spell of halcyon days, to people of his kind.

But people of a kind almost endlessly subdivide, and there was another particular—developmental, this time—in which Tindale and Anderman differed. Tindale's sexual orientation had, almost certainly, been from the first as it now was. This was why women alarmed him; they did so as small girls had once done. Anderman—but I was to learn this only at a later date—had a wife and children behind him. He had experienced, at a somewhat earlier age than the phenomenon is said commonly to occur, a complete change of sexual impulse; less, perhaps, a matter of something repressed breaking free than of the coming into being of a state of affairs with no existence hitherto, and this as the consequence of an obscure organic mutation. Such men are said frequently to go on sleeping with women in an intermittent way. Whether Anderman was one of these, I don't know. He undoubtedly retained an interest in women: his observant and confident eye hinted a kind of amused connoisseurship which Penny, for one, responded to. She may have felt that Anderman could and should be rescued from anything so dismal as the relationship she imagined to subsist between him and Tindale. Or she may have been attracted by some fantasy of giving an additional kinky twist to an existing kinky set-up. Where this might have taken her I can't say. Where we did all arrive was on territory I simply hadn't thought of.

When I meditate about Penny I see that all her frailties were comprehended within what, in another context, would be a virtue. It was her instinct swiftly to follow up hypothesis with experiment. This can win people Nobel prizes. With Penny it was unfortunately a matter of actually having a go at behaviour which respectable persons only indulge—and even then on a system of decent rationing—inside the security of their own heads. Yet the same mechanism could operate in her on an innocent level. Harmless things that it would be nice to do she commonly contrived to bring about. One of these was that dream of sailing the Tyrrhenian and Ionian Seas. Here, in quite a short time, an obvious resource unfolded. A yacht of our own was impracticable for the present; having neither of us the slightest nautical skill, we should have been too much in the hands of unreliable persons. But Anderman owned both a yacht and a wide knowledge of the waters involved. This was the simplest reason why Penny judged Sir Ulric worth being attentive to. We were to go sailing with him.

It might have been expected that Tindale, with his aversion to feminine society, would take a poor view of the idea—the more so as our presence on board the *Ithaca* might set a constraint upon what were presumably some of its customary freedoms. But this proved not so. Nervous and wary as Anderman was not, he seemed to spy a certain element of useful chaperonage in the occasional presence of a young married couple. And here I must explain what the customary course of things on the yacht turned out to be.

The *Ithaca*, although commodious, was very handlable, so that Anderman and Tindale could easily sail it unassisted at need. At times they would set out alone from Amalfi, and later pick up a suitable crew farther up or down the coast. At other times they would recruit at Amalfi a couple of respectable youths (recommended by the *parroco*), cruise with them for some days, and then send them home, adequately remunerated, by bus, while themselves departing to other hunting-grounds in the deep south. It must have been rather like travelling post in horse-drawn times: another stage accomplished, there were always fresh animals to hand.

This manner of predatory voyaging, the businesslike conduct of which is unendearing, had not been invented by our two Englishmen. Wealthy Germans were frequently to be observed thus industriously exploiting the poverty of Calabria—a poverty so deep as to be more shameful than most sexual irregularities.

We made a couple of short voyages during which, granted these underlying conditions and interests, a reasonable decorum was observed. Our hosts were, I think, in a peculiar sense on holiday. They were known in many of the tiny ports and fishing villages into which we sailed. Old men, sitting in long rows on benches as if for a formal photograph, would raise an arm in familiar greeting; their sons or grandsons would come on board, sometimes in ones or twos seeking employment, and sometimes by the half-dozen, when they would scuffle and tumble around the deck—benevolently regarded by Anderman and Tindale, and with all the innocence of children on a Sunday School outing. In these maritime places young men were still plentifully in evidence; the sea and its perils continued to hold their allegiance; it was from the life of the soil, equally hard but much duller, that this whole age group was draining away. Those who crewed for us every now and then were probably prepared for a ready acquiescence in whatever turned up; either by previous experience or by repute they understood the tastes of their employers. There was nothing *louche* about them, all the same, and Penny would have been undisturbed by their conduct had she been my maiden aunt. Practised sailors, they gave themselves eagerly to mastering the particular mysteries of the *Ithaca*; they sang and laughed, and were as polite as they were undeniably easy on the eye. It was with surprise that one would glimpse them, when they judged themselves unobserved, treat each other to an obscene gesture or an indecent lunge. I recall Tindale as on one occasion seriously reprehending a lapse of this kind.

Remembering Penny's interest in such fisher-lads—an interest which, upon a wedding-journey, had been a shade out of the way—I wasn't without the fear that she would occasion embarrassment by setting up in competition with our hosts for the regard, although not necessarily for the favours, of these engaging youths. They weren't *en disponibilité* in the fashion they were because of any particular homosexual inclination in themselves, and it seemed to me that our hosts, however free with their money (which I suspected them of not being in any notable degree), wouldn't stand a chance against my wife if she chose to entertain herself by cutting them out. That my mind could move in this way at all is an indication of what was happening to our marriage before it was two years old, and may stand in for episodes, in England rather than Italy, which there is no need to recount. But on board the *Ithaca* Penny was on her best behaviour; as these casual nautical assistants came and went during our wanderings she did no more than contemplate them appreciatively from a deck chair. They repaid this attention liberally as they worked at the tiller or on the ropes, but without offensive boldness and without—so far as I could distinguish—making either Anderman or Tindale in the least cross.

But despite this general propriety of overt behaviour it was all a little uncomfortable, nevertheless. I was relieved when, in due season, Penny grew tired of yachting, or of yachting under the inhibiting circumstances I have sketched.

'I think,' she said one evening as we sat on our diminutive terrace watching the sun go down behind Scala, 'I'll go and visit the Duthies. It's a long time since I've seen them.'

'Who are the Duthies?'

'Darling, you must know the Duthies. They're Scotch.' Penny took an irritating pleasure in uttering small stupidities of this sort. At least I had come to find them irritating; no doubt they had charmed me at first. 'I'll send Cynthia a telegram in the morning. It will be a good idea, don't you think?'

I had no means of telling whether it would be a good idea— nor of finding out. I'd just learnt all I'd ever learn about the Duthies. Penny made a point of thus naming unknown persons when she was proposing emancipated absences of this sort. I don't doubt that they existed, for she had a large acquaintance with people I'd never met. She simply judged it entertaining to lend them what air of unreality she could.

'I'll get some work done,' I said, with perhaps unnecessary grimness.

'Darling Dunks, you've been doing an awful lot of work.

You must go off with Ulric and his off-white Rabbit. They'd simply love to make a voyage with you *en garçon*. Tremendously *en garçon*.'

I hated routine camp remarks of this sort—the more so because I owned some skill in perpetrating them in dialogue. But what I said at once was 'Very well, I will'. For Penny had extraordinary finesse in manipulating my responses. She remained curious about our friends down in Amalfi, and wanted further information. It would probably be forthcoming under the changed shipboard conditions she proposed. In fairness it must be said that this indelicate inquisitiveness was something I had a share of myself. And a writer is licensed to peer around; indeed, he has a duty that way. Nevertheless it was against my better judgement that I carried a suitcase across the gang-plank of the *Ithaca* a few days later. I was going to be, it seemed to me, what the Italians call a *terzo incomodo*.

And so it proved—since I was quickly made aware of how much Anderman had thought was owing to the presence of a lady on his yacht. Now decorum was off. He took it decently for granted that I had no active interest in the pursuits in hand—but equally that I had this time come aboard as a man of the world prepared to take in his stride whatever blew around. This was fair, and if it cast me in the role of voyeur it couldn't be pretended I was such a fool as not to have asked for it. My situation was perhaps demeaning, but essentially it was harmless—particularly, I told myself, as I had no intention of sailing in the *Ithaca* again. And had this turned out to be the case all would have been well. But there were to be some further short trips in the yacht, and the last of them was to bring disaster.

XIV

Quis te, Palinure, deorum
eripuit nobis medioque sub aequore mersit?
dic age. namque mihi, fallax haud ante repertus,
hoc uno responso animum delusit Apollo. . . .

ANDERMAN CHANTED THESE lines solemnly as we
rounded Cape Palinuro by moonlight. For one who had put
in much time at Cambridge practising for the mile he appeared
to be reasonably grounded in the ancient languages. Hence
(I supposed) this Norman Douglas touch. It was a hot night,
and our helmsman, a dreamy-looking lad called Gino, still
wore only a pair of ragged shorts, so that over his slim torso
reflected light from the moving waters was at play caressingly.
He was a little too young, perhaps, to be Aeneas' companion.
But he would have made a creditable Trojan stripling, and
was certainly with us on that account.

'Have you ever gone in for any branch of archaeology?' I
asked—for no better reason than that Troy had been in my
head.

'You mean have I ever done a stroke of useful work in my
life.' Anderman laughed softly. 'I can't say that I have,
Pattullo.' For some reason I hadn't got on Christian name
terms with Anderman, although Penny had done so. 'Nor
that I feel in the slightest degree guilty about a life of idleness.'

'You've never done any gun-running, or set about
liberating an oppressed country? You'd make a capital
soldier of fortune.'

'Ah, now you're laughing at me. Am I to figure in a play?'

'Definitely not.'

'A presuming question. I apologize. But now it occurs to
me that I do have a life's work. I look after Henry.'

'He needs looking after?' Tindale was below, and certainly couldn't hear this conversation. 'Is he liable to be impetuous and indiscreet?'

'You know very well that he isn't. What he needs from time to time is a pull or shove. I had to yank him out of Oxford—a shocking place, if Cambridge is anything to go by. Don't you think? Can you imagine yourself, Pattullo, willingly going back there?'

'Good heavens, no!' This notion amused me. 'But I sometimes do in nightmares. I have to take some examination again.'

'All life is an examination, according to the religiously inclined. And if the dogmas are in decay the ethos is still around. You have to go quite some way to get clear of it.' Anderman's glance had strayed to the stern of the yacht. 'Gino wouldn't subscribe to it. But to return to Henry. There's a touch of the frustrate ghost about him.'

'And of the unlit lamp and the ungirt loin?'

'That last has always struck me as an ambiguous expression. But, in general, yes. And he's not a happy man.' Anderman paused and again looked at Gino—but, this time, absently. I realized that he was now talking quite seriously. 'I've tried to make a pagan of him, but it hasn't come off. I don't know why. Plenty of his mouldy old popes were as pagan as they come.'

'Not in Henry's period, perhaps. Zosimus and his contemporaries were too near the real thing.'

'Perhaps so. Henry would have done better to have a go at the Borgias. Gino—*vai all'orza!*'

This sudden instruction—concerned with I don't know what point of good seamanship—had to be followed by others, and I hoped that Anderman's anatomy of his friend would be broken off. He returned to it, however, a few minutes later.

'Henry's a nympholept. Wouldn't you say?'

'Hardly precisely that.'

'Well, that general notion. The unattainable ideal, and so on. The quest of the supersensible, and the dream of experience released from the bondage of the flesh. Oh, idle aspiration! Can I go down and get you a cigar?' Anderman was on his feet as he spoke; he was invariably the punctilious host.

'I don't think so—thank you very much.' Gino, I noticed, had a packet of cigarettes beside him. They were probably part of his tariff. I felt yet more indisposed to discuss Tindale with Sir Ulric Anderman. Although I had exclaimed in a facile way against Oxford there was college loyalty at the bottom of this. Tindale had been an accepted if very minor fact of life on Surrey Four: a dim decent donnish man, unfortunate in being attracted to youths who for the most part weren't in the least attracted to him. He hadn't perhaps been, like Arnold Lempriere (then unknown to us), a strictly non-playing member of his club. But he had managed to lead a useful and orderly life—Zosimus helping him along—and if his reserve had been of a nervous order he had maintained some dignity behind it. Many men had made themselves distinguished university careers under such conditions: for example, the poet Thomas Gray. But now Tindale was committed to aimless courses and to practices which brought him no happiness and which he may even have struggled against as sin.

I felt ashamed of once having rather disliked the White Rabbit. It had been for the snobbish reason that his manners were uncertain, and for the puritanical one that his glance used to stray fleetingly to my floppy hair. Perhaps I ought now to concern myself with not rather disliking his friend. In 'yanking' him out of Oxford (if that had really been the way of it) Anderman had probably acted with the best intentions; his conduct certainly had been disinterested, since he was a wealthier man than Tindale by a long way and owned no impulse to go to bed with him.

'Have you always got on well together?' I asked.

'Henry and myself? Oh, well enough. A joint household has its practical advantages. Of course we don't lurk in one another's pocket. And when I speak of looking after Henry I'm not referring to a full-time job. When he goes swimming—you'll have noticed he's fond of swimming—I don't sit worrying about whether he's been drowned.'

I was silent before this disclaimer. It seemed to be prompted by a certain honesty that Anderman commonly commanded; he was saying, in effect, that no depth of friendship was in question between Tindale and himself. I had met such deep friendships: a couple of bachelors, or a couple of spinsters, important to one another in a totally unerotic way. But here on board the *Ithaca* with me were two lonely men. Anderman could take it; he was the type of hedonist who can make do without whole areas of common human relationship. Tindale was perhaps another matter.

Presently we turned in—something which on the *Ithaca* meant the gaining of an agreeable privacy. There were three cabins: one fore and two amidships. The crew, when there was one, curled up in sleeping-bags in the stern. Or sometimes they did this. On the present cruise I had learnt not to do much prowling in the night.

Frediano turned up on us almost at our planned farthest out. It was at a little port somewhere south of Paola, crushed between the sea and abruptly rising mountains the savagery of which made our familiar *Costiera Amalfitana* seem tame. Or it ought to have been a little port. In fact it was in process of horribly transforming itself into something different: a *marina* in the emerging sense of that beautiful word, backed by chunky concrete hotels. It was a dire metamorphosis which the picturesque traveller was getting used to even farther south than this, although he could as yet scarcely have foreseen the extent to which the entire region would be 'opened up' as the *Autostrada del Sole* pressed resistlessly on towards Sicily.

Frediano was helping to build the *marina*, which we had gone on shore to inspect. Our first glimpse of him was with some appropriateness sheerly physical, being of straining buttocks tightly sheathed in faded levis (a species of garment which was then moving with the motor-way towards the sun) and a rippling spine glinting with sweat. He had just heaved an enormous boulder triumphantly into place, and now he straightened up and turned at our approach. He was smothered in the fine white dust which the building operation caused to hang like a cloud over the scene—so that whereas most youths of his sort suggested (as I have recorded) some Graeco-Roman bronze rescued from the sea-bed, his own momentary note was of marble similarly retrieved. Sizing us up, he instantly smiled. The statue vanished and we were at gaze with one more modern Italian boy.

There would be no point in enthusing over Frediano. He was a fisherman's son from a place called Campora S. Giovanni, and had been at sea since childhood. Now (and with all his fingers still intact) he was earning better money constructing this basin for fleets of pleasure-craft yet unlaunched. He was very good-looking indeed, and very perfectly framed. I was to judge him rather intelligent and as possessing more than an average share of the elusive quality we call sensibility. All this added up to quite an endowment, no doubt, and I could see that Frediano was, in a simple phrase, better value than any such youth we had run into so far. Yet he was fundamentally as the others were: a venal and ignorant lad, unlikely to arouse in anybody anything other than a very specific form of desire. So I was unprepared for the strange sequel to this encounter.

Anderman conversed with Frediano on the quay, and at once with the assumption that he might be looking for a change of casual employment. He asked him his name, his age, his sailing experience, looking him up and down the while with an arrogant openness of intent. The levis represented every stitch Frediano wore, and it wasn't to be doubted that in imagination Anderman was removing them inch by voluptuous inch, and presently passing a notional tape-measure round naked hips. Frediano wasn't discomposed; he had been in this situation before. But did I see him faintly smile; almost imperceptibly—yet with an arrogance of his own—shake his head? I can't be certain. Looking back, one easily fancies such things. Frediano may have been in some ways a choosey, even a fastidious, youth. There is nothing in the rest of his story to negative this.

Not being much pleased with Anderman's performance, I moved aside with Tindale. Tindale was thus withdrawing, it was to be supposed, to make his own observations of Frediano from a discreet remove. In Oxford he had never been one for bold appraisals, and he had taken his old habits with him into his expatriate life. On the present voyage, and without a lady on board, a certain frankness about my companions' behaviour, even if it didn't in set terms declare itself, seeped into the general atmosphere. But Tindale remained kittle and cautious. It may almost be said that he never looked at one of those accessible boys unless the boy wasn't looking at him—and unless he thought I wasn't either. Nothing had made me more doubt the good sense of my coming on the trip than the particular discomfort I seemed to occasion him at such moments. It was natural that he should hate the bobbing up out of his academic past even of an uncensorious and circumspect witness to his present way of life.

Wariness is catching, and it was covertly that I glanced at Tindale now. I expected him to be taking in Frediano only, as it were, by snatches and amid much appearance of interest in barrows, cranes, lorries, concrete-mixers and similar miscellaneous evidences of the enterprise going forward.

But it wasn't so. He was looking at the youth openly, steadily, and gravely. And Frediano, although still answering Anderman's questions, was looking back at Tindale in a very similar way.

We sailed that afternoon for Tropea, with Frediano and Gino on board. Frediano, unlike two or three of his predecessors, made no immediate attempt to please. On the contrary, he was rather withdrawn. If I am right about his intelligence, he may already have been reflecting upon an unfamiliar situation.

Anderman made no attempt to draw him out, or to disturb him in any way. Indeed, for the rest of the voyage he seldom addressed Frediano except with some brisk but polite order about the yacht, apart from this paying little attention to him at all. Crudely expressed, he had shoved the boy into his levis again and forgotten about him. There must have been some clear understanding between my two companions in these matters. Frediano belonged to Tindale.

Only he didn't. Or if he did, it was in the sense that Islay or Tiree belonged to my father: as sensible objects which, if contemplated aright, will reveal supersensible things. This may have been only the first stage in a developing relationship, but that it alone existed for a time I have no doubt whatever. Tindale had looked at this only slightly out-of-the-ordinary youth and said: 'This is it, this is it at last'—without, perhaps, clearly holding in focus what 'it' was. But the interval in which he was thus meditating was one of very calm inner weather.

This last point struck me most of all. During our cruise, and to a lesser extent during the previous cruises, there had been sufficient opportunity to observe Tindale living alike in the prospect and the immediate recollection of his closer approaches to young men. What, if anything, these came to I don't know, and it scarcely matters. The significant point is that the ghost was not merely frustrate, as Anderman had asserted; it was agitated, anxious, depressed as well. But now his entire comportment had changed. He sat on a deck-chair for hours on end—blamelessly, as Penny had done, but contemplating not several personable youths but Frediano alone. Once or twice, catching my glance on him, he made a small unembarrassed gesture—much as if he were saying: 'Isn't the lad quite delightful? I can scarcely take my eyes from him!'

It was very odd. 'Infatuation' wasn't the word for it. Nor did it answer to my sense of the early stages, the prodromal period, of a love-affair. It was more like a release from bondage: that, and the discovery of something thought lost. I woke up one night asking myself whether Tindale believed that he had found a son. Even an actual, long-lost son—since this, after all, was a chronological possibility. But that, of course, was nonsense. The meagre Tindale would have had to espouse a high-ranking divinity if a young demi-god like Frediano was to result.

I don't imagine Frediano told himself he had found a father. He didn't know what he'd found, and he was thoughtful, puzzled, bored—and perhaps conscious of a certain lack of occupation. He may, that is to say, have been piqued by what he judged an inexplicable backwardness on Tindale's part. But, on the whole, I think not. There was a certain lack of grossness in Frediano which constituted one element in his charm.

In one episode that might be termed gross Frediano, however, was involved. It happened at Palmi, where I had gone ashore with my two companions to seek various stores, and with the intention of lunching in a *trattoria*, known to Anderman, among the fisherman's huts on the beach. This was to have taken us some time. But we found difficulty in securing fresh supplies of Butagaz without surrendering a couple of empty containers which we had thoughtlessly left on board. Tindale and I therefore returned to the *Ithaca* together to retrieve these heavy objects. The result was that we caught Frediano and Gino, not napping, but entertaining each other (in the mildest and laziest manner) to a bout of mutual masturbation. Aware of our presence, they were sufficiently considerate to roll over on their backs, put their hands behind their heads, and smile at us sleepily from the deck. They were thus behaving with decorum according to their lights, and they can scarcely have expected a row over what was their own leisure-time affair. But Tindale was more than outraged; he was profoundly shocked. For moments, indeed, his anger was paroxysmal. Had there been a rope's end to hand, I believe he would have laid into both boys indifferently. Or perhaps only Gino would have suffered, as plainly the corrupter of Frediano's youth. I wondered where Tindale had been to school, and also what repercussions would follow upon this absurd if painful affair. In the issue it proved not all that traumatic. Gino was impudent, and probably made a joke of it with Anderman. Frediano struck me as distressed; as not understanding what could be wrong, but as willing to defer to Tindale's mysterious feelings in the matter. This was a sign of distinct good-will in him, and Tindale seized on it with pathetic—almost with ominous—speed. In no time Frediano was being judged immaculate again. He was assuredly nothing of the kind. But I don't to this day—curiously, as it may transpire—think particularly ill of him. Curiously, too, his great personal beauty comes back to me more and more. I even at times see him—vividly, and with no sense of resentment—in my dreams.

At Reggio di Calabria, where we were to turn about, we lost Gino in obscure circumstances to a citizen of Hamburg, over from Messina for the day. As a replacement, and through some quirk of temper, Anderman took on a grubby old creature who, anxious to impose himself for the rest of his days upon a granddaughter living in Salerno, was willing to work his passage to that end. This annoyed Frediano, who had enjoyed unobtrusively bullying Gino from time to time. He appeared to regard the old man as not quite fair game.

We turned north. Frediano was to disembark where we had taken him on, presumably to return to his occupation as a labourer. I wondered what sort of farewells there were going to be, and whether, either at that parting or earlier, any clearer light would play upon the enigmatical relationship that had so rapidly built itself up on the *Ithaca*. And one further small incident did take place. We spent the night before the youth's departure moored to the crumbling quay of what appeared to be a deserted village. According to Anderman it had been devastated by an earthquake many years before. I was curious about this, and got up unusually early with the idea of an exploratory walk before breakfast. As I left my tiny cabin I ran into Frediano leaving Tindale's. He went past with an unembarrassed but oddly absent smile. It seemed to me that he was bewildered. I felt bewildered myself, although it wasn't the response that the situation might have been expected to elicit. Had Frediano left a Tindale who was murmuring: 'The dawn—ah, God!—the dawn it comes too soon'? I found I didn't believe it. Had they spent the night together playing Snakes and Ladders—or on their knees, praying to the Blessed Virgin? I hadn't a clue, I never was to gain a clue, as to this aspect of the affair. Later that day Tindale and Frediano said good-bye to one another. It was after a short—and, as I judged—serious conversation. Frediano wasn't mentioned again—except by Anderman, who casually remarked to me that the name was an uncommon one, and that its main association was with the criminal quarter of the city of Florence.

This didn't prove, however, to be the boy's epitaph, for he

turned up in Amalfi some months later. Tindale, it seemed, was sending him to school. It can't have been exactly a children's school, since Frediano was too old for that. And it had no ecclesiastical character, so he didn't have to dress in a quasi-monkish fashion. (His clothes were clearly provided— and a little too lavishly—by his patron.) Perhaps Frediano had been placed in what would elsewhere be called a college of further education—although any education he'd had to start off with had certainly been negligible. However, he was clever enough to make do.

He lodged somewhere in the town. Anderman and Tindale, when at home, were ministered to by a couple of respectable elderly women, and were far from holding themselves out as running any sort of youth club. (In this they differed from my old friend Colonel Morrison, whose housekeeper had always enjoyed the assistance of one or two young men.) I suppose that Frediano went, as it were, to tea from time to time, but it was clear that he was by no means under Tindale's wardenship round the clock. I glimpsed him several times in a bar, and on each occasion in the company of a different girl—a circumstance confirming me in the view that he commanded a very normal sexual orientation at need. Once, aware of being thus under observation, he gave me a look of alarmed appeal, as if begging me not to tell tales. Tindale's radical feelings about the other sex, I reflected, were such that he would regard his protégé's 'going with a woman' (which had been Colonel Morrison's forbidding phrase) as a very deep treachery indeed.

But Tindale continued to turn up at the Villa d'Orso from time to time, and he talked to Penny as much as to myself. I think this was partly because, unlike his housemate, he was nervous of public opinion and fearful of gossip, and had got her into his head as a respectable association. There may have been some deeper prompting one could know nothing of. I was now almost sure that about Frediano he was in a high old muddle: the sort of muddle in which sons and lovers become telescoped conceptions. He might be in some similarly odd muddle about my wife. That their relationship, such as it was, remained quirky and unstable was all that I could be certain of.

Apart from their longer cruises in the *Ithaca*, Anderman and Tindale did a good deal of pottering about the Gulf of Salerno. They took Frediano with them from time to time—sometimes, but not always, accompanied by one of the *parroco*'s pious young men. Occasionally, indeed, they took the *parroco* as well; he was inordinately fond of fishing. In several of these day-trips, as they were, Penny and I had joined. I saw them as a kind of civil tailing-off of the nautical phase in our Italian life, since I was determined that we shouldn't again go on a long cruise down the coast. Penny was more enthusiastic, although it was clear that the sea in itself now bored her. As soon as Frediano turned up in Amalfi I had given her an account of his history as it was known to me. For by this time I had got into the way of doing a certain amount of thinking about young men in relation to her, and I must naïvely have supposed that she would refrain from developing much interest in one seemingly committed as Frediano was. Naturally the information didn't in fact work that way. And as Penny made several of these short expeditions without me I'd have been a greater fool than I was if I hadn't sometimes wondered whether she was a little trying the enigmatical boy out. What I failed to recall was the perverseness (and ingenuity) of her imagination.

Anderman owned an informed interest in the fauna and flora of the region, and had recently taken up its herpetology (a study pursued by Douglas, if I remember aright). He had now heard a rumour that on one of the few minute islands west of Capri—it was called the *Piccolo Gallo*—there had lately been discovered a new variety of a blue and black lizard (*Lucerta muralis faraglionensis*) of considerable zoological curiosity. He was eager to confirm this, and we set off accordingly on one very fine late September morning: Anderman, Tindale, Frediano, Penny and myself. We were all suitably and soberly equipped. Anderman had paraphernalia for securing and transporting specimens if he found any. I, as being more interested in *uccelli* (of which there were few) than *rettili* (of which there were many), took binoculars. Tindale had a garment in which he could swim with decency. Frediano had fishing tackle and may have hoped for his old adversary, *pesce spada*. Penny, whose reading was always at random, had provided herself with a small volume called *The Memorable Thoughts of Socrates* (rather, it occurred to me, as if Socrates had been Chairman Mao).

We anchored off the island, and Anderman and I rowed over to it in the dinghy which on these occasions bobbed along behind the *Ithaca*. We left Frediano already fishing, Penny deep in her studies, and Tindale letting down the rope-ladder by which he would regain the deck after his swim. The *Piccolo Gallo* proved, when we disembarked, to be long and narrow, with a rocky spine which rose at its western extremity to a sort of comb or crest from which the island presumably took its name. We worked along it for about an hour. Anderman found this and that, but not his lizard. I had a similarly thin time with birds. Eventually we scaled the crest, and commanded a considerable view. I swept the sea with the binoculars and then let them rest on the *Ithaca*, which lay nearly half a mile off. Anderman observed the action.

'Are they up to anything?' he asked in his casual manner.

'Nothing out of the way,' I answered, and swiftly restored the binoculars to their case. The truth of my reply might have been a matter of opinion. Amidships on the yacht was a small deck-house the roof of which made an agreeable spot for sunbathing. Penny was lying on top of it now, and might have been described as fully exposed to the sun but for the fact that Frediano was in turn lying on top of her. As both were stark naked there couldn't be much doubt about what was going on. But it wasn't quite all that was going on. The rope-ladder had been drawn up, as if Tindale were already back on board. Only he wasn't. His head was bobbing on the surface of the sea a dozen yards from the *Ithaca*. Helpless to intervene, or to do more, I suppose, than cry out with heaven knows what emotion, he might very well have been described as permitted to watch this small drama from the pit.

I don't think Penny had thought about the binoculars, or about their owner either. I had no part in the atrocious fantasy she had so brilliantly and economically actualized. I don't suppose she had bothered her head about the performance's sequel, although she may have supposed that Frediano would be silent, that Tindale would have no choice but to swallow his humiliation, and that the brief *divertissement* would remain three people's secret to the end.

I didn't in the least puzzle over Penny's part in the affair. But what about Frediano? Perhaps there is no great puzzle there either. Even supposing him (and I do so suppose him) to have developed decent feelings in response to Tindale's devotion, he can't have done other (or be blamed for having done other) than harbour a certain impatience and resentment in face of the bewildering role in which he had been cast. And, again, what young man, not of morbid mind, could resist having Penny when Penny was suddenly on offer to him? There remains Tindale, bobbing impotently in the sea. Frediano—for it was that sort of moment, after all—may simply have forgotten about him. Or Penny may so have spun out her enticements that Frediano's sense of time became confused and he believed that his patron must still be swimming a safe half-mile away. In any case, Penny had them both just where she wanted them.

Come son' crudele, le donne! I don't recall these words as impudently spoken, and they suggest to me that Frediano, although his lapse would have pained the *parroco*, was not a conspirator. But I may be wrong. Perhaps I have too much kindness for him—for the queer reason that he rang down a curtain so resoundingly on an unsatisfactory marriage. I drove to Naples that night, and was in London on the following day. There seemed nothing else for it. *Crudeltà* was the only word for Penny's last experiment. And that she could carry it out after nearly three years of marriage meant that I had been no use to her at all.

XV

Between Frediano and the Sheldrake twins even the physical resemblance may not have been all that striking. The memory of Frediano had undoubtedly stirred in me just below the level of consciousness at the moment of my first glimpsing Mark Sheldrake outside my rooms in Surrey. But that might have been largely because Frediano had remained for me—again in a scarcely conscious fashion—the archetype of good looks in a young man. And a little, no doubt, it had been because those rooms had been Tindale's long ago. The odd experience on the Cherwell had followed. I couldn't, as a result, be ignorant of the nature of Penny's current conduct.

It was conduct which was blessedly no longer any business of mine—or at least so it would be rational to conclude. Yet there was one aspect of her Oxford foray that I couldn't help reflecting on as I walked back to college from that river picnic. The plurality of the Sheldrakes was the circumstance that must most attract one with Penny's peculiar turn of mind. She was finding amusement in the thought of having—and in so unusual a manner—two strings to her bow. That might be almost innocent in itself. But the situation would undoubtedly set her imagination to work. And there was little likelihood that she had outgrown her liability to convert undisciplined fantasy into fact. Of course it was scarcely possible that the twins, being as they were, lacked experience on how to cope with predatory persons. But then Penny was more formidable than most.

Passing through the college gate with these thoughts in my head, I came upon Charles Atlas. Although a young man, he had some old-fashioned tastes and habits, and he was now engaged in strapping a small pile of books to the carrier of his bicycle. He took a glance at my clothes.

'Duncan,' he said, 'how pleasant to see that even a university reader can snatch a brief period of leisure now and then.'

'I've been on the river most of the day, as a matter of fact. Holding the fort with the Bedworth children, among other things, while Cyril supports the college on his shoulders.'

'What about supporting the affair above our heads at this moment? How is that committee getting on?'

'The committee on the tower? Not too rapidly, Charles. Of course I lack experience of the pace at which such deliberations are conducted. But I'd say not too rapidly at all.'

'Is Edward dragging his feet?' As he asked this question Atlas looked round rapidly—I suppose to insure that nobody could possibly overhear our Provost's being referred to on a critical note.

'Yes, he is—but I feel with some deep intent. I have a notion he's going to spring a mine of some sort.'

'Surely nothing could be less appropriate than that.' Atlas, who liked mild jokes, paused to appreciate this one. 'And it seems it's what the undergraduates are going to do anyway with their tiresome *Tamburlaine*. I suppose you're producing it, Duncan?'

'No, I'm not. But it looks as if Albert Talbert is.'

'Albert?' Atlas giggled joyfully at this absurd idea. 'Preposterous!'

'Well, he seems to think he is, but it's possible the young men will head him off. As for the tower, there's nothing to report.'

'It's becoming clear there must be an appeal—but just to the old members, at least in the first place. A number of people are coming to think that way, Duncan. And we have an idea that Arnold Lempriere should be in charge of it.'

'Arnold?' It was my turn to be incredulous. 'I'd have thought he wasn't at all the man to organize such a thing.'

'Well, jointly with the Provost, of course. Arnold has the

advantage of being terribly concerned about the venerable pile. And he's had more of the nobility and gentry and affluent classes generally as his pupils than any half dozen tutors in the college bundled together. Just wait for his memorial service, and you'll see.'

'I hope I'll have to wait a long time for that. But I take your point.'

'It might get his mind off all those schools, as well.'

'Schools—what schools?'

'All those places of primitive education I have to deal with as Tutor for Admissions. Arnold believes in visiting them.'

'So he does, Charles. He's been on at me about it. Wants me to go talent-scouting to Loretto and Glenalmond and God knows where.'

'Unfortunately he has been rather stepping it up himself.' Again Atlas looked rapidly round, and I knew there was gossip to come. 'Proposing himself to headmasters like mad. Provided they have swimming-pools—open-air ones. And a spot of *puris naturalibus*, as he likes to say. Arnold goes and blamelessly goggles. It takes the place of Parson's Pleasure. He's dropped that this term.'

'That wretched Mumford boy!'

'Quite so. Mind you, one can be sure Arnold always behaves perfectly. It's an embarrassment, all the same. I've had a tactful letter or two—simply as being the man the headmasters generally correspond with.'

I don't know how I'd have reacted to this disconcerting news if we had not been joined at this moment by the Estates Bursar, Geoffrey Quine. Quine was not seen all that frequently in college, but this didn't mean he was lacking in devotion to his job. He had to keep his eye on a large number of agricultural properties scattered over the kingdom, and when he wasn't discussing the crimes and follies of various government departments with disgruntled tenants he was likely to be conferring with persons of influence in the City of London. These may have included, for all I knew, the egregious Cyril Mumford himself.

'Chatting about the tower?' Quine asked genially.

'Well, yes,' I said. 'And I was saying to Charles that our plans don't seem to be advancing very fast.'

'At least the legal position has come clear. These are rather absurd places, you know. Oxford colleges, I mean.'

'Just what's absurd now, Geoffrey?' It was with a trace of irritation that Atlas asked this. Quine remained to a certain extent an outsider. Despite his skills being held in high regard, he was expected to be moderate in any censures directed upon our ways.

'I gave you all a hint at that G.B. meeting, didn't I, that there might be a certain element of personal discomfiture ahead of us if things go wrong? Well, I'm going round in my unobtrusive way being more explicit about that now. It's those troublesome Statutes again. They make it clear that the maintenance of the fabric is a first charge on the revenues of the college. And now I've had counsel's opinion on the ramifying consequences of that. If the tower really begins to totter the college would be in breach of Statute if it paid any of us a penny until it was clear we had the means to prop it up again. How do you take that, Charles?'

It was clear that Atlas took it seriously. I'm not sure he hadn't turned pale. All right-thinking members of Governing Bodies regarded being in breach of Statute as the ultimate sin that mortal man can commit.

'Of course one would accept some element of sacrifice,' Atlas said. 'But what you suggest is quite outrageous. And a statute can always be emended or abrogated by the Queen in Council.'

'With the sanction of the University nowadays, my dear Charles.' Quine chuckled happily. 'And everybody believes us to be as rich as Croesus. We'd have to move uncommonly cautiously. *Pedetemptim et gradatim*, as you learned folk would say.'

Here, too, was disconcerting intelligence, although it upset me less than hearing about the unfortunate conduct of Lempriere. This wasn't because sudden academic penury would affect me less than some other people. It was simply that I didn't believe what Quine said. It is true that one learns from *Hedda Gabler* the fallaciousness of insisting there are things people don't do. But here was something that doesn't happen. Whatever might befall a college tower it was certain that, so long as the general social fabric held, no large body of Oxford scholars would find itself suddenly on the dole. Reading of such an event in one's newspaper, for example, was totally inconceivable.

This robust faith of mine was never, as it happened, to be put to the test. For a time, indeed, it looked as if it might be. But crisis was to be averted in the end. Only, however, by what is called—extremely strangely—an Act of God.

Perhaps Ibsen has come into my head because, during the remainder of that summer term and the early weeks of the long vacation, something not altogether unlike a play unfolded. There was a real centre of interest; the action disposed itself into several distinct acts or phases; and between these were intervals during which we all may be said to have left the auditorium, suitably recruited ourselves, and pursued this or that extraneous interest until the bells rang. I don't know that the piece ran to a *peripeteia* in the solemn Aristotelian sense. But there were certainly surprises, and one of them I'd judge worthy of being termed a *coup de théâtre* in the most robust melodramatic context.

My first intimation of anything of the kind was of a tenuous sort, and occurred immediately after my taking leave of Quine and Atlas. Traversing the Great Quadrangle, I noticed an untoward vehicle drawn up before the senior common rooms. 'Untoward' is, I think, fair enough, since it had the appearance of a prison van. I wondered whether one of the pantry boys had been apprehended in the act of making off with the college plate.

Then I found that I was mistaken. The van belonged to a Security Service, and was manned by two outsize men probably described as guards. They were gauntleted, wore enormous helmets, and moved stiffly within garments of what seemed extremely inflexible leather. They were also draped with chains and thongs and straps and sinister holsters presumably intended to suggest to the ignorant minds of criminals the weapons which, in fact, they certainly weren't allowed to carry. An unfortunate race, I told myself, perpetually getting themselves reported in the press as being bound and gagged and shoved into cupboards in humiliating circumstances. The college plate might still be the explanation of this odd phenomenon. It was being removed, with an imbecile display of maximum publicity, to receive the attentions of a skilled silversmith.

Speculation on this minor curiosity was driven from my head when I reached my room, since it was to find Nicolas Junkin curled up in his favourite attitude on my sofa. Junkin had advanced well beyond that point at which an undergraduate waits diffidently outside his tutor's door. There wasn't anything unseemly in this. Junkin had a flair for the due advancement of an intimacy; his judgement in such matters would have done credit to the most polished of men; and he now gracefully acknowledged my seniority (and proprietorship of the room) by momentarily dropping his feet to the carpet.

'Hullo,' I said—and added, 'Where's Moggy?' For Junkin's mistress, although not a member of the university, was being variously active in the interest of the forthcoming production. She frequently sat in on her lover's consultations with me.

'Moggy's gone to London to see if she can hire some leopards.'

'Whatever do you want some leopards for?'

'Well, it's like this.' Junkin considered. 'Can you remember ever looking at a thing in the National Gallery called *Bacchus and Ariadne*? It's one of those Old Master affairs.'

'I confess to some dim memory of it.'

'To Jesus, Duncan! You do talk like a don.'

'It's what I'm around for. But go on.'

'There are leopards in it. They've been drawing the chariot the chap's jumping out of to lay the girl. Well, we thought that, when we harness up the captive kings to Tamburlaine's bus, we'd have them take the place of a couple of leopards. The leopards can then run around.'

'Among the audience?'

'That's the idea. Create a bit of participation. We thought of handing out bows and arrows for people to have a shot at that Governor tied up on the tower, but we decided there might be too much competition.'

'How does Talbert regard these robust innovations, Nick?'

'Not too kindly. I'll give it to him that he's an enthusiastic character, but his ideas are utterly out of the ark. Of course it's only to be expected at his age.'

'Of course.'

'The problem is to give him the brush off with any sort of politeness. It's what I've come in to see you about, as a matter of fact. We thought you might do the job for us. Come easily between colleagues. That sort of thing.'

'I will most certainly do nothing of the sort.'

'I thought not.' Junkin was resigned at once. 'But, you see, the trouble's his wife. Always being around too, I mean. It makes it pretty well impossible to tell Talbert to get knotted—even in quite a civil sort of way.'

'It is a difficulty, I agree.'

'Incidentally, I've found out something about the Talberts that's rather touching. It explains why they're so keen on us. They played together in *Tamburlaine* at Cambridge.'

'It's not possible! And how could you discover such a thing?'

'I thought I'd find out about earlier university productions. You know how interested I am, Duncan, in the historical side of things.' Junkin had become rather tediously fond of this joke. 'Of course I didn't look into it myself, being much too busy. But I set a really brainy freshman on it, and he did some deep research in the Bodleian. You may have met him. Matthew Sheldrake.'

'No, I haven't—only his brother. Are the Sheldrakes brainy?'

'Fearfully bright—and, of course, pretty neurotic as a result.'

I don't know why, but the first part of this information (which alone I credited) surprised me. I had somehow thought of the twins as being polished and agreeable but rather thick. It is pleasant to believe with the poet that all that fair is is by nature good, but patently unrealistic to add that all that fair is is by nature clever.

'Go on about the Talberts,' I said.

'It's just what I said. They played Tamburlaine and Zenocrate in some dramatic society's production over there round about the date of Waterloo. No possible mistake. Matthew checked on Mrs Talbert's maiden name in *Who's You.*'

'I can't believe it, Nick. If chronology is to come in, there's the fact that he's a good deal older than she is.'

'Talbert may have gone on hanging around, looking for a don's berth like that sort do. And she may have been a fresh young thing, waiting to be introduced to passion. And it happened. A mutual flame. If all the pens that ever poets held, and so on. Incidentally, I haven't told anybody else. Matthew is rather strong on that. He says it wouldn't be on to spread it around that we'd been poking into the old creatures' amorous past.'

'Matthew's quite right.' This strange information about my old tutor had disturbed me, and I changed the subject. 'Have you seen that armoured van and those security people in the quad, Nick?'

'Oh, yes. They've been around all day. Everybody knows why.'

'I don't.'

'It's because a young Sheik has come among us for a spot of higher education. He'll be studying petroleum technology, or something like that. And he has to be guarded round the clock. There are to be a couple of chaps with sub-machine guns on either side of him at lectures. At tutes too, I expect.'

'I see.' I was impressed, not for the first time, by the bright speed of undergraduate inventiveness. 'And now you'd better go away. I've a woman coming to talk about Bernard Kops.'

'To Jesus, Duncan! You're a fiend for the daily round and common task.' And Junkin, unoffended, took himself off. It was often possible to work out his current reading from his vocabulary. His latest pious ejaculation was straight out of David Storey.

Walking over to hall that evening, I met the urbane Dr Seashore of the Ashmolean with his gown slung over his shoulder.

'Ah, good evening, Professor!' he said, and fell into step beside me. It was one of his affectations to be a little vague about who was who (or Who was You, as Junkin had it) in the purely academic waters lapping round him. 'Your Provost has very kindly asked me to dine. And several of my colleagues as well, I believe. Or I should say, rather, my *confrères*. But perhaps that term sounds a shade pretentious in English? I wouldn't know. Would you address Mr Beckett as *cher confrère*?'

'I think not. It wouldn't be so much pretentious as damned cheek.'

'Well, there they are to be—grand metropolitan *Kunster-*

fahrenen, by whom I shall be quite overwhelmed. They include, I understand, a Metropolitan one in the special sense.'

'From the Metropolitan in New York?' This obliquely delivered information must have made me stare.

'Yes, indeed. And somebody from the Brera. And that delightful little Cesare Marotta from Urbino. He is the prime authority, after all. And a very senior man. Your father would have known him, no doubt.'

'Dr Seashore, will you tell me just what this is in aid of?'

'You don't know?' Seashore glanced at me with a sudden wariness. 'Well, among other things, I'd say it displays your Provost as owning a pronounced dramatic sense. Perhaps he's right—from a certain point of view. But you won't accuse *me* of having failed in circumspection.'

'No, I don't think I shall.'

'Mine was only a guess, after all. Or call it an informed guess. No more than that. There was everything to be said for keeping quiet at the moment.'

'You decidedly managed that. And has the Provost himself kept quiet ever since—or do some of my colleagues know about whatever it is that's to be known about?'

'My dear Professor, I'm really rather in the dark as to that. But there has certainly been discretion in the handling of the affair. Now—later this evening—there is to be this small surprise. And there will be a special article in *The Times* tomorrow morning. I have been allowed the honour of contributing it, as a matter of fact.' Seashore smiled at me blandly. 'But there is the Provost! I must hasten to present myself.'

I entered hall wondering on just what the glance of this cagey person had momentarily paused in the last dusty moments of that treasure hunt. It certainly hadn't been on Hans Eworth's lost portrait of Provost Pagden. However replete with satyrs and quaint devices, that masterpiece would not draw together *Kunsterfahrenen* (as Seashore learnedly described them) from New York and Milan—to say nothing of the delightful Signore Marotta from Urbino's windy hill. Something of much greater artistic significance must be in question.

Whether the undergraduates in the body of the hall were looking around them in the expectation of spotting the newly-arrived Sheik I couldn't tell; but I did know that it was nothing of the sort that had been responsible for the appearance of those security guards and their van in the Great Quadrangle. The picture Seashore had discovered must have been removed from college for a time and had now been returned under the protection of these men—perhaps after cleaning or being subjected to some form of expertise elsewhere. Whatever had resulted from any scrutiny hadn't presumably been a drastic demoting, for in that case it would have been brought back unobtrusively, and there would have been no reception committee of the august kind which the Provost appeared to have gathered together this evening.

It was an unwritten, indeed unspoken, rule among us that at dinner we didn't sit down too often beside our particular cronies or more intimate friends, since this was the common meal of a society in which everybody was to be presumed equally agreeable to everybody else. But it was some time ago that I had last talked to Bedworth, and I took my place beside him now, intending to give him an account of the day's river picnic. Then it occurred to me that the Provost, although so prone to mature his policies deep in unfathomable mines, could hardly long exclude from his confidence his own Senior Tutor. Bedworth must have some notion of what was going on. I approached the subject cautiously.

'There seem to be a good many guests tonight,' I said. 'Can you put a name to them?'

'I don't think I can.' Bedworth was glancing in some perplexity round the table. 'Except Seashore of the Ashmolean up at the end there.'

'Yes—and I've just been talking to him. It seems that several of these strangers are in the same line of business as himself. The rosy-faced man beside the Provost, whom you might call a thoroughly Nordic type, in fact comes from Urbino. His name's Cesare Marotta, and it rings some elusive bell in my head. What Seashore says about him is that he's the chief authority on whoever painted the picture we've just discovered as in the college's possession. You must know more about that than I do.'

'Well, no, Duncan.' Bedworth was detectably upset. 'I've heard very little. The pictures are very much Edward's thing, you know. He looks after them, and we simply pay any bills. It's not an area you could strictly call college business.'

'I think it possible that this affair may be big business—quite big enough to be important to us. These gallery directors and art historians—for that's what they are—don't come scurrying across the continents after peanuts.'

'But why are they all here tonight?' It sounded as if Bedworth was becoming quite agitated. 'I don't understand it at all.'

'We're going to be shown the picture.'

'Good heavens!' It was with a slight clatter that Bedworth put down his knife and fork. 'Does everybody know about this except myself?'

'No, no—it's not like that at all.' I saw that Bedworth's injured feelings must be assuaged at once. 'I myself know only because I happened to get it out of Seashore. And you've only to look round the table to see that nobody is in the slightest expectation of anything out of the way. I don't think anybody's even tumbled to wondering about this batch of guests. We're much too accustomed to odd bods for that. No—it's just to be a small surprise in the course of the evening. Call it one of those casual and gracefully achieved effects that Edward is fond of. But the light and elegant gesture conceals a master-stroke. That's his style, wouldn't you say?'

'I suppose it is.' Bedworth, regaining composure, resumed his meal. 'Duncan,' he presently said, 'do you mean there might be money in this?'

'Why not? Pictures are often worth quite a lot of it. The committee on the tower, as a matter of fact, has had half a mind to tot up what the existing college collection might fetch. It's a category of property we'd be perfectly entitled to alienate in a serious crisis. What would you say our most valuable picture is, Cyril?'

'I've no idea. Might it be the Cuyp?'

'I suppose it might. And what could it fetch, would you say?'

'I haven't a clue—only I do know people pay the most absurd sums for such things. Would it be several tens of thousands of pounds?'

'Yes.'

'Well, I don't suppose any pictures fetch significantly more than that.'

I was silent for a moment, since this innocence surprised and interested me. Cyril Bedworth was by no means a narrow specialist. In the fields of English and French literature he was very widely read. But he must be capable of extraordinary inattention even to matters of common report if they didn't happen to interest him.

'It isn't quite like that,' I said. 'Suppose Cuyp's cows weren't cows, and weren't by Cuyp. Suppose they were leopards, and by Titian.' The occasion of Moggie's visit to London had recurred to my mind. 'In short, suppose the college owned the *Bacchus and Ariadne*. We could rebuild the tower on the proceeds of that—and probably put up another one at the opposite side of the Great Quad.'

'I don't think we'd want to do that, Duncan.' Bedworth may have said this either with a humorous intention or in reproof of my frivolity: it was impossible to tell. But he was thoughtful for the rest of the meal.

The ordering of things in common room, at least so far as introductions and the proper disposal of guests went, was normally the prerogative of Arnold Lempriere, who could be tiresomely tyrannical about it. But on this occasion he hadn't been dining, and we were presided over by the next most senior fellow. He introduced me to Marotta—about whom he seemed not notably well informed—and we sat down together. Marotta had caught my name, and immediately gained a further good mark by asking whether I was by any chance related to Lachlan Pattullo—one of the greatest painters of our time, he immediately added upon receiving an affirmative reply. We got on excellently after this, and the discovery that each of us was more than tolerably proficient in the other's tongue led us into a sort of contest of politeness that lasted through dessert. Marotta showed no sign of being puzzled by English conventions (or Oxford conventions, which can be particularly odd). But he was a little puzzled by the Provost—and so, I believe, were the other guests whom he might have termed his *confratelli*. Edward Pococke had settled into a modest seat nowhere in particular, and was conversing in a courtly manner with a very young man but recently promoted among us. The talk round the big table was of the usual rambling, carelessly learned, anecdotal sort: there was this and an occasional fishing for general topics on which our visitors might care to pronounce. Nobody talked about pictures for the simple reason that—apart from the Provost, Seashore, Bedworth and myself—nobody had pictures in their head. Marotta and his fellows must have felt that, invited on a professional occasion, it wasn't for them to turn to the matter perpending until their host had taken an initiative. And as the Provost's sense of propriety required that anything of the sort should attend upon the consumption of a couple of glasses of port this didn't happen for some time.

Such waiting on the event continued until the butler removed the decanters. I then saw what was in the Provost's mind. For it was our custom to take this clearing of the board as a signal to move into the adjoining room, in which coffee was served. And we didn't do this *en masse*, but at a sort of elegant leisure and by twos and threes. It was clear to me that this was how Seashore's discovery—momentous as one could now be assured it was—was to be manifested to the yet unknowing world. We were simply to stroll into the next room, and there the thing was to be. Since it was up to anybody to make the first move, I resolved to plump for it myself, got on my feet, murmured to Marotta an invitation to accompany me, and ushered him through the door.

I have no doubt that in the smaller common room a servant was already pouring coffee as usual, and the under-butler deploying bottles and decanters and cigars with his customary morose devotion. But all I saw for a moment was one of the leather-clad security men. He was posted with a decent unobtrusiveness in a corner. His presence, nevertheless, was somehow as startling as would have been that of a white rhinoceros or a baby giraffe.

'Ah!' Marotta exclaimed softly—and I turned and saw the picture. It was perched on an easel which, I imagine, commonly supported a blackboard in a lecture-room somewhere in college. Just so would the latest bad portrait of a retired fellow be briefly distinguished before some obscure wall received it. Or even, perhaps, a group photograph of a victorious college eight.

But this was neither of these things. I had been brought up among pictures, and I hadn't much doubt of what I saw. Yet, when I turned to Marotta, I didn't know what to say. At the same time, I suddenly remembered why his name had rung that faint bell in my head; on just whom he was a prime authority.

'Is it the real thing?' I asked.

'Beyond a shadow of doubt.' Marotta glanced at me, and must have realized that I was feeling my question to have been crudely phrased. For he added, with instant courtesy, 'Is it not your own opinion, sir?'

'Yes, it is—although this is my first glimpse of it. And I'm not an authority.'

'Only an amateur, Dr Pattullo, in the noble old sense of the word.' Marotta may have felt that he had now done his best for me, since he turned back to the picture with an absorbed gaze. But this was only for a few moments; then, rather surprisingly, he took my arm and guided me to another part of the room. 'I hope,' he murmured, 'to look at it many, many times. But there is one sense in which a single look is enough.'

'Its turning up here is almost unbelievably strange. An unknown work by such a painter! But *is* it unknown? Can you give it any provenance?'

'Ah, Dr Pattullo, you are a little the sceptic, I can see. Then let me put the philosophical question. Does it matter at all whose hand achieved it?'

'Of course it doesn't. Or only in the light of certain down-to-earth considerations.'

'There indeed you are right! But your college, I believe, is not ill-endowed?'

'You mean, signore, that it's extremely wealthy. But we happen to have a somewhat embarrassing liability at the moment.' I paused on this, for I was perhaps speaking out of turn. And Marotta, I suspected, had just undergone a very powerful experience indeed—a fact which seemed attested by his disinclination to remain in the vicinity of the picture, which was now being milled around by a miscellaneous crowd of instructed and uninstructed persons. He had exchanged a single significant glance with the man from the Brera, but seemed to have elected to keep me company for the present. 'Let me put an absurd question to you,' I said.

'Suppose, Signore Marotta, that you were very hard up. And suppose that your good fairy offered you either this picture or Titian's *Bacchus and Ariadne* to take along to Sotheby's——'

Marotta interrupted by touching me on the arm. He was amused—and apparently grateful for this ridiculous diversion of his feelings.

'My dear Dr Pattullo,' he said, 'this one would be the better choice—either for your earthly pocket or to lay up in heaven.'

'I'm sure about heaven.'

'Good, good—we are agreed! But to take your point about a provenance. There is none. It is a masterpiece hitherto unknown. So a name must be found for it. I think you will choose *The Madonna of the Astrolabe*. Yes, that is it! *La Madonna del Astrolabio da Piero della Francesca*. It is beautiful, is it not?'

I found no reply. Partly, I suppose, the painter's name (although I had been certain of it) silenced me—but partly, too, I was puzzled by what Marotta had just said. For he had seen more than I had. We had looked at the picture for an equal space of time—but, as if in Kim's Game, he had been the more practised player. Challenged, I'd have said that the infant Christ held a bauble, or perhaps the links of a chain depending from his mother's neck. It was in fact a silver astrolabe, delicately miniaturized, and inscribed (it was just possible to distinguish) with Arabic characters.

'Iconographically,' Marotta said when he had explained the point, 'it is, I believe, unique—as unique as the pose of the *Madonna del Parto* at Monterchi. And yet how simple the symbol and how sublime! The infant Redeemer holds in the palm of his hand the instrument that metes and measures the stars. Cunningly reduced to this scale, it was known as the mathematical jewel. How inevitable, after all, that it should be thus employed by the artist who wearied of painting and occupied his declining years with abstruse geometrical studies.'

'Yes,' I said.

'A further thought of some interest comes to me. There was undoubtedly a period in which Piero interested himself in *intarsie*—in which you will have noticed how often mathematical and musical instruments appear. It is a significant point, that.'

I agreed to this too, but not without a feeling that the eminent art-historian was turning a shade informative. As it happened, his colleague from the Metropolitan now came up to him with an obvious wish for urgent conference, and it seemed proper that I should move away. The group of men in front of the Piero was dominated by the Provost. Not that the Provost wasn't full of all reasonable diffidence in the presence of this majestic thing. But he was permitting himself an occasional restrained gesture, all the same. He certainly knew all about Piero's mathematical mania. I had an awkward, if momentary, impression that he was explaining the proportions of the composition to the *Direttore* of the Brera himself.

The oddity of this small spectacle struck me as I watched. When, I asked myself, had it begun to occur to anybody to bring Italian paintings of this sort into England? I thought I could recall Albert Talbert telling me impressively that the poet Spenser had been able to view 'Renaissance masterpieces' when he gained the *entrée* to Leicester House. But what could be vaguer than that? And how utterly mysterious this object's centennial seclusion amid the lumber of an Oxford college! Freed from that now, the *Madonna del Astrolabio* was due for instant fame. Seashore's article would be in *The Times* in the morning, and within days collectors all over the world would be agog. The Provost—there was no denying it—had acted with his maximum of propriety in affording this quiet and restricted preview to his colleagues and a few eminent persons from great public galleries. But that this was so, and that the entire present company consisted of men devoted to disinterested studies and intellectual pursuits, didn't quite obscure the fact that Mother and Child had tumbled out of darkness to encounter the market place. They would, as the phrase is, come under the hammer and be knocked down during some festival of the higher acquisitiveness in a London sale room. Fortunately both looked as if they would stand up to it. The Child was tough, even a little threatening; by no means likely, one would have supposed, to grow up meek and mild. The Virgin was a peasant girl who had received the highest conceivable promotion and distinctly knew where she stood: a Queen of Heaven whom one couldn't imagine being presented with a bouquet or going round with bobs and smiles. Taken together, they constituted a composition evoking something more than awe, although awe was there. Doubtless because Piero could do sums, and knew just where to place what, time had here been swept away, and the vast liberation of eternity existed for us as we looked.

Walking back to Surrey, and with my eye on the tower, I had some more prosaic thoughts. Would the Provost and Scholars of the college corporately have to prove their title to this extraordinary find? If they couldn't, might it not legally be some species of treasure trove—like a golden helmet, say, that a man digs up in his back garden? Or suppose that some person of ancient lineage, alerted by Seashore's article, came forward with evidence that just such an aid to devotion had been carelessly mislaid by an ancestor of his in the sixteenth century? But these seemed unlikely contingencies. And, even so, I had little doubt that Edward Pococke had already taken the measure of them. There had been one slip between cup and lip in the matter of the Blunderville money. Nothing of the sort would happen again.

XVI

I WAS SOON to learn that nothing must be taken for granted
about the future of Seashore's discovery. Through several
of the remaining weeks of term, and until the question
appeared to be settled for us in a startling way, there was a
great deal of debate about the Piero. People took issue over
what was to be done with it, and often so vigorously that the
word 'divisive'—popular in various contexts at the time—
might fairly have been applied to the influence the picture
had on our society.

Charles Atlas, always a stickler for constitutional pro-
cedures, felt obliged to disapprove of the Provost's having
divulged its existence and placed it virtually upon public
exhibition without a prior resolution of the Governing Body.
Nobody paid much attention to this, the general opinion
being that which Bedworth had propounded to me: namely
that the Provost, having always looked after artistic or
aesthetic matters of no academic consequence, had been
entitled to continue doing so now that a matter of some
weight in that area had turned up. There was a general belief,
too, that Edward Pococke's persuasive air of moral elevation
was by no means at war with his being a shrewd business
man. He had taken the best means to our driving the best
bargain over the astonishing windfall that had tumbled in on
us, and that was the important thing. Atlas himself was
constrained to concur in this view—perhaps because nobody
would be more affected than himself if the dire predictions
of Quine came true. There was, in fact, clearly a majority
holding the opinion that the Piero should be turned into
cash with all possible expedition, and work on the tower put
in hand forthwith. The Piero was something we hadn't
known the existence of; it had in no sense been any part of the
life or sentiment of the college; it symbolized for nobody

the corporate life of the place. The tower did; a surprising proportion of old members might be shown to have print or etching or photograph of it hung in some domestic sanctum of their own. So the tower must be saved, and to that end the Piero had been sent us by God. This, I say, was the majority view. Equally important was the fact that the Provost, very obviously, had no other conclusion to the matter in his head.

Still, there were other voices. Some people believed that it would be unbecoming to sell the picture, and that the problem it presented us with and the problem of the tower must be regarded as unconnected in any way. Whether the Piero went to public auction or were privately disposed of, somebody would soon gain an export licence for it, and we should thus incur the odium of having alienated what ought to be regarded as a national heritage. These people added—perhaps not very consistently—that the grossly inflated value of such things at present would compound the near-felony we should commit. The only proper course would be to present the *Madonna del Astrolabio* to the National Gallery. I found that I was myself expected—again without much logic—to support this proposal because there were now so many of my father's paintings in the Tate. James Gender went one better. With a streak of imagination which I was ashamed to admit finding unexpected in him, he urged that the picture should be donated to the *municipio* of Borgo San Sepolcro, so that it might there hang in the *Palazzo Communale* in company with Piero's *Resurrection*, regarded by many as the greatest painting in the world. Those disconcerted at the thought of this splendid gesture to Piero's home town murmured darkly that pet foods had made Gender an unobtrusively wealthy man, and that none of us would be less affected by what had come to be known as Quine's Curse.

Amid all this conflict of views I waited with curiosity for the opinion of the formidable Dr Wyborn. This came to us at a Governing Body meeting largely devoted to inconclusive

231

debate on the issue. Wyborn acknowledged the splendour of our newly recovered aid to devotion as absolutely as he had declined to see any merit in the elegance of the tower. (Indeed, he had formed the habit on the one hand of presenting himself before the picture apparently for the purpose of more or less private prayer, and on the other of pausing in the quad or in the street to regard the tower with frowning disfavour.) It was self-evident to him that the only proper home for the Piero was the college chapel. I felt there was a great deal to be said for this proposal. It received no support, however, except from Lempriere, who approved of it because—as he said—'it would put us one up on King's'. This was a reference to the Rubens owned by that noble Cambridge foundation, and might be regarded as very much a college man's point of view. The Provost, a member of the higher clergy, was put in an awkward situation by Wyborn's case, but at once resourcefully adduced the grave problem of security. At present the Piero was guarded round the clock, something that couldn't go on for ever. Nobody could walk off with the Rubens, for the reason that it was, one might say, the size of a tennis-court. But Piero's *Madonna del Astrolabio* was very little larger than his *Flagellation* in Marotta's Urbino, and everybody knew what had happened to that. In short, a portable object worth many hundreds of thousands of pounds was not a practical proposition in an Oxford college.

Meanwhile, and as this debate went on formally and informally, the picture was admired by Oxford at large. Or not quite at large, since it was decided that the privilege must be restricted for the time being to persons known to and conducted by a fellow of the college. Some condition of the sort may have been necessary, but the arrangement hit upon proved to be as vexatious as might have been guessed at the outset. *The Times* had inevitably given the discovery instant celebrity, and Oxford is full of people who will pursue such an interest at the drop of a hat. Ladies were particularly prominent in the queue. There was even at times a queue in the literal sense, my colleagues conscientiously lining up with women who until that day had been virtually unknown to them. But as a recent arrival it happened that I escaped this particular *Frauendienst*. The only person I can recollect conducting into the presence of the Madonna was Jimmy Gender's pupil-to-be, Peter Lusby.

As on the occasion of our first meeting, Peter had come to Oxford for the day, but this time unaccompanied by a batch of schoolfellows. That he should think to call on me in the course of his expedition was entirely agreeable. Though he had lately been discovered by Gender to be almost alarmingly religious, and had even corresponded with Wyborn, mysteriously denominated Pastoral Fellow, on matters presumably arising from this habit of mind, Peter wasn't in the least a prig—and he was sensitive enough to have gathered that I wasn't myself at all in the van of the godly. So I didn't expect that his call would resolve itself into any sort of *santa conversazione*. I chatted in a general way while making coffee for him just as on our previous occasion.

There was a certain constraint about Peter, all the same, and quite soon I was suspecting that I was myself in some way the main reason for his coming to Oxford that day. As he hadn't acknowledged this at once he felt himself to be in a false position, and he wasn't a boy to take anything of the sort in his stride. The duty of absolute truthfulness was without doubt one of the inconvenient things he had to live with.

'I've left school, you know,' he said suddenly.

'That's quite usual, isn't it, when one has got one's university place?

'Oh, yes—I don't mean they've expelled me.'

'I'd hardly have expected that, Peter.' For Peter, I felt, this had been quite an effort after a joke, and it increased the effect of an acute strain in him. 'Are you putting in a month or two seeing the world?'

233

'Well, not much of it, really. But I've got a job. It's not a terribly exciting one. But they pay quite decently, and the money's going to help. Of course I manage to go on studying at the same time.'

'What kind of a job is it?'

'It's in an office in Lombard Street, and I'm temporary office boy. I address letters—I think the ones to unimportant people who aren't on the addressograph. And I lick stamps. I lick them till my tongue hangs out. But then I'm tea boy as well. That's useful in the circumstances.'

'I see.' This continued facetiousness on Peter's part held a hint of desperation. 'What sort of an office is it?'

'It's called a Discount House—but I don't know what that means.'

'No more do I.' I managed to say this casually as I poured the coffee—and then I decided that the casual was no good. What had bobbed up was another of Chance's artistries rather than a meaningless coincidence. 'Peter,' I said, 'out with it.'

'Well, you see——' For a moment Peter looked at me helplessly. Then he squared himself. 'Do you know anybody called Mumford?'

'I know several people called Mumford. One of them is an old friend of mine.'

'No. I mean somebody of about my own age, who was at this college.'

'That's Ivo Mumford, my friend's son. He had the rooms above these last year. He's in this office of yours, is he?'

'Yes, that's it. He seems to be the nephew or something of one of the top men. I don't know how to begin about this.'

'It doesn't matter how, Peter. Just go ahead.'

'He spoke to me once or twice in my first week there—not very politely.'

'So I'd suppose.' I wondered whether I could keep the tone of this relaxed. 'Does he give himself airs and expect you to call him "sir"?'

234

'I wouldn't do that.' Peter took this seriously. 'Of course I call the older people that way. But I don't think I'd ever say "sir" to somebody my own age. It doesn't mean I'm discontented and insubordinate. I don't resent licking stamps all day. It's a useful lesson in humility, I suppose.'

'It's nothing of the kind. But never mind that. Go on telling me about Ivo.'

'He must have seen my name on a pay-packet or something. Because one day he asked me if I'd had a brother at Oxford— and he named this college.'

'What did you say?'

'I said, Yes I had.' Peter's chin went up. 'And that I was coming here too.'

'Good man! And that's all?'

'Of course not, or I shouldn't have——' Peter broke off. 'You see, it's about this I've come to see you, really. I hope that's all right.'

'Of course it is. Go on.' If I uttered this injunction confidently I was concealing a sense of the awkwardness of the situation into which Chance, again, had manœuvred me. It was my impression that the Lusbys—Peter and his parents—had never heard the full story of what had led to Paul Lusby's suicide. It had remained for them a matter of some perhaps ill-judged behaviour on the boy's part which had led to his failing an examination and taking the failure disastrously to heart. But the whole college had come to know of the element of responsibility borne by Ivo Mumford, and Gender and I had both worried about the possible effect on Peter were he to learn the facts when he himself came into residence. Ivo's abrupt departure from our midst had mitigated this anxiety—but the problem had not, so far as I knew, been wholly resolved. It was essentially Gender's problem. But now I had been pitched in this odd way into the firing-line. I had better learn just what had happened.

'A couple of days ago,' Peter was saying, 'this chap

Mumford came into the sort of cubby-hole where I make the tea. He must have been looking for a chance to get me alone. There was something very queer about his look. I wondered whether he was drunk.'

'It wouldn't be an impossibility, I'd say.'

'But he wasn't. He mumbled something I couldn't catch. It wasn't at all his usual way of speaking. And then he suddenly looked straight at me and said, "I'm damned sorry about your brother".'

'I see.' For a moment I was more struck by this totally unexpected revelation of Ivo's state of mind than by how the incident might have affected Peter. 'And how did you take that?' I asked.

'I don't think I liked his saying he was damned anything about Paul.'

'Well, I suppose it was a bit crude, Peter. But, you know, it was perfectly proper. He and Paul had been up together, and now he'd heard that you were coming to the college. He couldn't very well have said nothing.'

'But then, you see, he said something more.' Peter was looking at me almost sternly, and I felt ashamed of my attempt to ride away from the issue in so pusillanimous a fashion. 'Mumford went quite pale. He really was terribly upset. And what he said was, "How could I have known the bloody silly bet would end that way?" And then he seemed to lose his nerve—it really was like that—and bolted from the room. I was upset myself. So I want it explained, please—if you can explain it, sir. Can you?'

For this instant Peter Lusby had become a skilled interrogator, and I could make only one reply.

'Yes, I can. It's not at all pleasant, but at least it's not complicated. Just before Paul's Prelim Ivo Mumford threw a silly sort of dare or challenge at him: to stay up all night, gate-crashing on the Commem Ball.'

'A Ball! Paul?' Peter stared at me. 'Paul would never——'

'Well, that was how it was. Paul was pretty well flat-out already. He'd been over-working, and the sleepless night and general strain of the thing wrecked him in the Examination Schools next morning. That's the whole story, Peter.'

Peter was silent—for so long that my thoughts went back to the wretched Ivo. I remembered intolerable things he had said about Paul Lusby long after the tragedy was over. I reflected that his second utterance to Peter had hinted at a shallow self-justification not alien to his habit of mind as I knew it. Still, in a small way the Furies had been at work on Ivo. I could recall hinting to him—although in different words—that it would happen. For the rest of his days he'd have something to live with.

'Do you mean,' Peter asked, 'that but for this man Mumford Paul would be alive today?'

'That is the probability. Only, Peter, "but for" thinking doesn't mend things.'

'Mr Lempriere never told me about this.'

'Mr Lempriere was concerned to see you through the college entrance examination; he wouldn't want to come out with something that could only distress you.'

'That's true, I suppose.' Peter was again silent for a time. He was quite as distressed now as I had feared he would be. 'I can't go back to that office,' he said. 'I'll write and tell them so.' He smiled at me wanly. 'The tea boy tenders his resignation.' He stood up as if to take his leave of me—and then said something quite surprising. 'And to this Ivo Mumford. I'll write to him too. Thanking him for what he tried to say. Something like that.'

'I think he'll be grateful. He's rather a mixed up young man.'

'Only I don't think I'd want to meet him again. Will he be coming back to the college?'

'Definitely not. He hasn't just been rusticated or something like that. Ivo's days here are over.'

'I see.' Peter moved to the door, and then hesitated—

perhaps wondering whether we were due to shake hands. And I myself felt that here was rather too abrupt a parting.

'Look!' I said on impulse. 'There's something I'd like you to see before you go. It's a picture the college has just discovered it possesses. I think you'll like it.'

'A picture?' The boy was only half attentive, but was instantly polite. 'Thank you very much, sir.'

We walked over to the common room. There happened to be nobody there—or nobody except one of the security men. He was imposingly tough, but I caught myself wondering what would have happened if Peter Lusby and I had burst in with guns in our hands.

'Here it is,' I said.

Peter looked at *The Madonna of the Astrolabe*. I thought for a moment that it was almost unregardingly. But I was wrong.

'Oh!' he said—and after a long pause asked, 'Sir, could it be by Piero della Francesca?'

'It certainly is. All the authorities say so.'

'It's terribly beautiful.' Peter was now round-eyed. 'Does the college have a lot of things like this?'

'No, indeed.' I might have been surprised by Peter's knowledge if I hadn't remembered what a picture gallery can be to a boy or girl—what, for example, the Scottish National Gallery had been to me. There was no Piero there: only Vermeer's *Christ in the House of Mary and Martha*—in front of which, surely rather profanely, I had first kissed Janet.

'The Virgin isn't like the one in the *Nativity*,' Peter said. 'Not a bit.'

'In the National Gallery? No, she's quite different. But they didn't think it odd—did they?—to keep on painting the Virgin now from one woman and now from another. I suppose it was part of the idea, in a way.'

'Yes, of course.' Rather comically, and to a slight effect of anti-climax, Peter was betraying surprise that I should prove not without rudimentary religious knowledge. 'She's every mother. But glorified. Thank you very much for showing me the picture, sir.'

We went out into the quad, and I accompanied Peter to the gate, much as I had done upon our first encounter less than a year before.

'Did you call on Dr Wyborn?' I asked, remembering that Peter had corresponded with our Pastoral Fellow.

'No, I thought I oughtn't to bother him. You see, I see him occasionally in London now. I don't mean to talk to. But he has connected himself with our mission at St Ambrose's—that's my church—and he sometimes celebrates Holy Communion. Does he do that every day here?'

'I don't think so.' This was an awkward question, since my knowledge of what went on in the college chapel was sketchy. 'We seem to have a good many clergymen around. And there's a chaplain of course. He's quite a young man. I hope you'll like him.'

'Dr Wyborn said in his letter to me that I should always go to the chaplain, and that he is thoroughly sound. Doctrinally, I suppose he meant. Would you agree?'

'I wouldn't know, Peter. I'm not entitled to an opinion. I'm an old-fashioned agnostic, you see.'

As I said this, I remembered that Peter, only minutes before, had shown that he already possessed some awareness of the state of my case. And I felt that I might have left 'old-fashioned' out, since it suggested a whimsical lightness of air which he didn't deserve. He now received my explicit confession in silence. I felt, without resentment, that he was probably making a mental note to pray for me. When I had said good-bye and was walking back to Surrey I was conscious of an increased discomfort about *The Madonna of the Astrolabe* as a potential article of commerce. I was even prepared to vote for Wyborn's view of what ought to be done with it. I'd have liked to feel that Peter Lusby, when he came into residence, would be able to do some of his praying in front of it.

XVII

An event now took place which drove Piero della Francesca and the unstable condition of the college tower alike clean out of my head. It even banished my altogether more intimate unease before the thought that the Penny Pattullo of the *Piccolo Gallo* was at large in Oxford. Rather unfairly, perhaps, Penny and sexual depravity had become interchangeable notions for me; the thought of her prompted humiliatingly crude imaginings; I was perpetually seeing her as triumphantly bringing off the *tour de force* of bedding simultaneously with two young men who were entirely nice and brothers into the bargain. But this (which was to prove not Penny's idea, after all) sank into some region of my mind that it ought never to have risen from as soon as J. B. Timbermill's cerebral disaster became known to me. Timbermill was dying.

It was I who discovered him in his stricken state, and it happened on one of my duty visits in Linton Road. I am ashamed to have to call them that, but it is true that keeping an eye on the Wizard of the North had become something I had to bring myself to face up to. Timbermill had come to expect my presence almost as much as he had come to expect Fiona's. But, paradoxically, he seemed scarcely aware of us when we did turn up in Heorot, and when he spoke it was querulously and reproachfully. Once or twice we found ourselves visiting him together—although by no pre-arrangement—and I was made aware of how much better Fiona managed what Wyborn would have called a work of corporal mercy than I did. Visiting the sick—the really sick—isn't easy. One has to repress in oneself that sizeable chunk of one's unredeemed nature which prompts one simply to get away. And Timbermill was sick in his head, although not yet in the physiological manner soon to overtake him. I don't know that Fiona felt this evil impulse of rejection at all. I had, in a sense, loved Timbermill when I was a boy; she loved him now, and in his decrepitude. I wondered whether I loved Fiona. If I was drawing nearer to something of the kind it wasn't least rapidly on these occasions, which revealed a Fiona not commonly on view. Shaw's Vivie Warren was out; and I'd sometimes have been inclined to say that here were first cousins to Lear and Cordelia, had I not been aware that the comparison was altogether too august to be applicable to these two academic persons, old and young. Unfortunately the increased warmth I felt for Fiona while in Timbermill's company during this final phase of his life was not recip- rocated. Perhaps Fiona felt that she and I (being January and May) were in a frivolous relationship which rendered inappropriate our simultaneous attendance at Timbermill's bedside. Or perhaps—I told myself alternatively—she considered that I had been no sort of faithful pupil, and oughtn't to be pushing in now. These were unsatisfactory conjectures. But Fiona often had me guessing about how she felt we should respond to one another.

Usually I had been finding Timbermill alone in his vast and shadowy attic. The place had always been untidy and dusty; now it had become dirty as well. Dirt can turn a formidable adversary in old age. I had reasserted my right— first claimed in my final year as his pupil—to wander about the place as I chose; and on one of these visits I let this liberty extend to glancing into the three small rooms tucked beneath the subsidiary gables of the house. They were no improve- ment on the main chamber. Cobwebs were thick in the bathroom, and thickest of all in the bath, which had become a kind of spiders' club. Not many months before, it had been within my knowledge that Timbermill had admitted the ministrations of a cleaning-woman once a week. It was clear that this no longer obtained. His becoming a nocturnal wanderer in the streets had been coincident with his embracing a complete domestic seclusion. What he lived on, I didn't know: tea, perhaps, and bread and butter and boiled eggs. The eggs were more than a conjecture. Sometimes he wore an old sports jacket, sometimes a dressing-gown, and sometimes merely his pyjamas. There was a good deal of egg on all of them.

These signs betokened an ominously swift decline into dotage, as did his inability or indisposition to enter into any sort of rational talk. Nevertheless it was evident that he still regarded himself as engaged in learned pursuits. Here the main sign of change was a retreat, a thinning out, of the books and papers and journals which had formerly been piled up around him, and their replacement by an advancing chaos of broken pottery, rusted iron and crumbling bronze. It was obvious that Timbermill put in a lot of time handling these multifarious memorials of Anglo-Saxon culture, probably with some thought of reassorting them on their shelves in fresh typological sequence. Of the pottery, at least, a good deal that had been painfully pieced and glued together over the years—by myself, some of it—must have been dropped and broken again during those fumbling efforts; more than once I even thought I detected, littered on the floor, the fragments of some pot or urn, costrel or skillet, which I had actually held intact in my hands many years before.

This return, as it were, to the midden from which they came of evidences to the study and interpretation of which Timbermill had given much of his life was not inspiriting. Fiona and I had agreed—she on the basis of a much fuller knowledge—that there was nothing to be done about it; there would have been an impossible officiousness in our attempting to organize the interest and interposition of fellow-scholars of Timbermill's with whom he had long ago lost touch. I did feel that a simple clear-up would be useful, since the spectacle of Timbermill shambling around in carpet slippers among a thick scattering of knife-edged shards was extremely alarming. Going to work in a Draconian spirit with a dust-pan and brush, I quickly found that Timbermill had really lost interest in the pottery; he watched without protest or interest while I did what I pleased about it. But it was otherwise with certain other objects in his collection. The coins were in fair order, but even of them a good many lay scattered around. My attempt to cope with these made Timbermill uneasy at once. And violent agitation followed upon my putting my hand on the Petersfinger *scramasax*.

Timbermill, I imagine, would have placed this short sword or long dagger a good way ahead of *The Madonna of the Astrolabe*, and I had done right in proposing to pick it up from the floor and restore it to its prescriptive place behind glass. Although he possessed a mass of material of great archaeological interest and considerable value, the *scramasax* was his only major treasure, and must have been worth a very large sum. It was to turn out that he had bequeathed it to the Ashmolean Museum, where it would rank with the Alfred Jewel and the Minster Lovell Jewel.

Timbermill snatched it from me and fondled it. It had fascinated me in the past, and it did so now. The fascination wasn't entirely aesthetic, since it partly consisted in a contrast between the exquisite artistry of the pommel and the sinister character of the blade. The pommel displays a gold panel with an interlaced filigree wire ornament superimposed, and it further incorporates some exquisite animal heads which lurk amid bunches of grapes made of tiny granules of gold. (These gold blobs had at one time incongruously reminded me of Tony Mumford's superior swizzle-sticks, given to him by an indulgent aunt.) So much for art. The blade was entirely real life—or death; it showed a long groove, believed by some (Timbermill had told me) to have been smeared with poison to effect an enemy's more certain despatch.

I have somewhere recorded that Timbermill's scholarship was at times a little touched by imagination, as one might expect of the author of *The Magic Quest*. His persuasion that the White Horse of Uffington had been cut in the turf by a non-Belgic tribe called the Dobunni was an orthodox belief at the time of his communicating it to me, although scholars may well have changed their minds about it now. But that the Bunns of Uffington village (butchers, not bakers) were descendants of the Dobunni was a theory difficult to judge persuasive. Timbermill similarly believed, or professed to believe, that his particular *scramasax* had figured at the assassination of some royal personage whose name I forget—although I remember reflecting that the date of this killing must have been quite close to that at which my father's young Picts had watched the arrival of Columba from Iona. I was disinclined to believe that the weapon was quite as old as that.

It could no longer be called lethal, since the blade would probably have shivered had it been used to impale a sparrow. Nevertheless the sight of Timbermill mindlessly fingering it was disquieting, and on the next occasion of my running into Robert Damian I was prompted again to mention my old tutor's condition.

'Oh yes, indeed,' Damian said. 'I took your hint, Duncan, and went to see the old boy.'

'You managed that?'

'I put on a turn as the old-style family doctor—who called on you regularly, just like the men who wound the clocks and swept the chimneys. And do you remember the tailors' touts, who used to tap on one's door in college and murmur a desire to be of service to you?'

'Yes, I do. But tell me about your seeing Timbermill.'

'It wasn't a striking success. He turned me out of the room. We didn't have the confidence to do that with the touts, did we? Just ordered a gent's suiting right away.'

'I suppose so. So it was no good?'

'I wouldn't say quite that. At least I had a look at the old chap. He'd clearly ordered his final gent's suiting long ago. Nothing to measure him for, Duncan, except a shroud.'

'He won't last long?'

'Well, not all that long. A little embalming might be possible, supposing him willing to submit to it. But it wouldn't answer for long. Does anyone look after him?'

'I don't think so. Or not in a regular way. Would you say he ought to be in a home or something?'

'No, I wouldn't. The van will call in the end, I suppose. And I'll continue to look in from time to time. He may get used to me.'

I suppose I must have shown my distress at this prognosis, for I became aware of Damian smiling. It would not be his usual response to the glum or stricken faces of a dying man's relations. But, unlike most of these, I counted as an old friend. '*Morbi tristisque senectus*, Duncan,' he said. 'That's Latin for the van at the door. Cheer up.' And Damian walked away.

Three days after this conversation I went out to Linton Road again. Anything characteristic of Oxford has faded away by the time you get to Linton Road; you might be in any substantial suburb in England. It is true that at the farthest end of it old Mrs Triplett's house has been knocked down, and a whole new college built in its place. But that is screened and out of sight. The average age of the surrounding inhabitants has dropped a good deal, since in this part of North Oxford nearly all the big houses have been turned into flats for the younger members of the learned and scientific community. I thought it odd that this humdrum locality had once spelt romance for me, had been a kind of Lyonnesse, bringing magic to my eyes. Penny had been chiefly responsible for that, but Timbermill had played his part. Timbermill had in a quite real sense formed my mind. Any seriousness in me (and it was only because I did have a little seriousness that I was able to write comedy) he had injected. And now I had some responsibility to him that I didn't see how to discharge.

This last proved an abortive thought. It had come to me too late. I had an intuition of the fact as soon as I saw, planted by the old kitchen door which served as the entrance to Timbermill's staircase, two newspapers and two bottles of milk.

He had been, in his way, an orderly man, and I was sure that in his later years he had come down and collected his milk in its bottles as regularly as, long ago, he had taken his pitcher to collect it from Mrs Triplett's celebrated cows. I picked up the bottles and the two copies of *The Times* and went upstairs. The bottles, having been in the sun, felt warm to my hand. I wondered whether I should find Timbermill feeling so.

He wasn't dead. But he was lying, half dressed, on the floor of the big room in what I took at first to be a coma but which was in fact a semi-stupor and paralysis. His features moved as I knelt beside him, and his lips formed words which emerged as a mere gabble. Yet I knew instantly what he had tried to say. It had been his invariable greeting to me. *Duncan, son of Lachlan!* That had been it.

It wasn't a moment in which to be overwhelmed with distress. I smiled at him and said I don't know what—judging that his hearing might be more in working order than his speech. Then I ran downstairs and out of the house, as its idiotic botched architecture required before I could get to somebody's telephone. At the front door I rang a bell. It brought a predictably cool and competent young academic female, with two curly-headed little boys grinning hospitably behind her. Yes, they were on the phone. Damian himself answered my call. I went upstairs again, able to feel that the proper wheels had begun to revolve. But, meanwhile, was there anything that it was vital I should be doing myself? I wondered about trying to get Timbermill on his bed, but decided I didn't know enough about the hazardousness of moving him. I fetched a pillow and a frayed eiderdown, and while doing what was possible with these noticed that his left hand was moving in what seemed designed as a meaningful gesture. But it wasn't interpretable, and I found myself looking at him inquiringly, although it seemed not a tactful thing to do. His gaze suggested a mind lucid at least for the moment. I had never before encountered an imprisoned intelligence: present but bereft of the instruments of communication. To a person in this condition one gives pencil and paper, and sees if anything can be elicited that way. I don't know why I shrank from the attempt; perhaps it seemed too brutal an acknowledgement of his helplessness; in any case it was a matter for the judgement of the doctors. I continued making my one-way remarks from time to time, and was fairly sure that Timbermill understood them. But it wasn't easy to say much that didn't sound irrelevant, or impertinently of the cheer-up sort. I wondered about drinks, hot-water bottles. Then, blessedly, Damian arrived. It had presumably taken him about ten minutes from his consulting rooms in Beaumont Street, but it had felt much longer than that.

As Damian examined his patient he behaved much as I had been doing: offering occasional spare remarks and admitting no inconvenience in the fact that any response was ruled out. Then, holding a clinical thermometer as if proposing to rinse it, he went into the bathroom and unobtrusively beckoned me after him.

'We'll have to make do,' he said. 'It would take the fire brigade to get him out of this damned garret.'

I thought of the ladder-like staircase up which weary housemaids had once clambered to their repose, and took the point.

'It can be done?' I asked.

'For a short time, yes. If there's any use in hospitalizing him we must take the risk of moving him. It's marvellous what those ambulance wallas can do at a pinch. Away ahead of the furniture removers. Meanwhile, you'd better contact the relatives, Duncan. They're entitled to be in on the act, if they see it that way. I'll get agency nursing. And a home help. Queer place for a home help.'

'Just what is a home help?' This was an idle question. I was wondering if there *were* any relatives. I'd never heard of any.

'Something laid on by the welfare shambles.'

'I see. But I don't know anything about brothers or sisters or nephews or nieces. I doubt if anybody does. Would it be decent to ransack his drawers—that sort of thing?'

'Bugger decency! It's up to you. Why isn't there a telephone in this daft place?'

'Timbermill has given up the telephone. But the woman at the bottom has one. I used it to get you.'

'Then I'll go and use it. Just stand by.'

So once more I was left alone with J. B. Timbermill. I knelt beside him again.

'J. B.,' I said, 'would you like me to get Fiona?' This seemed to me a sensible idea. Fiona had been much closer to Timbermill than I had ever been, and something of his family background might be known to her.

Timbermill made a noise which could be taken to be a reply. And the question hadn't really been necessary. It was self-evident that Fiona must be got hold of at once.

'Fiona's in Copenhagen,' Margaret Mountain said on the telephone. 'She loves the place.'

'Copenhagen?' I repeated stupidly. It was still term-time. That Fiona might be out of Oxford—and without telling me—hadn't entered my head.

'At a conference. And she's been asked to give a lecture by Steenstrup.'

'Who the devil is Steenstrup?'

'A professor there. Fiona took you to a lecture by him at the British Academy.'

'So she did. It was quite too awful.' Impatience had possessed me. 'Look, Margaret—Timbermill has had a stroke or something, and isn't expected to survive. Fiona would want to know. Do you think she can be contacted?'

'I've no notion where she's staying. But I can find out who the conference people are, and get them to have her ring me up. That will leave you free to be with Timbermill if you want to be.' Miss Mountain was perceptive as well as reassuringly efficient, and it was evident that Timbermill's ill opinion of her hadn't entered her head. 'Where is he? And is he conscious?'

'He's at home, because it's felt he'd be difficult to move. And he's conscious in some fashion, I think. Only he can't talk. Do what you can about Fiona, Margaret. She'd be a comfort to him.'

I rang off, and for some moments found Fiona's absence from Oxford strangely confusing. I had an impulse to ring up Janet, and then wondered how such an irrelevant idea could occur to me, since her acquaintance with Timbermill must be either minimal or nonexistent. Moreover I knew perfectly well that the McKechnies had left for the United States a couple of days before. So it looked as if I myself badly wanted feminine support—which seemed an extravagant reaction to the impending death of a very old man who had made me learn Anglo-Saxon verbs long ago.

There was still the question of finding relatives. I started this hunt with *Who's Who*. It named Timbermill's parents and told me that his father had been a merchant banker. But these people were centenarians if they weren't dead; there was no mention of marriage or of any other connections; and there wasn't another Timbermill in the book. *The Times* would be holding a full obituary, and the colleges of which he was an honorary fellow must similarly be possessed of something in the *curriculum vitae* way. But they would scarcely run to nephews and nieces prepared to turn up and mourn on call. It was borne in on me that a scholar of the first distinction could live out his life in Oxford without anybody knowing the first thing about him in a human and family way—or that it could be so, at least, if he was a reticent and reclusive man. Timbermill must have a bank manager, and probably a solicitor who had drawn up and now held a will. But gaining any information expeditiously looked like being a job for a professional private eye. As for hunting through Heorot for private papers, that didn't seem to me to be on—particularly as there would be Timbermill himself, conscious even if as definitively *incomunicado* as he seemed likely to remain. If he were going to die he would have to be seen through the mysterious occasion simply by two former pupils. And that was that. At least it wasn't likely that there would be other persons for whose presence he felt an urgent need.

But this quite quickly took on the appearance of a fallacious assumption. Damian called me later that evening, and told me that Timbermill had recovered some very slight command of speech.

'You mean he's improving?' I asked. 'He may come through?'

'No, Duncan. It isn't that at all, I'd say. In fact there are other signs that point to the contrary. We'll have him in hospital tomorrow morning, if he lasts that long. They'll take out a window-frame and lower him on a stretcher. But he is uttering, as I say. Somebody's name.'

'Mine?'

'Yours? No, it isn't yours.'

'I see.' It felt as if I had said something rather foolish. 'It's just that he did name me—when I went in and found him. Or I did think he did, although it wasn't really distinguishable. He likes my father's pictures.' I realized that this was an incomprehensible remark. 'I mean he calls me Duncan, son of Lachlan.'

'Oh, I see.' I had a sense that Damian was glancing at his watch; he had more hopeful patients than Timbermill to be thinking of. 'It's a woman's name.'

'Fiona?'

'No, not Fiona. Anna. Have you got a line on any relatives yet?'

'I'm afraid not. But I'll keep trying.'

'Good. Duncan, if you want to see him again you'd better run out to Linton Road tonight. But after nine in the morning ring the Radcliffe. They'll have got him there by then.'

This was all Damian had to say, and I called a taxi at once. As I was driven through the near-midsummer dusk I wondered who on earth Anna could be, and whether she was likely to be still alive. Probably not: a person thus invocated by a very old man on his death-bed was likely to have existence only in a deep past. But this wasn't certain; Timbermill's Anna might be a living woman—an early love or a favourite sister—from whom he had been long estranged, and whose presence would be important to him now. This problem was still troubling me as I mounted that final narrow staircase to what Damian had called Timbermill's garret.

Timbermill was on his bed, which had been moved out into the big room, perhaps because the bedroom was too cramped for nursing purposes. I had arrived at a moment when one nurse was packing up and another preparing to settle in for the night. There was also the sound of somebody pottering in the little kitchen; presumably this was the home help, and it seemed improbable that she was facing any long assignment. There was something disconcerting in Timbermill and myself being thus outnumbered in this celibate haunt by the female sex. The incoming nurse, moreover, disapproved of my visit at this hour, and I had to explain that I had turned up on Dr Damian's authority.

Perhaps Timbermill had been sedated in some way and it wasn't a good idea to disturb him. He was certainly lying peacefully enough on his back, and I'd have had a sensation of merely trespassing awkwardly on his normal repose if it hadn't been for what his stricken brain had done to one side of his face. It had set a leer on it—comical rather than malign, so that the effect was of a cheerful vulgarity such as one might come upon in a strip cartoon. I wondered whether death would wipe this away and recompose Timbermill's features along lines of youthful serenity and noble calm. I had always felt this—if it happened—to be a poor joke on death's part. But I found myself hoping for it now.

Quite a lot of stuff had been humped up into the room: oxygen apparatus and similar gear. It lent the place an incongruous air, seemed to be in collision with the dusty massive evidences on every wall and vacant space of a lifetime given to remote learned purposes. And I now noticed that Timbermill's left hand, which had been placed outside the coverlet, lay inertly on a leather-bound volume.

'He could rotate the left wrist,' the outgoing nurse said professionally. She had followed my glance. 'He seemed pointing at the books—so I gave him one and it seemed to content him. It can't have been the one he wanted, of course—supposing he did want one in particular.'

'No,' I said, 'it can scarcely be that.'

'They speak of dying with one's boots on. Perhaps for Dr Timbermill——'

'Yes, nurse; it's a good point. Has he been trying to say anything more?'

'He hasn't even been murmuring for some time.'

'Was there any attempt to see if he could write?'

'I think the doctors found there was no possibility of that. There has been a consultation, you know, this afternoon. Dr Damian brought the Regius Professor.'

'Ah, yes. Well, if your colleague doesn't mind, I think I'll

252

stay for a time. Dr Timbermill, you see, was my tutor long ago.'

'Oh, Nurse Jones won't mind. And it won't be difficult to find yourself a book, will it?'

This young woman went away. I had a little subdued conversation with her successor, and then sat down to a silent vigil near the bed. There seemed to be a feeling that Timbermill was unlikely even to approximate to articulate speech again. But I wanted to be within hearing if he did.

The night wore on. I must have dozed—because floating in my head was some macabre account, surely somewhere in Edgar Allan Poe, of misbehaviour on the part of the dead Schopenhauer's false teeth. Perhaps to a tiny sound, and with grotesque effect of *rictus*, they had popped out——

There was a tiny sound in Heorot, and it brought me to my feet and to the bedside. Timbermill's mouth was trembling, moving. I put my ear to his lips.

'*Anna!*' Timbermill whispered—almost inaudibly, but with extraordinary passion. And his eyes, which had been closed, slowly opened. But there was no speculation in them. The night-nurse, after certain tests, drew the sheet over his face.

I walked back to college in the small hours, with some very curious speculations dominating my consciousness. Instead of thinking about J. B. Timbermill's life and character and achievement—and in particular what he had done for me—I continued to be troubled by the problematical Anna. Could Fiona perhaps identify her? I asked myself this question only to answer that it was unlikely. Yet mightn't there be some connection unknown to me between Timbermill and Fiona's family, and mightn't it account for the very strong affection he had so obviously entertained for Fiona when his pupil? There was nothing irrational in this notion. But the same could scarcely be said of what next came to me. This was an impulse to haul into the picture, in what was surely an almost paranoiac fashion, the only Anna I myself happened to know. Wasn't it possible that Timbermill might have known my elder Glencorry cousin, who became Fiona's mother as Mrs Petrie of Garth? Fiona had never mentioned such a thing. But she seldom had much to say to me about family relationships, and I had even wondered at times whether she could have been told the story of my boyhood's comically chivalric offer to make an honest woman of her mother at the time of young Petrie of Garth's proving backward in coming forward as the unborn Fiona's father. But the unlikelihood of there having been any such disclosure of an embarrassing family moment was extreme. Moreover, this line of thought was all nonsense in any event. It was impossible that between Timbermill and Fiona's mother there could have been—even had they known one another—any relationship which would justify or explain the passion with which the dying man had uttered the name of Anna.

Fiona had caught the first available flight, and was back in Oxford not many hours after Timbermill's death. But there was now nothing for either of us to do. Solicitors and undertakers were in charge; there was to be a private cremation; in a few weeks time there would be a memorial service in some college or other, which a surprising number of aged or elderly scholars would attend. I gave Fiona what account I could of Timbermill's last hours.

'Can you think of anybody called Anna he may have been interested in?' I asked.

'Yes, of course I can.' Fiona's answer was decisive and immediate.

'Your mother?' Fiona's confident assertion had somehow brought my aberration back on me.

'My mother!' For a moment Fiona stared at me blankly—as was not, I suppose, unreasonable. But she seemed displeased as well. 'Duncan, I can't think what you're talking about.

J. B.'s mind had just gone right back. It happens when you've decided to die, I believe.'

'You mean this unknown woman must have been very deep in his past?'

'There wasn't any woman, you idiot. What his mind had gone back to was Sutton Hoo, and all the controversy the discoveries there touched off. It was the great archaeological find of the century, so far as Europe is concerned, and J. B. was very passionate about it. Have you forgotten your East Anglian kings, Duncan?'

'Definitely.' I was staring at Fiona in my turn.

'King Anna died in 654. He was strongly Christian, and J. B. was convinced the ship with its treasure buried at Sutton Hoo was a cenotaph which his loyal pagan subjects created to make sure his newfangled religion didn't count against him in the shades. J. B. must have harangued you about it vehemently enough long ago.'

'I expect so,' I said humbly. 'Look—let's drive out somewhere and have a drink.'

And that was the best I could do. I was finding that this odd conclusion to the affair upset me a good deal. It was ridiculous, like the trick-ending to some silly short story, but it was something else as well. I had been eleven in 1939, and could quite clearly remember my father's delighted interest when the first pictures of the Sutton Hoo treasure appeared. Probably I had told Timbermill of that on some occasion when he had talked to me about the discovery. But King Anna had passed utterly from my mind. Irrationally now, I felt this forgetfulness to have been a kind of treachery to Timbermill. When he had whispered that impassioned 'Anna!' to me I ought to have been able to reply to what was perhaps a still receptive ear: '654, J. B. And his court must have been the most brilliant in Europe.'

Fiona would have brought off that in her stride. It was a pity she had been lured to Copenhagen by the wretched Steenstrup.

XVIII

HAD NICK JUNKIN not proposed a production of *Tamburlaine* there would have been no consultation with Talbert, no calling in of Seashore and no luncheon party for him, no discussion of Hans Eworth's lost portrait of Provost Pagden, and therefore no discovery of Piero's *Madonna del Astrolabio*. So much is mere reiteration. Had Junkin's production when it took place not been marked (as tends to happen on such occasions) by a totally unrehearsed effect, it is probable that the subsequent history of Piero's picture would have been other than it turned out to be.

Tamburlaine is a tolerable read because the verse, although primitive and monotonous, combines vigour and speed in a way that carries one along. As a stage play it is pretty hopeless, but offers scope for a romp. Junkin, despite his hankering after leopards and a free hand-out of bows and arrows, was far from intending anything of the sort. He regarded all theatrical enterprises very seriously, and was regularly furious when casual attitudes or unseasonable levity manifested themselves in his cast. Because of this, I expected that he would come round to regarding Albert Talbert as an invaluable ally, even granted that his ideas belonged to the age of Noah. And something of the sort did happen. For most of the time the well-known Talbertian *gravitas* was prominently on the scene. But so was a great deal of enthusiasm—this on both Talbert's own part and that of Mrs Talbert—and the spectacle won them considerable good will in the Dramatic Society at large. In the later stages of rehearsal Talbert actually became something of a romper himself. It was as if that imprisoned gaiety occasionally to be detected in him was breaking surface and taking command. It had to be concluded that in the distant era in which the Talberts had sustained the principal parts in Marlowe's declamatory drama the *gravitas* had not yet established itself. Albert and Emily had been clever and joyous young people with as yet no thought to the textual quiddities of *Lust's Dominion* and similar masterpieces of Elizabethan rim ram ruff. I found the thought of these Cambridge lovers and their idyll attractive but rather awesome.

The Sheldrake twins had been enterprisingly cast as Mycetes, King of Persia, and his brother, Cosroe, whose quarrel dominates the opening of the play. In Marlowe's time these must already have been stock stage characters: the weak monarch and his ambitious kinsman at a bitter enmity. But nobody, I imagine, had ever ventured to present them physically as alike as Tweedledum and Tweedledee (and a Tweedledum and Tweedledee raised, moreover, among the demigods), and I wondered whether it had been to Talbert or to Junkin that this freakish idea had come. As for Mark and Matthew, I thought of them as temperamentally somewhat aloof youths whom it was surprising to find mucking in with the enthusiasts of the Dramatic Society. But I was pleased that they had done so, judging that this absorbing and time-consuming activity might provide a wholesome distraction from Penny. The rehearsals showed them throwing themselves into their parts. They were hating each other like mad.

Amateurs tend to be wary of a professional man of the theatre in their midst, and for this reason I was relieved to be no more than tenuously connected with the production. Timbermill's death was continuing to affect me, so that I was not in any case much inclined to be involved in gambols. Nor, for more constitutional reasons, were the majority of my colleagues. During the days immediately preceding the production they were to be observed hurrying through the Great Quadrangle with averted gaze, muttering to one another that these affairs were getting altogether out of hand. Buntingford, peering into the pool around Bernini's fountain, was heard to aver that the hullabaloo was very evidently fraying the nervous condition of the great chub.

Not all our senior members, however, reacted with this sort of irritation. Some of the younger among them were even actively involved—the Dramatic Society, like most similar undergraduate concerns, being entirely acceptive of persons distinguishably beginning to decline into the vale of years. A college play, moreover, appeared to rank with major athletic occasions as requiring a decent turn-out of senior-common-room people together with their wives and children. In Eights Week (now behind us) abstracted scholars who scarcely knew one end of a boat from the other would wander amiably down to the Isis, watch the watery proceedings politely, and even offer mild supporting vociferations as the college boat went by. This was an entirely agreeable duty; one needn't stay long; and one could gossip with one's colleagues about less incomprehensible matters while waiting for one labouring crew or another to appear from the direction of Iffley Lock. Attendance at dramatic spectacles was more testing, particularly when they were presented in open air. They might begin only after irritating delays; last for hours (and the two parts of *Tamburlaine*, however mercifully cut by an intelligent scholar reading English, might well establish a record); and draw to a close in steadily worsening climatic conditions more discouraging to the audience than they were to the swarms of stinging insects also in attendance. Everybody brought rugs and the more apprehensive brought umbrellas. Occasionally, one knew, some tremendous thunderstorm would bring the dramatic venture to a dramatic close. But more frequently the gods (as if they were morose anti-theatre puritans) simply arranged for a steadily increasing drizzle to accompany the entire latter part of a play.

Conscientious men like Bedworth and Gender, as also their equally conscientious wives, strong in the conviction that the young should be countenanced in all feasible enterprises, and faced with the natural reluctance of their contemporaries to endure the rigours of the night, were accustomed to do a certain amount of whipping in. Just as when, on the occasion of some eminent foreign savant's coming to deliver a lecture in Oxford, accompanying cocktail parties are frantically arranged on the unspoken assumption that the guests will feel honourably bound to show up at the *conférence* or *discours* as well, so now Anthea Gender was mounting a buffet supper in her husband's rooms in college which was to take place immediately before the first-night performance. It was understood that the more eminent members of the cast had been invited. And they would probably have the civility to turn up.

Giving an eye to the play, I felt that the more elderly in the audience would need any preliminary recruitment they could get. All sorts of violent things happen in *Tamburlaine*, including an ingenious diversity of incendiarisms which it seemed that Junkin and Talbert had done little to mitigate; that Talbert had alerted the city's fire brigade to the hazards of the night struck me as an instance of the sagacity that distinguished him. Yet the intermittent violence of the action is as nothing to the sustained violence of the language. Marlowe was limited in the number of soldiers he could set bashing one another, but quite unlimited in the noisy fecundity of his speech. Tamburlaine's first victory is with words—'Won with thy words' somebody takes care to say in the first act; and after that the remorseless logomachy goes on and on. *Tamburlaine* was eminently the sort of play, I thought resignedly, that it is better fun to take part in than to listen to.

I arrived at Mrs Gender's party a little late, and there was already quite a crowd. The first people my eye fell on were Mark and Matthew Sheldrake. Not yet made up for their parts, they were standing at either end of the room, each with an admiring little clump of young women around him. And then I saw Penny. She had an admiring clump of young men.

How Anthea Gender, the most socially expert of all the

college ladies, had contrived this solecism I was never to learn. It seemed possible that the Sheldrakes had casually brought Penny along, without troubling to inform their hostess of their intention. Yet I couldn't believe that either was that sort of young man. Anybody would have said at a glance that one accurate word for them was 'correct'. The stresses of their twinned condition (as real, one imagined, as its satisfactions) would be in part responsible for such a comportment. But however this might be, here Penny was. It was a confused moment. What was alone clear was that we couldn't with any good sense ignore each other.

It would be foolish, I saw, to regard the situation as particularly difficult *vis-à-vis* my colleagues and their wives. Few of them could know much or anything about my domestic history. And none of them, if catching Penny's name and being thus apprised of the bobbing up of a Mrs Pattullo in our midst, would be other than circumspect in anything they thought to say. It was different with the scattering of young men and girls around the room. The Sheldrakes were in the know, and might have made it a talking-point among their fellow-undergraduates—in which case any of these youths might, in conceivable immediate circumstances, behave in an alarmed and awkward manner. Those around Penny now, for example, might embarrassingly bolt if I approached her. This wasn't a substantial anxiety, and for that matter it was my guess that the Sheldrakes—being again 'correct'—would have kept their piece of commonplace knowledge under their hats. In any case all this was as trivial as coffee-spoons. I walked across the room to Penny. As I did so it occurred to me that, actually and literally, I hadn't spoken to her since the moment at which I had left the *Ithaca* with Ulric Anderman to explore the *Piccolo Gallo*. I found myself wondering whether my instant walk-out, my refusal to utter after that grotesque revelation, had been uncivilized and even unkind.

'Hullo, Penny,' I said. 'I'd heard you were in Oxford. And I had a glimpse of you on the river only the other day. You look flourishing.' These last words, although notably true in fact, were false in feeling, since I had no honest impulse to commend Penny's looks. And my retreat upon a foolish conventional utterance amused her.

'Duncan,' she said, 'how nice to be able to talk to you! You were so silent the last time we met.' She paused on this, and I saw that the young men who had been surrounding her were edging away in much the manner I had been imagining. It may have been that they felt something odd in the air. Or not even that; they may have been doing no more than obey a notion of correct party-going behaviour. 'I was on the river with Mark and Matthew Sheldrake,' Penny was saying. 'Aren't they sweet? I expect they're great favourites of yours, Duncan.'

'They seem very nice lads. But I scarcely know them.'

'But Duncan, how wasteful! Surely you feel they'd be marvellous favourites? Have you *changed*, darling?'

I was startled by this sally, which confirmed something I'd picked up about Penny's version of the failure of our marriage. She'd found herself amid a nest of expatriate perverts and been obliged to quit. But the story, if outrageous, had long ago passed as water under the bridge, and I wasn't going to react to a quip based on it now.

'You seem to be a favourite too at the moment,' I said. 'I'm sorry to have driven all those attractive young men away. And aren't the Sheldrakes making you *their* favourite? Look how bored each is with his little bevy of younger and fresher women.'

This was a disgusting thing to say, and I knew as I uttered it that this sad little encounter must be cut short. But it was at least factually true. Admirers still surrounded the twins, and it struck me that their reputation for fabulous good-looks must have spread through the women's colleges by now, so that even a casual conversation achieved with one or the other would be a point of prestige. It was also true that Mark and

Matthew, thus severally besieged, were being no more than adequately polite. One would have said that they had other matters on their mind. And now I saw them exchange a cold glance, which they were tall enough to do over the heads of most of the company. They didn't like their own celebrity one bit. They didn't seem to like even each other.

Penny's only response to my last speech had been that slight movement of the mouth which probably now, as long ago, represented the sharpest barb in her armoury of seduction. Perhaps she had turned it on consciously and ironically. Or perhaps it had degenerated into a kind of habit spasm. I made a movement to part. But Penny detained me.

'Duncan,' she said, 'I'm thinking of getting married. Should you most terribly mind?'

'Don't be silly.'

'Aren't you even interested in who?'

'Of course I'm not interested in who. Your marriage may be a great success. I hope it will be. Such things happen.'

'Not even interested if I tell you it's a colleague?'

'A colleague?' No doubt I stared at Penny. This had rather shaken me.

'So we'll have lots of dinner-parties together. And delightful witty exciting affairs like this one. It's dear Mr Penwarden. Surely you know dear Mr Penwarden?'

'Of course I know Penwarden.'

'Isn't he charming? Like whoever it is in Beatrix Potter who's always bursting his buttons. I only met him half an hour ago. But it's destiny—a fated thing.'

I had a sudden searing recollection that precisely this sort of rubbish used to enchant me in Penny Triplett. And I turned away, acknowledging a shameful disposition to weep.

Outdoor productions in the Oxford summer term usually start rather late. The idea is that you get interesting effects out of a gathering dusk, and then turn on all sorts of ingenious lighting with expensive equipment hired for the occasion. Undergraduates—it has to be given to them—are extremely versatile. No dramatic society is without its complement of resourceful technicians. This was to be a factor in what was looming ahead of us. The situation was later to strike me as not unlike that in Thomas Hardy's terrifying poem, 'The Convergence of the Twain'. In our case the *Titanic* was represented by a boy called Julian Wright, who was a little prone to getting things wrong. The iceberg was constituted by the laws of electrodynamics.

The production showed itself from the start to be a thoroughly efficient affair. The text was taken at a spanking pace, and the Virgins of Damascus had been haled off to death, and Bajazeth and his consort had vigorously brained themselves, before the artificial lighting was required. Then there was a longish interval, and by the end of it darkness had fallen. At this point Julian Wright got to work. Zenocrate died, and at once the entire south side of the Great Quadrangle burst most satisfactorily into avenging flames. These faded at a turn of Mr Wright's rheostat. Minor conflagrations followed: a lady incinerated her husband and son; there was a bonfire of books carried out in a hearty Nazi manner. And now came the big moment when the Governor of Babylon was to be hoisted on the college tower and shot at. The preliminary dispositions for this pleasing spectacle were effected in a sinister near-darkness, but with many nasty noises. What was to follow was to be highly dramatic, for the tower was suddenly to be deluged with blinding light. And this happened. For a moment we were all dazzled. Then there was a yet more blinding flash, a loud report, a hideous smell of burning rubber. And by the time this last pheno-menon was appreciable the audience had, appropriately, only its nose with which to entertain itself. The entire college had been plunged into total darkness. So had a substantial part of the city of Oxford.

XIX

It was during this great darkness that *The Madonna of the Astrolabe* vanished. The first theory of the picture's disappearance turned on a hypothetical swift opportunism on the part of the thief or thieves. Professional criminals had been lurking in Oxford, awaiting their opportunity and generally 'casing' the college. Julian Wright's unfortunate error (whatever it had been) had given them their chance. They had gone swiftly to work, seized their spoil, and departed undetected in the murk.

But this theory didn't stand up for long. It was refuted—or appeared to be refuted—by the story which the night watchman had to tell. This security guard was indeed sadly confused—and very apprehensive (as apparently happens in such cases) of being suspected as an accomplice in the theft. It was more probable that he had simply been not too quick on the draw. Not that he had, of course, anything to draw in the literal sense. Weapons, whether termed offensive or defensive, were forbidden him. What he was equipped with was a powerful whistle and an electric torch. He had, according to his statement, just settled down to his spell of duty in the small common room where the Piero still stood. One of the two doors of the room had opened, and the blackout had followed an instant later. It was clear to him that he faced a crisis. What ought his first reaction to be? He obeyed orders, fumbled for his whistle, and blew it. But he had to contend with a great deal of noise from the quad, where the barbarous hordes of the Scythian Shepherd were howling for the Governor of Babylon's blood. So he went on blowing like mad. By the time he changed his mind and switched on his torch he was in an empty room and looking at a vacant easel. The Piero had gone.

If this was a true account of the sequence of events it was plain that the unfortunate Mr Wright was blameless. The blackout and the robbery had to be seen as deliberately synchronized actions, and the thieves were responsible for both. Swarms of experts, it appeared, would have to investigate the college's complicated electrical set-up before this aspect of the affair could be clarified.

The performance of *Tamburlaine* had naturally come to an abrupt close, with players and audience dispersing in a confused and indeed alarmed fashion. Torches of various sorts had been available, including the flares and smoky brands with which the rude soldiery had been disporting themselves. The headlights of parked cars and the more powerful beams from fire-engines had played their part. The Provost, with great address, had possessed himself of some loud-hailing apparatus used in the production, apologized to the audience, announced that no fresh danger was to be apprehended, and implored everybody to be calm. By the time we heard of the disappearance of the picture all the fuss was over. By midnight the audience had departed, and in college we had gone to bed—either that or were gossiping in our rooms over this untoward event.

Bedworth came in to see me at noon on the following day. He was predictably upset.

'Duncan,' he said, 'I don't like it. I don't like it a bit.'

'I'd suppose not.'

'It's going to cause a great deal of trouble.'

'No doubt.'

'I suppose you care a lot about what's happened to that damned picture?'

'Care about it?' I had to consider this. Bedworth appeared to feel that my family connection with artistic matters must be a point involved. 'Well, yes—I think I do, Cyril. I keep on telling myself that stolen works of art of great value are seldom destroyed. The thieves mayn't be aesthetically inclined, but the mere vague notion of enormous monetary worth somehow inhibits them. Even if they're cornered and find their enterprise no go they generally abandon the picture or whatever where it will be found by some fortunate dustman.'

'Yes, I suppose so. A Golden Dustman.' Bedworth, a devoted Dickensian, paused on this thought. 'Meanwhile, it's going to split the college.'

'Split the college?' I stared at Bedworth uncomprehendingly. 'What on earth do you mean?'

'I mean——' Bedworth broke off, as if shying away from something too dreadful to contemplate. 'Duncan, what are such things stolen for?'

'Ransom, almost invariably. There's a myth about mad collectors who will pay enormous sums for stolen masterpieces just for the pleasure of hiding them away in strong-rooms and cellars. That's poppycock, I believe. Ransom is almost always the idea. Insurance companies will sometimes play ball in a quiet way.'

'You know the thing isn't insured?'

'No, I don't.' This news surprised me. 'Surely the Provost wouldn't miss a trick like that? I don't know a more prudent man.'

'Insuring that Piero—particularly under the conditions in which we've been showing it—would be enormously costly. Not in terms of college finances, of course. But it can't be done. It would be totally *ultra vires*.'

'Good God, Cyril! Statutes again?'

'Yes, of course. We don't hold our pictures and so on in the interest of piety and learning. They merely conduce to our splendour, or whatever it's called. We have to be very careful when expending even moderate sums on them.'

'What utter nonsense!' Quite suddenly I was comically indignant. 'There's as much learning and piety in being able to look at——'

'Yes, I know. I know you must take that view.' Bedworth said this in a respectful tone, also comical. I was coming to have to reflect at times on what it must be like to bear a surname such as Wordsworth or Coleridge. 'But there we are, Duncan. If we lose the Piero we lose the hell of a lot of money—in fact, about the largest windfall the college has ever had. And you know perfectly well how much it's needed. Simply put, we send the Piero to Sotheby's, and clear ourselves on the tower.'

'Instead of which, we may have to shell out cash in some covert fashion for the picture's recovery?'

'I can't imagine our doing that.'

'Then we must just hope the police find the thing. Cyril, tell me what you mean about splitting the college.'

'It's writ large over the whole situation. There's already a good deal of criticism of the Provost.' Bedworth said this as if announcing Doomsday. 'There's a feeling he took too much upon himself about the confounded thing.'

'But haven't you told me that pictures and so on are something that the college has tacitly agreed to be entirely his concern? It wouldn't be fair to go back on that.'

'I agree with you absolutely. Only, in this case, there's the sheer order of money involved. It can be argued it ought to have been a Governing Body matter from the start. Nothing should have been done except by order of the Governing Body. Nothing at all. Charles is being rather hot on that.'

'Bother Charles!'

'Well, yes. But Charles is a highly conscientious man. And he can't be criticized for trying to ensure that we don't play fast and loose with our own rules. The business of putting the thing on show in that common room, for instance. The Provost has no authority in common room matters. They're entirely for the body of the fellows. The Provost enters common room only as a guest, even if he just hangs up his hat—let alone an enormously valuable picture. I don't think

267

that could be disputed. The Bye-Laws make it clear, even if the Statutes don't.'

'Cyril, what unutterable twaddle!'

'Well, yes—but people have their point of view.' Bedworth looked at me unhappily. 'I know it must all sound terribly parochial to you, Duncan. You've lived out in the world, and so on.'

'A make-believe world, Cyril. Phantoms that strut upon the stage, as Johnson has it. And here's a whack, I suppose, of vehement real life. What happens if a Provost is seriously criticized in a formal way?'

'I don't know. It hasn't happened in my time.'

'Nor will it, if you ask me. Of course that's only a guess, and I dare say I don't yet in the least understand the place. Still, hot air tends to rise and blow itself away. We just have to keep our cool.' I was conscious of a certain impertinence in thus—and with an air of superior sagacity—essaying to calm down a Senior Tutor. He knew far more about the temper of our colleagues than I did. On the other hand he had presumably dropped in on me, even if not quite consciously, in search of reassurance. To me Cyril Bedworth would always be the raw and nervous youth I had first bumped into outside Tony Mumford's rooms while terrifying young men were howling hideously in Surrey Quad. On that occasion I was by a hair's breadth less bewildered, already more at home in the college, than he was; and that far-away time was still faintly operative in our relationship. 'Do you think anything falls to be done?' I asked. 'Right now, I mean.'

'Nothing except fight off reporters and camera men. The picture has been so tremendously publicized, you know. All part of Edward's plan, of course, eventually to get the best market for it.'

'We may get that yet.' I felt that the Provost's having become 'Edward' again suggested a certain slackening of tension in Bedworth. And I wondered under what circumstances he had first nerved himself to address Edward Pococke in this familiar if prescriptive way. Between these two there must also linger the dim memory of a first encounter in untoward circumstances. Bedworth, just before making my acquaintance, had escaped being brained by a champagne bottle; the Provost hadn't been so lucky—Bedworth's brassie-shot having found its billet—but his urbanity on the traumatic occasion had been unflawed: a circumstance constituting my own first vivid impression of him, and remaining with me still. And this quality, as it happened, I was to find sufficiently illustrated, once more, that afternoon.

I lunched frugally in my rooms. After Bedworth's leaving me I had discovered that my degree of caring about the loss of the Piero was surprisingly intense. In fact I had got it mixed up with the death of Timbermill, and I found myself—a habit growing on me—muttering not particularly applicable scraps of Shakespeare. *So quick bright things come to confusion.* . . . In this frame of mind I hadn't wanted to lunch in company, and at about two o'clock I went out with the idea of a solitary walk round Long Field. There weren't many people in the Great Quadrangle, but among those there were was the Provost. He might have been described as taking the air. Indefinably, too, he had the appearance of blessing it, of honouring vacancy with a benevolent regard, certainly of being comfortably—although sensitively—at home in his own house. The van of the security firm had departed, I suppose in a modified disgrace, but its place had been taken by two cars saying 'Police' in large letters, and by a third and grander car, not similarly distinguished or disfigured, which I had an intuition about as coming from Scotland Yard. What are called intensive investigations were doubtless going on.

The Provost, despite an absent and musing manner, spotted me at once and made a sign—a sign which I had remarked as characteristic of him and as combining summons and

269

benediction in an economical gesture. I made my way to him, skirting the staging and scaffolding which nobody had yet turned up to dismantle. These objects too, although now holding unfortunate associations, he seemed willing to bless. Edward Pococke, in fact, was showing the flag. Like one of those Russian generals in *War and Peace* who murmur 'Excellent' and 'Just so' and 'Convey my congratulations to the commander' to aides dashing up with news of one or another unexpected tactical disaster, he was very adequately masking any sense of discomfiture which his part in the present posture of college affairs might have occasioned.

'My dear Duncan,' he said, 'can I possibly prevail on you to take a turn with me round Long Field?'

'Yes, indeed. It's what I was thinking of myself.' I fell into step beside the Provost. 'I hope,' I said at a venture, 'that the fuzz haven't been harassing you?'

'Not in the least.' The Provost indicated with a smile how charming it had been of me to venture upon this juvenile expression to an older man. 'And they have even ceased badgering that ill-named security guard. Some of our colleagues, however, may be described as harassing themselves. It is much to their credit, no doubt. They feel the thing keenly—as, indeed, you and I do. The Senior Tutor is perturbed.'

'Yes, he came to see me this morning. Cyril is anxious that we should all pull together. At least I think his attitude may be expressed that way.' It was easy, when talking to Edward Pococke, to fall into his own diplomatic patter. 'How lovely the tower looks against that clear sky.'

'Long may it continue so.' The Provost came to a momentary halt, politely concurring in my sense that the tower rated for at least brief contemplation. 'I recall, my dear Duncan, your father's whimsically telling me that it was to the tower that we owed your first coming among us. He took a fancy to it, and interviewed me on the spot.'

'And you talked about Dürer.'

'He made me ashamed of my small knowledge of the subject. But he was informative in the most tactful way. He was also—if I may venture the recollection—well-seen in claret.'

These and a few similar amenities took us into Long Field. The straight path down to the river was almost deserted, there no longer being troops of young oarsmen making their blithe way to servitude in their galleys. We talked about the state of the trees on either hand, some of them over-mature but fortunately not yet afflicted by Dutch elm disease. Anxiety over this threat might have been the sole cloud on the Provost's horizon. I wondered whether he was going to say anything at all about the fate of *The Madonna of the Astrolabe*. It had a better claim on our present attention than the art of Albrecht Dürer.

'It appears, Duncan, that the police—those who have appeared with so commendable a haste from London—hold elaborate dossiers on gangs of art-thieves. They assure me that such persons are being raided—if that is the term—at this moment.' The Provost had made a businesslike transition in the blandest manner. 'I hope they are on the right tack. Alternative possibilities must have occurred to you.'

'I can't say they have.'

'Might not the theft—if it is to be called that—be a more domestic matter?'

'An inside job?' This new line occasioned a certain bewilderment in me.

'For example.' The Provost, who was carrying a walking-stick, delayed to poke at an abandoned cigarette carton with disapproval. 'For example, may we not have to reckon with the sometimes disconcerting character of undergraduate humour?'

I hadn't thought of this one—and didn't know that I thought much of it now.

'It wouldn't have surprised me,' the Provost said pleasantly, 'if those going into hall for breakfast this morning had found the Piero to have taken the place of some former college grandee on the line.'

'But it hadn't.'

'That has to be admitted. It would have been a good joke in its way—although we should have had to treat it with some severity, no doubt.'

'I suppose so.' It was hard to believe that the Provost had seriously entertained this notion.

'The Blessed Virgin may still be within the curtilage of the college, all the same. Consider how little we know about many of these young men and their backgrounds. They constitute a rapidly shifting population, almost like guests in a hotel.'

'Are you suggesting, Provost, that one of our undergraduates may have taken the picture not as a joke but with the intention of actual theft?'

'Perhaps not quite clearly to one effect or the other. We are not, after all, without our share of mixed-up kids.' It was the Provost's turn to dip into demotic speech. 'It would be sad if there had to be some public exposure, even protection, of a boy who was merely in the grip of neurotic illness. If one of our junior members, for example, should be proved to have been a systematic pilferer, I should have my own way of dealing with the matter adequately. And it would certainly not include an appearance in a police court.'

'Edward, a painting by Piero della Francesca can scarcely be described as an object liable to be pilfered. And if a young man has made off with it because out of his mind, what we confront is a very grim situation indeed. He may take it down to the boiler-room and stuff it into the furnace. But I don't myself think that a demented undergraduate is a substantial probability.'

'No more do I, my dear Duncan.' The Provost allowed himself a faint surprise that he could be judged to think otherwise. 'My point is simply that any one of a number of unlikely explanations may conceivably be the true one, and that therefore we ought to treat the affair with the greatest discretion. Circumspection should be our watchword.'

I received this in silence, and we pursued our walk along the river bank. There was no reason to be surprised by the Provost's remarks. Circumspection—or plain wariness—was, after all, his habit all along the line, and nothing in the world would distress him more than any occasion of grave scandal erupting upon the college. But if I wasn't myself surprised I was at least irritated, since here was the familiar spectacle of Edward Pococke's talk being not quite faithful to what he had in his head. Just what that was, I found myself unable to fathom. Perhaps I'd have tried to do so if we hadn't, at this moment, come upon Burnside.

Our archivist was sitting on that seat, commemorating the loyal satisfaction of college servants at the coronation of Elizabeth II, on which Arnold Lempriere and I had sat just before his telling me of the momentous fact of our relationship. That had been almost a year ago, and within a fortnight the annual Gaudy would have come round again. I wondered how, in his traditional after-dinner speech on college events, the Provost would contrive to deal with the unfortunate loss we had sustained. I also wondered how Burnside felt about it.

But Burnside proved to know nothing of the matter. He had only just arrived from the British Museum, and having characteristically not sought anybody's conversation had not heard the sensational news.

'It has been removed,' the Provost told him with uncustomary abruptness when the subject turned up.

'Removed, Edward?' We were now sitting on either side of Burnside, and he glanced from one of us to the other in mild perplexity.

'The picture, I am sorry to say, has been removed, quite

273

without authority, from the common room in which it was on display.'

'Dear me! Who has removed it, and for what purpose?'

'That's what we'd like to know,' I said. 'The police are now seeking answers to both these questions. The Piero was there last night and is there no longer. And the plain English for that is theft.'

'Oh, dear me!' The simple dismay that Burnside registered was oddly mingled with discreet amusement; he hadn't failed to notice the impatience which had made me rudely call a spade a spade. 'Its whereabouts are quite unknown?'

'Totally so, my dear Christian.' The Provost, who apparently felt that he had been a little short with his honorary archivist, was all benignity again. 'We must pray to St Anthony, must we not? St Anthony of Padua, that is.' This amplification was presumably for my benefit as one born in the darkness of a Calvinist faith.

'Yes, indeed,' Burnside said. 'Whatever we are bidden to believe about the intercession of the saints, Edward, I have myself frequently found an application to St Anthony of marked psychological efficacy. I suddenly remember where I have vexatiously mislaid something. However, the Piero is another matter. For the moment, it seems, it has departed even as it came. Out of nowhere and back again. It is almost an allegory of human life.'

This view of the matter, although interesting and even edifying, made no present appeal to the Provost, and he now turned to me.

'Duncan, you are quite right. The Piero, somewhere or other, is in human hands——'

'Unless,' I said, 'St Anthony has sent it miraculously flying through the air and dumped it in Borgo San Sepolcro, like the House of the Virgin at Loreto.'

'No doubt that is one of the improbabilities not to be excluded out of hand. But if we stick to human agency,

274

somebody has possessed himself of it. And, if it isn't theft, the onus is upon that somebody to prove the fact. Yes, we are entirely at one. Only, circumspection is required, as I have said. Christian, I am sure you agree with us?'

'Oh, yes—indeed.' Burnside offered this concurring judgement absently, as if thinking of something else. 'But perhaps not quite from nowhere,' he said. 'It is premature even to be hopeful. But a promising line of investigation has undoubtedly appeared.'

'On what has happened to the thing?' The Provost hadn't quite followed. 'Where it's to be found?'

'No, no. But—what is equally interesting—where it came from.'

'That,' I said, 'would certainly be very interesting indeed. But, in the present state of the case, not exactly useful.'

'Unless,' the Provost emended, 'there is some relationship between where it came from and where it went. As there is, I believe, in the case of human life, Christian. But let us abandon speculation. Are we to understand that you have something positive to report about the provenance of the Piero?'

'Far from that. But there is one small clue—for it may be that—to which my attention has been drawn, very kindly, by Gregory Wyborn. As you know, he takes a keen interest in the college archives. But what he has pointed to, in this instance, is simply an interesting provision in our present Statutes.'

I am not sure that, at this juncture, I didn't feel an impulse, like Dr Johnson on some similar occasion, to remove my mind and think of Tom Thumb. From Bedworth I'd had the college Statutes once already that day.

'*With these as with other matters indifferent it shall be as heretofore.*' Burnside enunciated this declaratory statement with considerable pleasure; it was evident that to him the language of Statutes was entirely agreeable. 'The context makes it clear that this includes the disposition of various chattels deemed too inconsiderable to be reiterated in a detailed way.'

'And among such inconsiderable chattels,' I said, 'there might be included a major painting by Piero della Francesca?'

'Just so, Pattullo, just so. The significance of such things changes with the centuries. And I don't suppose, you know, that the Piero came to us along with Bernini's fountain. Indeed, I think it must have been a pre-Reformation acquisition.'

'And later judged to be an object of false devotion,' the Provost said, with a detectably sarcastic intonation he didn't often use. 'Really, Christian, this seems a tenuous clue—if clue it can be called.'

'There, alas, I agree with you. Still, it is worth following up. Only, it may take some time. Many of our minor documents, as you know, are still sadly uncalendared. I do my best, but progress is necessarily slow.'

'My dear fellow, your labours are as of Hercules, and most deeply appreciated.' The Provost came out very promptly with this, and as he did so got to his feet. 'And now I have one of those detestable teatime committees. Shall we go back? A longer walk and talk would have been delightful on so pleasant an afternoon.'

We strolled back to college, discussing other matters. I felt that Edward Pococke had admirably masked a certain impatience with the mole-like enthusiasms of our indefatigable archivist.

XX

The seventh and penultimate week of full term had arrived with no news of the missing picture. The police cars had followed the security van into retirement and with the same implication of dubious efficacy in coping with crime. But as the police had not been told of the Piero's existence until after it had vanished, and thus bore no responsibility at all should it be judged to have been inadequately guarded, they were not disposed to apologize for themselves. The Provost professed to be on excellent terms with the Chief Constable and other of their top brass. Several 'leads', it appeared, were still being followed up, and at any time something might 'surface' in a useful manner. It was thought that the Provost or some other college authority might soon receive demands for ransom money. Various contingency plans were drawn up to cope with this according to whatever channel of communication the thieves chose to adopt.

The behaviour of my colleagues during this stage of the affair on the whole vindicated my own sense of the matter as I had expressed it to Bedworth. At first there was a good deal of talk about the enormity of carelessly letting something like half a million pounds (far from an exaggerated figure) depart down the drain, and there may even have been among some a sense that heads ought to roll. Yet a certain unreality attended the whole brief history of the Madonna in our midst. It wasn't our sort of thing; we could associate it with none of our customary preoccupations; we disliked both the amusement and the commiseration of our friends in other colleges— as also the impertinent intrusions of journalists and similar impossible persons. Moderate regret and underlying unconcern established itself as our public stance, and when we spoke of the financial aspect of the theft it was with an air of decently dissimulating the fact that it didn't mean much to us. Quine (who was secretly appalled) was reported as having taken this line when dining in New College—throwing up his hands in a theatrical despair and asserting so vehemently that we should all be finding ourselves on the bread-line that everybody gained the impression that we had never as a society been so disgustingly affluent throughout the many centuries of our corporate existence. Quine was much commended among us on the strength of this primitive guile. We felt it would have done credit to Arnold Lempriere himself in Washington DC. It almost looked as if, when Michaelmas Term came round, the whole episode would be as forgotten as a last year's detective story.

Lempriere on the few occasions he spoke about the thing professed to believe that the picture had been an ingenious fake anyway, and that if cleaned it would reveal itself as having been executed on top of a representation of Queen Victoria presenting a Bible to a black man as the True Secret of England's Greatness. I found this witticism hard to take— a masterpiece by one of the world's supreme painters being no fit subject for escapes of donnish fun. When I expressed this opinion to Lempriere rather late one night he was delighted with me: a response which was a tribute to his sense of our mysterious family relationship. And then one morning I ran into him under the tower. I had never seen him look so grave, and supposed that he must have fancied himself to hear those fatal sighs and groans from the im- perilled structure above our heads.

'Dunkie,' he said abruptly, 'there's a very serious situation in college—very serious indeed. Say nothing to anybody, but come to luncheon in my rooms tomorrow.'

'I have an engagement, I'm afraid.'

'Cancel it. One o'clock.'

'Can't you tell me now what the trouble is?'

'Very well—since it will certainly persuade you to turn up.' Lempriere looked about him cautiously, and his hand went up to the side of his mouth. 'Two of our young men have quarrelled—bitterly, it seems. There's even talk of their fighting a duel.'

'Arnold, what nonsense!' I was distressed by this exhibition of my kinsman's advancing senility.

'Nothing of the kind. It does happen, you know, from time to time. On Port Meadow. I was once a second in such an affair myself.'

'Then it must have been when Queen Victoria was still handing out Bibles to blacks.'

'Don't be a fool.' My joke hadn't been a success. 'But it oughtn't to happen between boys in the same college. That's bad—very bad indeed.' It was now clear that Lempriere felt the monstrousness of this supposed situation keenly. 'Brothers, too. It must be stopped.'

'Certainly it must. But——'

'Twins, at that.'

'Twins?' I felt a real chill. 'In heaven's name what are you talking about?'

'Two of our men called Mark and Matthew Sheldrake. Nice lads, they tell me.'

'And just what have they quarrelled about?' This was something I didn't need to ask. I knew.

'About going with a woman.' Lempriere named this not unusual activity as if it represented an ultimate in human depravity. I was reminded of my boyhood's friend Colonel Morrison, whom I have recorded as having, in morbidly anxious moments, employed the identical words in a warning manner.

'What are you going to do about it?' I asked. 'Tell them they mustn't?'

'Mustn't what?'

'Go with women.'

'That might be misconstrued.' Lempriere managed a throaty chuckle, although it was evident that he wasn't feeling jocular. 'They mustn't quarrel over a bit of skirt. My father used to say that was a rule. He was in a damned good regiment, you know.'

'I'm sure he was.' This military background of Lempriere's was news to me. 'And you're going to prevent it, Arnold?'

'Of course I am.'

'But just how?' A quick fire of questions was for the moment my only means of going on talking—which was what I had to do while trying to collect myself in face of this fresh complication in my revived life with Penny.

'I've told you. I've asked them to lunch with me.'

'You haven't told me that, as a matter of fact. And do you know the Sheldrakes?'

'Never set eyes on them.' Lempriere chuckled again, and with complete innocence. 'Or barely.'

I nearly said (prompted, I suppose, by this last word), 'They must have been a marvellous sight in a school swimming-pool.' But this facetious grossness was spared me. Instead, I asked another rational question.

'But you feel it's all right to summon them?'

'To invite them, you mean. Of course.'

I knew that this was an article of faith with Lempriere. As the most senior of senior members now in college, he considered such invitations out of the blue as a command, and had thus bewildered and alarmed innumerable young men in his time. He liked young men. He understood them very well through intuitive processes I envied him; and as often as not, I didn't doubt, he was as useful to them as he was terrifying. If he was at times a little too curious about their privacies, it was reported that he would always shut up if they told him to. But none of this was relevant to the present formidable situation.

'And you're inviting me too?' I asked. 'Just why?'

'Dunkie, you know very well just why.'

'Who told you?'

'Our kinswoman in common, Anthea Gender. She had it from a woman called Fire-escape, or some such.'

'Mrs Firebrace. Penny's staying with her. Making her a base for operations, so to speak. And what good am I going to be? Serve as an awful warning?'

'You're an interested party.'

'I'm nothing of the kind. I'd only serve enormously to embarrass these young men. Enormously embarrass them yet further.'

'That may be good for them.'

'I've no ambitions as a do-gooder, Arnold. None at all.'

'Not true, Dunkie. You'd do a lot to get these decent boys away from the lady. So will you come?'

'Yes, I'll come.'

'As I said, one o'clock.'

And Arnold Lempriere walked away. Or tottered away. He was now never without his stick, even within the walls of the college. He did, I felt, have the power of hanging on, and was determined that, if he could help it, no unforgivable thing should happen among us. I didn't for a moment believe in the threatened duel on Port Meadow. That was a typical piece of undergraduate embroidery upon an observed situation. But it was true that the situation itself appalled me. The essence of Penny's present ploy was now clear, and it shocked me more than the simple if depraved sexualities I had at times been compulsively visualizing. These had been summed up in a word I had heard from Nick Junkin. Tripling. Penny Triplett tripling. But the cardinal point about Penny was that she was more malicious (or mischievous, if one was to be over-charitable) than lecherous. The Frediano episode instanced this. What had taken place on the sun-deck of the *Ithaca* had been much more for the fun of humiliating Tindale than of fornicating with a personable fisher-lad. That was what I had been unable to think of forgiving and forgetting. Cats mustn't be judged deliberately cruel to mice. But then cats aren't human beings. And there were kinds of cruelty which Penny's imagination found irresistible.

My own imagination didn't stretch to the Sheldrakes in their present situation. The fact of their having quarrelled I had to admit; it had peeped out through much theatrical nonsense when Cosroe confronted Mycetes. But could it conceivably amount to anything justifying an old gentleman's shoving in an oar—and an unknown old gentleman at that? I didn't know. I ought to know about brothers, since I had a brother of my own. I had been jealous of Ninian's precocious sexual successes, but we had never in any sense been rivals. I had no more tried to steal his mistresses (if they were to be called that) than he had dreamed of casting an eye on Janet. It wasn't to be doubted that in endless families brothers quarrelled bitterly over girls. But surely—although this was perhaps an irrational thought—twins were a special case? I knew nothing about twins, about the psychology of twins. I had a dim impression that studies of animal behaviour showed that among twins there was always a dominant partner. Did Mark dominate Matthew, or Matthew Mark? If so, it was certainly something that didn't appear in the comportment of the brothers.

Or did it? I realized that I was judging only on the strength of a most superficial view. In Matthew's case it was literally a view, since I'd never so much as spoken to him. And with Mark I'd had no more than those casual chats, standing in a doorway. My sense that they were 'nice' lads, agreeably reserved, sexually virginal and fastidious in disposition if not in common schoolboy history: my sense of this—which I called instinctive—was really no more than a function of their extreme good-looks. *All that fair is, is by nature good.* Once again it was no more than that. If Matthew had a squint, and Mark a heavy and unsightly jowl, it would never occur to me that I had an insight into the 'niceness' of their underlying feelings. I told myself—on a solitary walk to Godstow that afternoon—that the fact of these boys' having got tangled with my ex-wife didn't make them any business of mine, and that equally they were no business of Lempriere's. But this way of thinking didn't work. Lempriere mightn't be in the picture, but I was. My mind went back to the moment when I had discovered Penny to be in communication with Mark Sheldrake. Just because it had been an awkward moment, I had, with a fatuous conventionality, told Mark that he would find my former wife charming and entertaining. I ought to have told him nothing of the kind, and then cultivated his acquaintance so as to be in a position to say something quite different at need. And this must be what Lempriere was designing I should do now. I judged it unlikely that he hadn't given careful thought to his luncheon party.

'I'm Matthew Sheldrake.'

Standing in Lempriere's doorway, Matthew Sheldrake made this announcement with a faint implication that it ought to occasion surprise, produce explanations. When I had asked Ivo to lunch with me (with the fond thought of chatting him up or dressing him down) he had appeared in my doorway and said 'I'm Ivo Mumford' more or less in the same fashion. But not quite. Ivo had simply been defiant in a wary way. Matthew was conveying a sense that here was a situation in need of a little elucidating. *All that fair is, is by nature thick.* This cynical perversion of the Platonic view was another dubious truth. Matthew Sheldrake wasn't without brains, and this presumably went too for his brother. Junkin was probably right about them.

'You must take after your mother,' Lempriere said. 'How do you do?'

For a moment I found myself supposing Lempriere to have asserted that Matthew's charms were of an effeminate order;

283

then I realized that he was simply saying he had known Matthew's father. Lempriere hadn't mentioned anything of the kind to me. But it was quite probable that the senior Sheldrake had been his pupil, and that the Sheldrake family sent their sons to the college as a matter of course.

Matthew said 'How do you do, sir?' and for a moment nothing more. There was no reason to suppose that he cared for comment on his personal appearance as an opening conversational gambit on the part of a more or less unknown old man. But chiefly he was engaged in glancing at me and taking me in. As he did so he flushed faintly—precisely as his brother had done when first realizing that here was Penny's former husband.

'I expect you've met Mr Pattullo,' Lempriere said casually. 'He's a kind of freshman too in his way, although they tell me he was around the place long ago.'

'How do you do, sir?'

Matthew said this instantly, and waited alertly to be shaken hands with. We achieved this formality.

'I've got to know your brother,' I said, 'since he came over to Surrey Four.'

'I'm high up in Howard. There's a perfectly splendid view.'

'Of open country, and not of the dreaming spires? That's most satisfactory.' I said this while wondering if it was deliberately that Matthew hadn't responded directly to my mention of Mark. I also wondered when Mark was going to arrive, and why the brothers hadn't turned up together. To this second question I got an answer at once.

'Talking of your brother,' Lempriere said with an amiable and chatty air not habitual with him, 'I've asked him too—as you probably know.'

'I didn't know. How nice of you.'

This didn't sound promising. Lempriere busied himself unconcernedly with sherry, and then found it necessary to confer with his servant at some length. I realized that I was expected at once to take a full part in the entertainment.

'The end of *Tamburlaine* was a bit of a shambles, wasn't it?' I said to Matthew. 'But it was great fun while it lasted. Had you done much acting before?'

'None at all. But Mark and I were just told we must have a go at it.'

Here at least was Mark's name. I supposed that the pressure or compulsion had come from Junkin and other senior persons—and then I suddenly thought that perhaps it had come from Penny, who had been in Oxford long enough for that. As this speculation came to me I think something mildly telepathic happened. Matthew and I hadn't been exactly easy, and now I could feel his discomfort grow. Penny was in both our heads. I had to consider how to cope with this. The Sheldrakes were very young, absurdly young, and not in the remotest degree hardened amorists. If they had been in bed with Penny (severally, as I now felt with some relief it would have had to be) they would judge it dreadful and demeaning to have to traffic socially with her former husband even although he belonged to an era when they were still at their private school. If I was to establish any confidence with them I had a long way to go.

Mark arrived. I believe he would have said 'I'm Mark Sheldrake' if it hadn't been on his brother that his eye fell first. For a moment he stiffened and simply stood. There could be no doubt that the brothers were literally not on speaking terms. Lempriere's temerity in inviting each to luncheon without telling the other appeared for a second or two in an almost lurid light. But that was absurd. A short period of masked social embarrassment was the worst we could be in for, and I had some faith that my posited 'correctness' in the Sheldrakes would stand the test. It was even just conceivable that the enterprise might pay off.

But no approach to frankness was remotely possible yet. I couldn't say, 'Look, I'm not entitled to mind, and I very much don't mind, if you've both been making love to Penny—but it does seem to have got you into a silly sort of fix.' As for Lempriere, I was now sure that he wasn't going to acknowledge by a flicker any consciousness that he and I weren't in the company of other than two devoted siblings. And here he had his known habits on his side. Everybody in college was aware that he entertained in this way a good deal, troubling himself very little as to whether he had ever set eyes on his guests before or not.

And the luncheon did at first run on these lines. Lempriere talked a good deal; he made me talk; he made the boys talk too. I found without surprise that he possessed an unerring sense of how to recommend himself to young men. He was never other than the much older man, and never other than the fellow-collegian either. He was authoritative rather than deferential, but anything either youth ventured was received with consideration and brisk requests for amplification on one point or another. He told anecdotes of eminent people without a hint of name-dropping and of simple people on his Northumberland estate without condescension. He moved from one topic to another—and would then go back and show that he remembered precisely what Matthew or Mark had said ten minutes before. They weren't boys who needed to be told that this is how gentlemen talk, but I think they were drawn to remember how it is civilized to behave at somebody's table. Sitting facing each other at this one, they had begun by ignoring each other and speaking directly only to Lempriere or myself. Later they appeared to decide simultaneously that this wouldn't do; they talked a little to one another, but with the particular sort of politeness one accords to a stranger. This was sufficiently absurd, but I think Lempriere felt he was making progress. He redoubled his efforts—although not obtrusively—glancing rapidly now at Mark and now at Matthew in an effort to increase their interplay.

I think it must have been this swift looking from one youth to the other that, towards the end of the meal, almost proved Lempriere's undoing. He became oddly confused, showed signs of losing his grip on the situation. And the reason was plain to me. Matthew and Mark Sheldrake were inexperienced lads, who had been drawn into a silly and rather shameful quarrel for the amusement of a seductive and malicious middle-aged woman. As such, they were to be brought to their senses and persuaded that there are certain ways in which one just doesn't behave—or not when one has the good fortune to belong to the college one does. This was all perfectly clear to Lempriere, and he knew exactly what to do. But Mark and Matthew were also demigods (it is the term for which one has to settle)—and here they were, as like as two peas (or roses on a branch), one on Lempriere's right and one on his left. And this—for it was very simple—was becoming too much for him. If one can imagine a Gustave Aschenbach who has encountered in Venice not only Tadzio but a twin brother of Tadzio's as well, one is imagining something like the experience now overtaking my elderly colleague. No donkey between carrots—to put the thing more coarsely— was ever in greater plight.

He recovered himself—as it had been certain he would do. What, if anything, Mark and Matthew had been aware of, I don't know. I imagined them as likely at once to be uncomfortably conscious of any sort of unacceptable admiration. But this may not have been so now. Lempriere, for one thing, was as incapable as the Sphinx (or Aschenbach, one imagines) of a loose or lascivious glance. And the twins may have been so accustomed to stirring adoration whether dim or lively that they had ceased to register the phenomenon long ago unless it took on some outrageous form. Moreover they were probably preoccupied in wondering whether this was after all an innocent social occasion, promoted in ignorance of their being at odds with one another, or whether—polite chat being over—they were due for admonishment on the score of an unbecoming bearing to one another upon public occasions. Despite the extreme amenity of Lempriere's manner—or partly, even, because of it—they might judge it really conceivable that something as archaic as that was in the wind. In which case they'd have to work out what was the adequate response to so arbitrary an intrusion into their personal affairs.

I wasn't, however, to be afforded this interesting spectacle. The luncheon came to an end; coffee had been drunk; the moment had arrived when the Sheldrakes might decently rise, express their thanks and depart unscathed. But Lempriere nipped in ahead of them, getting to his feet himself.

'I'm sorry I can't join in the walk,' he said. 'A touch of gout, as a matter of fact. But Mr Pattullo will do a Long Field with you.'

'Mr Pattullo' was perhaps a shade formal; the rest of this speech confidently conveyed the assumption that a walk round Long Field on these occasions was a law as immutable as Medes or Persians ever enacted. In no time I was out in the quad with the two young men.

They could still have rebelled, murmuring to me (as less terrifying than Lempriere) information on inescapable early-afternoon engagements. I could sense them communicating on this as by bush telegraph—which did at least represent the re-establishment of some process normal between them. They apparently decided that the walk had to be. We set out.

I had a good deal to think of myself. Lempriere had lobbed the ball into my court without notice, and no doubt retired for some customary nap. I was expected (as the ultimately responsible party—for hadn't the lady in the case been my wife?) to sort the twins out. It was a challenge not absolutely to be declined.

We crossed the Great Quadrangle in silence, a Sheldrake on either side of me. It was a configuration which promised to maintain itself round the very large stretch of semi-rural Oxford which calls itself, for some reason, a field. Trusting to the silence as being for a short space judged companionable, I devoted myself to hearing my own voice on my inward ear.

This is a bit of a plot, you know. That can't be denied, although I could plead I haven't been enlisted very willingly. But here goes, my dear Matthew and Mark. If I may so address you? Good. You've got yourselves into a jam—that's the nub of the matter—and I'm not unfairly to be credited with a certain inside knowledge—as a matter of anterior experience of my own, shall we say?—of just how it has come about. . . .

This was an impossible speech; it sounded like some bogus-colloquial performance out of Henry James. I was reminded of those never—actually—uttered outbursts which, although different in tone, Ninian and I had discovered ourselves as sometimes meditating the delivery of in a family circle. Better continued silence than anything so impertinent. That, or more small-talk of our lunchtime order. As we went through Rattenbury gate I made some remarks on the architecture of the building. We continued for a little with that sort of thing. Once or twice I detected Mark and Matthew as glancing one at another. It was something they were almost able to do above my head. They were, in a fashion, coming together in face of the interference they couldn't feel as other than impending. Without my uttering the fact, that is to say, they had concluded that there was indeed a bit of a plot. But if I was thus an adversary I felt that this didn't in itself sum up quite all that was between us, common to all three of us. Penny was that too. Quite what, if anything, this portended, I didn't know. But I decided that during the rest of our walk down to the river a continued reflective silence should for the most part obtain. The twins seemed to be of the same mind. So it was with only a few desultory exchanges that we reached a turn on the path and continued along the river bank.

'Lempriere's seat's in the sun,' I said. 'We might sit down on it.'

'Mr Lempriere's seat?' Matthew asked politely. 'Did he present it to us?'

'No, the inscription tells you who did that. I think it's the inscription that makes him fond of the seat.'

'The Oxford College Servants' Rowing Club,' Mark read aloud. 'It sounds as if they have one club between them. Do you know who they row against, sir?'

'Cambridge college servants, I believe. Perhaps House of Commons ones as well. I don't really know.'

'It has an old-world ring,' Mark said.

'Ring out the old, ring in the new would be in order, to my mind,' Matthew said. 'It's a social anachronism.'

I made no comment on this rather unexpected egalitarian statement. We sat down. Surprisingly, Mark and Matthew were now both on my right hand.

Look—Matthew, Mark—there's something I feel I ought to say—or just tell you. You can stop me if you think it's cheek. Call it a short narrative of a cruise, quite a long time ago, down the coast of Calabria. . . .

But that wouldn't do either—although not quite so bad.

'The river turns a bit dull after Eights,' I said. 'Nothing but those shocking motor cruisers.'

Both boys were now looking at me, and I couldn't be certain it wasn't gratefully. Mark stretched himself lazily as he sat; Matthew instantly did the same. I decided it would be over-dramatic to get up and leave them to it. We sat sunning ourselves for a time, and then walked back towards college.

'Do you know Italy?' I asked—of either twin indifferently.

'Not very well, I'm afraid.'

Matthew and Mark had produced the same words simultaneously.

'I went there for the first time in my first long vac. It was with a nice Australian called Fish. We'd bought a copy of *Lady Chatterley's Lover*, which wasn't easy to come by in England at that time. Fish used to read it aloud to me at night. He thought it was very funny. I remember his coming to a bit where Mellors goes over the top to Connie about things that have happened to him in bed. Connie says, "You do seem to have had awful experiences of women." I was quite upset, and made Fish chuck the book into his suitcase. It's a moment that sticks comically in my head. We were both young and innocent and so on, but had got rather involved with things that summer term. Fish is back in Australia now, growing millions of sheep. I can't say I think *Lady Chatterley* is Lawrence at his best.'

'Of course not,' Mark said. 'It's *The Rainbow* that's that.'

'No,' Matthew said. 'It's *Sons and Lovers*.'

This seemed a satisfactory disagreement. We parted in the Great Quadrangle, after I had made a suitably indefinite suggestion that the young men should drop in for a drink some time. They walked away together, divagated on their several paths, simultaneously halted, turned, and exchanged some casual remarks while for a few paces moving backwards. It was an almost precise re-enactment of the occasion on which I had first glimpsed them together. That evening they were sitting side by side in hall.

XXI

Dᴇᴀʀ Mʀ Pᴀᴛᴛᴜʟʟᴏ,

It was very nice seeing you in college again, and I greatly appreciated being shown Piero della Francesca's *Madonna of the Astrolabe*. I never thought I'd see it again so soon—and in the East End of London! But here it is, safely in the little crypt in St Ambrose's that is used as the chapel for our Mission. (At least I hope 'safely' is right. It's a little worrying, really.) I haven't seen Dr Wyborn, who of course must have brought it to us, but I want to tell him how much I, at least, appreciate and reverence it, and how kind I think it is of the college to let it come here, where beauty is so sorely needed.

I have left the Discount House, and written the letter we were talking about, and now I am doing the sort of Latin that is needed for reading Law.

Yours sincerely,
PETER
(P. L. Lusby)

P.S. I hope I am acting properly in writing this to you.

P.L.L.

My first thought on reading this letter—astonishment apart—was that Peter had done well in a tricky situation. What he had written was perfectly proper if all was fair and above board, and at the same time his postscript showed that this was something he was not so guileless as to feel assured of. I read the letter twice, gulped my breakfast coffee, and went straight over to the Lodging. The Provost received so early a call without surprise, and read the astounding communication with every appearance of calm.

'It goes to show,' he then said grimly, 'the prudence of

those eighteenth-century divines who recommended being religious without enthusiasm.'

'I suppose so, Provost. It also shows that you were right in supposing that the picture's disappearance might be a domestic matter. But we're not confronted with a mad undergraduate.'

'We're confronted with a mad fellow, which is a great deal worse. Just how do you imagine he got away with it?'

'I've been thinking about that as I crossed the quad. He had the habit of taking a look at the Piero several times a day. Presumably he was opening that common room door to do so in the very instant of the blackout. So—just on impulse—he picked up the picture and made off with it.'

'It must have been precisely that, Duncan. Moreover, poor Wyborn's theology has its primitive side. He would be capable of judging that sudden electrical failure to be a special act of Providence, pointing him to the course he immediately took. But why, in heaven's name, this particular church as the recipient of the divine bounty? St Ambrose's! I never heard of it.'

'I think it's in Bethnal Green—which, as you see, is Lusby's address. And the Mission centred there is probably something that Wyborn has much at heart.'

'Anything of the kind is greatly to his credit, no doubt. But this is a crisis, Duncan, and immediate action is required. I shall ring up the Commissioner of Metropolitan Police, and ask that a discreet and unobtrusive guard be at once mounted over the picture. If professional thieves got wind of this insane exposure of a priceless thing, it's safety would not be worth a moment's purchase. And I shall take the first train to town and retrieve the painting myself. With good fortune, the whole thing can be hushed up. It must be hushed up! And poor Wyborn must be placed in the hands of his doctors at once. Perhaps we can get him into the Warneford straight away. They have great experience there with demented dons, one must suppose.'

293

'But, Provost, Wyborn mayn't be in the least mad.'

'Not mad!'

'Not in any valid clinical sense. It might be represented that he is doing no more than going out and preaching to the poor and illiterate. Taking the Gospel story to them. That's what that sort of picture was originally painted for.'

'My dear Duncan, the Piero is simply not his property to do anything of the kind with. It belongs to the college. And this is no time for idle debate.'

I accepted this merited rebuke in good part, although Peter's 'where beauty is so sorely needed' was quite genuinely in my head.

'Are you sure,' I asked, 'that the vicar—or whoever he is—of St Ambrose's will let you walk away with it?'

'It is incomprehensible that he has not already communicated with me. We can only suppose that he is totally unaware of what this picture is—as, of course, everybody else will be in a humble neighbourhood of that sort. Except Lusby, indeed—and thank God for the boy! But, no doubt, the susceptibilities of this ignorant priest ought to be considered. Some quiet approach is desirable. Something in the nature of a deputation, shall we say? I can pick up the Bishop of London on my way. He is an old friend.'

I almost said 'Or his boss the Archbishop from across the river'—this because the oddity of the situation had a little unsettled me. But I was preserved from frivolity by the ringing of the Provost's telephone bell.

'Yes, by all means,' the Provost said into the instrument. 'Now?' This came with an inflexion of civilly muted surprise. 'Certainly, certainly. I have Duncan Pattullo here. We happen to have been talking about it. Most interesting. Pray do.' The Provost put down the receiver. 'Burnside,' he said. 'Our admirable archivist once more. Oddly enough, he is eager to communicate the discovery of something important about the Piero.'

'It can hardly be anything particularly opportune.'

'I fear it may be *à propos de bottes*.' The Provost smiled a little wearily. 'You know, Duncan, I am far from eager to turn this exquisite thing into money. But it has to be done. I see no other ready way out of our present difficulties. What can have possessed Wyborn? His suggestion that the Piero should have a permanent home in the college chapel was perfectly proper, eminently proper. But for various expediencies, that is to say.'

'Yes. But perhaps if Wyborn were promised that the *Madonna* would be hung in the college chapel and remain there for keeps, he would be willing to bring it back.'

'There can be no question of his being coaxed into willingness, or dictating to the Governing Body. We shall fetch the picture back. And that will be an end of it.'

'I doubt it, Edward. There would almost certainly be a scandal. If there were some quiet accommodation, on the other hand, we could get away with the story that the Piero had been briefly loaned somewhere on some reasonable grounds.'

The Provost stared at me rather as if he had suddenly been confronted with a talking horse. My politic suggestion must have been out of character as he conceived me.

'But in that event,' he said, 'we should be landed with Wyborn, a dangerous and irresponsible person, still permanently in our midst.'

'Shan't we be that in any case, even if you are successful in simply carrying off the picture? The position would then be that he had done something very high-handed and eccentric— but somehow connected with his notions of promoting the spiritual welfare of the inhabitants of Bethnal Green. I'm quite ignorant, of course, but I rather doubt whether there would be enough in that to oblige him to vacate his fellowship. The Statutes'—I paused on this impressive word—'are

295

quite clear that a fellow can't be turned out except on very
serious grounds indeed.'

'That is true.' The Provost frowned. 'Do you think,
Duncan, that James Gender is likely to be in college by now?'

'Almost certainly. He makes an early start to the day,
getting through his chores as Dean.'

'Then I think we should invite him to join us.' The Provost
moved back to his telephone. 'It may be unwise to take any
step without legal advice. Do, pray, for a moment excuse me.'
And the Provost made his call.

Gender and Burnside arrived together. Gender, feeling
that he had been summoned on formal business, had put on
a gown. This made me feel naked at once—and even
prompted, like Adam in ancient pictures of the Paradise
Garden, to place an occluding hand over my privities, the
fig-leaf expedient not yet having come along. 'You know our
ways,' the Provost had said to me reassuringly when there
had been the first question of my returning to the college.
But I was tardily picking up some of them still. Burnside,
although an anxiously correct man, hadn't thought of a gown
either. But he seemed not discomposed, perhaps because he
was too excited to reflect on the matter.

'My dear Jimmy, let me begin by hastening to congratulate
you,' the Provost said. 'We are all delighted.'

I hastened to look delighted myself, although without a
clue as to what this was about. It immediately transpired,
however, that Gender had been appointed to a readership,
and was thus to be in the same faintly anomalous position as
myself. He was to be Reader in the Conflict of Laws. It
sounded a harassing assignment, potentially full of *Sturm und
Drang*. But, if this were so, Gender was taking it well. He
produced some adequate murmur in his diffident fashion, not
omitting to say that he would have to consult my ripe
experience of the mysteries of reading. And then Burnside

took charge of the proceedings. He could contain himself no longer.

'A most delightful thing!' he said. 'The mystery of the Piero is solved. A line of inquiry to which Wyborn kindly prompted me has borne abundant fruit. The vital document is with me now.' He paused to fumble in a pocket, and I suppose that Edward Pococke and I stared at one another with a wild surmise. 'It was among the Allsop Papers. The Allsop Papers are almost virgin territory to me, I am ashamed to say. But Wyborn has been glancing through them.'

The Provost was not slower than myself to sense something ominous in this communication. But he remained unperturbed.

'Ah, Wyborn!' he said. 'Wyborn is in our present thoughts, as it happens. But tell us about this, Christian, pray.'

'The Piero, which is accurately described'—Burnside had produced his document—'even although the painter is unnamed, came to us with some other things now obviously lost under the will of Anthony Woodeville. And that is quite as far back as we have been imagining.'

'Certainly it is,' the Provost said.

'Or not exactly to *us*—if by "us" we mean the college. The chattels enumerated—all religious in character, it is apparent—are to be held in trust by the *Praelector Theologiae*— may I quote?—"being that fellow of the said college in whose charge the right devotions of the young scholars do chiefly lie, by him and his successors to be disposed as they judge shall best conduce to piety, whether within or without the said body collegiate". There is rather more, but that is the crux of the matter.'

'It is, indeed.' For the first time in my experience of him, Edward Pococke was visibly agitated. For a moment he sank back in his chair, and passed a hand over his brow.

'Is there any doubt,' he asked in a choked voice, 'who the *Praelector Theologiae* is?'

'Oh, none whatever.' Burnside was entirely happy about this. 'For some centuries we have been calling him our Pastoral Fellow, but the continuity of the office cannot be in doubt. Our present Statutes require that the Governing Body elect into the Pastoral Fellowship a Clerk in Holy Orders eminently well qualified to undertake the pastoral care of our undergraduates. Wyborn—it is a curious and most pleasing circumstance, is it not?—is undoubtedly——'

'Good God!' The Provost, bracing himself, had got to his feet and was pacing the room. 'Jimmy, Christian—you had better hear at once an extremely shocking piece of news about the Piero which has just come to us. Duncan has had a letter from a young man—obviously a thoroughly sensible and responsible young man—who will be coming into residence next term. His name is Peter Lusby. He is that dead boy's brother.'

'Peter Lusby?' Gender repeated softly. 'Whatever——?'

'Perhaps Duncan will permit you both to read the letter, as he has permitted me. And we can then consider what is to be done about it.'

Peter's letter was read in silence, first by Burnside and then by Gender.

'Jimmy,' the Provost then said, 'suppose I go directly up to town, make my way to this obscure parish church, and simply possess myself of the *Madonna del Astrolabio*. Shall I be justified and protected in so doing—legally, I mean—by the fact of my office?'

'I am afraid, Provost, that the answer is definitely not. In fact, and to put the thing brutally, I think it very possible that you might be chargeable with theft.'

'You tell me that this absurd and obsolete document——'

'It would appear very doubtful that it is either of these things. It's certainly precise. I'd say that Anthony Woodeville employed rather a good man of law.'

'Very well. Suppose that Wyborn dies, or resigns his

fellowship, or has to vacate it on the score of total and permanent incapacity. Would the control of this enormously valuable painting quite ludicrously pass to any successor we might elect?'

'Provost, I can't possibly hazard a guess there. We'd have to take counsels' opinion on the matter. And they'd love it. If the issue came to litigation—which heaven forbid!—it would make a case in a thousand.'

'No doubt, Jimmy.' Gender's professional enthusiasm had not been well received. 'I only remind you of how deeply grateful I should be for any guidance in the affair.'

'I can certainly mention a possibility. Were a new Pastoral Fellow to be elected, it might conceivably be held valid in law that he should abnegate this specific ancient trust when taking his oath in the college chapel. It might be held that it then passed to the Governing Body. Only he would then be depriving a successor of his own of a privilege he would otherwise enjoy. So it would be dodgy—decidedly dodgy. Of course there's the college Visitor. He's the arbitrator to whom one is expected to take domestic disputes. And this *is* a domestic dispute—or so it may be maintained. But I don't know that I regard that course as promising.'

'It certainly is not,' the Provost said grimly. 'The Visitorship of this college lies you perfectly well know where. And the bishop in question is, I am sorry to say, of a rabidly evangelical cast of mind. He might highly approve of this extravagant nonsense on Wyborn's part.'

There was a long silence. Burnside appeared not yet to have grasped why it was not 'a most pleasing circumstance' that he had brought to our notice. The situation bewildered him. I imagine that his mind was on escaping to the tranquillity of the British Museum as soon as possible. He had once spoken to me of the 'rough and tumble' of college life. Here, it was to be supposed, it was.

'Somebody must talk to Wyborn,' I said. 'He'll be around.

He isn't going to bolt when he discovers we know where the picture is.'

'You mean he'll brazen it out?' The Provost again caressed what was presumably his aching brow. 'But no; that one must not say. One must acknowledge that he believes in the rightness of what he has done. The recovery of the Piero is paramount, and its present possessor is insane. I hold by that. But let us not forget that he is a man acting according to his lights, wandering though they be.'

This was, perhaps, on the heroic side. It didn't make me think the less of our Provost, all the same.

XXII

WHAT OXFORD CALLS Trinity Term Cambridge calls
Easter Term—officially, that is to say. Colloquially one hears
of the 'Summer Term' in both places, perhaps as a consequence of people recalling the nomenclature of their schooldays. At neither university is it a summer affair in the
substantial sense. 'Full Term' may end only a week or two
short of the solstice, but in England it is at midsummer that
summer is getting under way. The two universities (as Uncle
Rory called them) 'go down' much earlier than schools 'break
up'. And as there is something autumnal about the feel of any
going down, Oxford and Cambridge—or at least undergraduate Oxford and Cambridge—thus in a sense miss out on
summer altogether. For nearly a third of our number the
sere, the yellow leaf has already declared itself; the last
tutorial has happened—or, like a trumpet, faded on the air;
means to an honest living must be found. 'Going-down'
parties hint future nostalgic occasions. The trees of Long
Field, although in full foliage, are avenues to be traversed as
if they were those bare ruin'd choirs where late the sweet
birds sang.

Term, then, was over, and the college Gaudy with it. Plot,
while feigning to be extremely busy in preparing for those
profane 'conferences' which would presently inundate the
college in its transformed character as a hotel, was in fact
leading a relaxed life on the staircase of Surrey Four. And I
was doing this too.

Although I still didn't feel like a don, I looked back on my
first year in the role with tolerable satisfaction. I had made
new friends. I had held down the job, and now didn't believe
Buntingford's assertion that the first ten years were the worst.
(Perhaps the last year of all would be that.) I had seen Junkin

off to the Middle East, to which he was journeying in the faith that the sheikdoms would in no time be ripe for extended tours by undergraduate dramatic societies. Janet had written me a long letter from Princeton. It was much more entertaining than those picture-postcards upon which she had once recorded the reading of a new novel by Joyce Cary and the like. It had finished with the words 'Our love', and I was willing to believe that this was how Ranald McKechnie felt towards me. There wasn't a flaw in the end-of-term picture—or, if there were, it concerned only an actual picture: the *Madonna del Astrolabio* of Piero della Francesca. It still wasn't where it ought to be.

Wyborn remained among us. He didn't dine—but then he seldom did anyway. People nodded to him and gave him the time of day in the quad. This I supposed to be the same sort of propriety operative when Christopher Cressy had dropped in and out of the place even after so nefariously making off with a letter-book of the fourth Marquis of Mountclandon. The Provost, it seemed, was marking time, circumspectly holding his hand after all. There was to be a consultation with legal big-wigs of enormous eminence (and devotion to the college, since they would undoubtedly be old members) as soon as it could be arranged.

On the Thursday of the ninth week—which was the day after the Gaudy—I went up to town on one of my still-existing theatrical concerns. While there I felt a prompting to make my way to Bethnal Green, seek out St Ambrose's Church, and take a look at the lie of the land there. That I didn't do so was a consequence of wholly irrational feeling. I'd be taking an initiative, I told myself, that wasn't properly mine—as I'd ventured to do on that earlier occasion in Bethnal Green when I had presented myself at the home of the Lusbys distinguishably in the role of a spy. That had turned out all right. But I somehow didn't want to be prowling round the same quarter of London again.

So I got back to college late in the afternoon, and sat down to write some letters. Then I found myself without envelopes, and walked over to common room to collect a few. The large common room was deserted. I passed through it and into the smaller common room, where there were several writing tables equipped with stationery. And at once I stopped dead. *The Madonna of the Astrolabe* was back on its easel.

There it was, and Gender was standing in front of it. I had a fleeting sense—this before I exclaimed in wonder—that in some unaccountable way he wasn't too pleased.

'Jimmy, in heaven's name! How on earth——'

I broke off. Gender (one of my new friends) was looking at me as if I were a stranger. Or perhaps he wasn't looking at me at all—or not so as to be aware of me. I realized that my impression of mere displeasure in him was short of the mark. It was as if something dreadful had happened to this poised diffident courteous man. I thought of some domestic calamity. I am always quick to remember that husbands, and fathers of families, have given hostages to fortune.

'Jimmy—what has happened?'

'The Piero has come back—as you see. Undamaged, they say.'

'Thank goodness for that! But just how?'

'Wyborn has returned it. He says that it's at the disposal of the college.'

'A change of heart?'

'Very radically that, it seems.' Gender had momentarily recovered himself. He glanced at a corner of the room, and my eyes followed his. The security guard was back. In fact he was back reinforced by a colleague. 'Duncan,' Gender said, 'come into the next room.'

We went into a third room, cumbersomely called the senior common room smoking room. This, like the large common room, was empty.

'Should it be like that?' I asked. 'Just stuck there again?'

303

'Edward's way of minimizing the whole incident, I suppose.'

'Incident? The Lord help us!'

'Wyborn has resigned his fellowship. And that evangelical Visitor, despite Edward's dark view of him, has been entirely reasonable. He has simply ruled that Wyborn's successor must abnegate any title to control the picture before we admit him. As for poor Wyborn himself, he says he's entering some Order—one of those closed affairs in which they put in all their time praying for us.'

'How very odd!'

'Wyborn took what had happened as a special sign, a judgement upon him, God's terrible voice in Bethnal Green.' Gender was now painfully agitated—which was an extraordinary circumstance. And then he said an extraordinary thing. 'At least they've extracted the bullet. But they say they still don't know.'

'From Wyborn? He tried to——'

'No, no. From Peter Lusby. He's in the London Hospital, with just this chance of pulling through. Good God, Duncan! First this place kills Paul Lusby, and now——'

'Peter Lusby attempted to——'

'No, no—thank God not that. It was thieves, professionals, trying to steal the Piero from that accursed crypt. Peter was there. I rather think he must have taken it into his head to guard the thing. He fought them off. Then the police arrived. It seems there were a couple in a vestry. Why only in a vestry, God knows. Edward's insistence on discretion, perhaps. Anyway, they caught the men. But not before one of them had lost his head and shot the boy.'

It was a week before we knew that Peter Lusby's life was out of danger, and that he would make a full recovery. It was a very bad week. But in the course of it the Governing Body had held a special meeting, and Piero's *Madonna* had gone to the sale-room.